IRONMIND®:
STRONGER MINDS,
STRONGER BODIES.

....

IronMind®: Stronger Minds, Stronger Bodies

Cataloging in Publication Data
Strossen, Randall J., Ph.D.—
Ironmind: stronger minds, stronger bodies by Randall J. Strossen, Ph.D.
1. Sports—Psychological aspects 2. Weight training   I. Title
GV706.4S.94   1994   796.01   94-73052
ISBN 0-926888-02-1

Published in the United States of America
IronMind® Enterprises, Inc., P.O. Box 1228, Nevada City, CA 95959

Printed in the U.S.A. First Edition
20 19 18 17 16 15 14 13

Acknowledgments

When I was sixteen, I drove to the York Barbell Company to buy the squat racks and bench that were the industry standard, in what would mark a major advancement in my basement gym. While there, I can remember seeing Steve Stanko and Bob Bednarski, which alone would have been pretty memorable, but what I remember most is that when asking if it would be possible to talk to John Grimek for a minute, I was brought up to his office, where he patiently answered every question I put before him. Can you imagine that?

That's the kind of good fortune I have had throughout my life: Access to top authorities, leading teachers, various experts and just plain positive influences. Without these people, this book would never have been possible.

Other IronMind Enterprises, Inc. publications:

SUPER SQUATS: How to Gain 30 Pounds of Muscle in 6 Weeks by Randall J. Strossen, Ph.D.

The Complete Keys to Progress by John McCallum, edited by Randall J. Strossen, Ph.D.

Mastery of Hand Strength by John Brookfield

MILO: A Journal for Serious Strength Athletes, Randall J. Strossen, Ph.D., Publisher and Editor-in-chief

Powerlifting Basics, Texas-style: The Adventures of Lope Delk by Paul Kelso

Of Stones and Strength by Steve Jeck and Peter Martin

Sons of Samson, Volume 2 Profiles by David Webster

Rock Iron Steel: The Book of Strength by Steve Justa

Paul Anderson: The Mightiest Minister by Randall J. Strossen, Ph.D.

Louis Cyr: Amazing Canadian by Ben Weider, CM

Training with Cables for Strength by John Brookfield

The Grip Master's Manual by John Brookfield

Dexterity Ball Training for Hands Course by John Brookfield

Captains of Crush® Grippers: What They Are and How to Close Them by Randall J. Strossen, Ph.D., J. B. Kinney and Nathan Holle

Winning Ways: How to Succeed In the Gym and Out by Randall J. Strossen, Ph.D.

To order additional copies of *IronMind: Stronger Minds, Stronger Bodies* or for a catalog of IronMind Enterprises, Inc. publications and products, please contact:

IronMind Enterprises, Inc.
P.O. Box 1228
Nevada City, CA 95959 USA
tel: (530) 265-6725
fax: (530) 265-4876
website: www.ironmind.com
e-mail: sales@ironmind.com

Contents

Dedication

This book is dedicated to all who are trying to make wise use of the gifts they have been given—not only to make the most of themselves, but also to help others do likewise.

1 Why IronMind®?

Build a nineteen-inch arm, bench a quarter of a ton, snatch 400 pounds—let's get physical! We're talking sweat and blood, heaping on slabs of muscle and moving piles of iron, so how can mental training help? After all, who ever heard of applying serious sports psychology to the Iron Game? When you know you want to win the Mr./Ms. Whatever title or the Heavy Hammer Lifting Championships, who needs a shrink, a black leather couch and a session of dream interpretation?

Nobody, probably, but what you might need is an opportunity to bring the same level of technology to the mental aspect of your training and competition as you put to use in your workout, your diet and every other aspect of your program. Just as training has gone beyond turn of the century one-set schedules and nutrition has gone beyond the beer-and-beef diets of nineteenth century Continental strongmen, psychology—as an experimental science—has made more than a little progress since Freud's day. IronMind® will show you how some of the research results can help you on the platform—whether you're posing or lifting.

"Mind over matter" is such a cliche that it's muttered all the time, and everyone has heard about supernatural-sounding feats of strength at one time or another. To go beyond conventional wisdom, each month the "IronMind®" column will get specific and relate how psychology applies to pumping and humping iron. So whether you hit the weights as a bodybuilder or as a strength athlete, this is the place to check for tips on how to really use your brain when you train.

"Sounds good," you say, "but I'm from Missouri, so you'll have to prove to me that what goes on between my ears influences my body. If you can do that, I'll listen."

Did you know that you can train your mind to control internal processes usually thought to be under automatic control? For example, you can learn to control your body temperature and heart rate, influence your circulation, etc. in a process called "autonomic self-regulation."

"Influence my circulation, huh?" you think, "does that mean I pump up my muscles without even hitting the weights?"

Sorry to disappoint you, but even if you become a master traffic cop of your internal functions, exercise will probably remain a necessary element in your training program. The point is that your new level of autonomic control will allow you to put more into your workouts and get more out of them, consistently giving you a small edge which will add up to big time results. As an added benefit, these same tools will be applicable to other aspects of your life, too.

"O.K., but I've heard about stuff like that before. Surprise me with some research from this fancy sports psychology stuff."

How's this one? Did you know the way you interact with other people probably influences your testosterone level?

"Huh?!"

You heard it right: Research on primates demonstrated that there was a positive correlation between social rank and testosterone levels. That is, the higher one's social status, the higher his testosterone level. This prompted the question of which caused which: Did leaders emerge because they had more testosterone or did leadership itself increase testosterone levels? The resulting experiments measured testosterone levels as social position was manipulated upward or downward, and you guessed it, the testosterone levels varied with the new social position.

"I'm impressed," you say, "but can you show me a little of this mind-body stuff in action." Fair enough. Try this harmless demonstration: Get a piece of string about a foot long and tie a key to one end. Hold on to the other end of the string, and with your elbow on a table, let the key hang straight down. Ready for the fun? Stare at the key and think "circles." Stare hard at the key, and concentrate on "circles" as if your life depended on it. Notice the key starting to move around in circles—pretty weird, huh? The next time you're bored, try to reverse directions, go for figure-eights, Mach I, or whatever.

You've probably heard about the little old lady who, in desperation, lifted a car off her son and you probably dismissed the tale as tabloid-style exaggeration. But did you know that, roughly 70 years ago, Peary Rader's life was saved when his father lifted an enormously heavy plow off him? Since Peary estimated that his father lifted about three-quarters of a ton, it shouldn't come as a surprise that he could never come close to repeating this feat.

This childhood experience, together with decades of Iron Game experience, gave Peary good reason to support scientific efforts to identify the chemical and mental conditions underlying superior strength; noting our vast untapped reservoirs, Peary wrote: "It is apparent that the human body is capable of several times the effort that we have heretofore been able to realize. I suppose this is the reason that records continue to go up and there seems to be no limit. Our limit is so far above what we now do that we will probably never reach it."

Every now and then, a world record is shattered by such an enormous amount that the door between our normal experience and the realm of possibility is opened just a crack. Paul Anderson's squats in the late 1950s were such an example, as was Bob Beamon's long jump in the 1968 Olympic Games.

Many of you have probably read Dr. Charles Garfield's widely publicized account of how Eastern European scientists used visualization techniques to enable him to demolish what he thought was his bench press limit, in the wee hours of a Milan morning a few years back. As Dr. Garfield explains, he had seldom benched more than 275 or 280 in training at the time of this demonstration, but when pushed by the Soviet scientists, he was willing to try for 300—which he made with "enormous difficulty." With the help of the Soviet sports psychologists' techniques, Dr. Garfield went on to crank out a 365-pound bench press, equal to his old PR, and instantly became a believer. After all, a 65-pound advantage isn't bad for one night's work.

And on the bodybuilding side, there was a fellow from a little town in a country most people couldn't find on a map, who caught everyone's attention while he was still in high school and went on to rewrite the book on the sport—Arnold Schwarzenegger. Reflecting on his accomplishments, Arnold explained, " The secret [of success] is contained in a three-part formula I learned in the gym: self-confidence, a positive mental attitude, and honest hard work. Many people are aware of these principles, but very few can put them into practice." Examining these and related principles of building mental muscle and power, plus showing you how to apply them, is what IronMind® is all about. So, have at it, go train, and next month we'll show you how it all starts in your brain!

2 Limits

If your brain is really critical to your training progress and your contest results, and if we have vast untapped potential, then two things should happen: 1) every now and then, someone will come along who completely devastates the old record, and 2) once a new standard has been established, a lot of people will quickly be performing above the old limit. In fact, this is exactly what happens, and bodybuilders and lifters should understand how this applies to them.

Last month IronMind® cited, in passing, the accomplishments of Paul Anderson and Bob Beamon as examples of people who redefined what's physically possible, since both men have performed at what would appear to be historically-impossible levels. To illustrate the process of how you can break old ideas about your limits and set higher standards for yourself, let's take a minute to review some phenomenal performers, beginning with Messrs. Anderson and Beamon, and go on to several bodybuilders who set new standards.

Our goal is to, first, identify some major trend-setters, and second, examine what happened after each made his mark. In coming months, we'll visit the psychology laboratory to learn why we sometimes limit ourselves for no good reason and how you can redirect your thinking to break all your old limits.

In the early 1920's Henry "Milo" Steinborn squatted with approximately 550 pounds, which—beyond being a record lift—was viewed as close to man's ultimate limit. Even by the mid-1950s, this standard had only been nudged up to around the 600-pound mark.

Enter the Canadian superman Doug Hepburn, who squatted 760 pounds in the mid-1950s, a prodigious performance in the history of strength, but one which Paul Anderson completely upstaged by cranking out 1160 in 1957. To properly accent the supreme nature of Paul's squatting ability, recall that in 1965 Dr. Terry Todd won the first "official" Senior National Powerlifting Championships with a 675-pound squat.

The fact that no one—even with drugs, squat suits, super wraps and super belts—has yet come within 100 pounds of Paul's mark is further testimony to his colossal squatting ability. Once Paul Anderson had completely redefined conceptions of leg strength, however, others followed him into previously untouched territory, and by the end of the 1960s, there were a handful of 800-pound squatters.

And just what sort of history was Bob Beamon setting on that fateful day in Mexico City? The legendary Jesse Owens' long jump mark of 26' 8 1/4" stood for 26 years, and at the time of Beamon's jump, the world record had crept up to 27' 4 3/4"—a gain of about eight inches in 33 years. Bob Beamon uncorked something unreal at those '68 Games, when he put nearly two feet on the old record, an accomplishment so unexpected and so stupendous that it might seem more at home in the world of psychic phenomena than sports. Twenty years later, Bob Beamon's mark remains the world standard, although Carl Lewis has drawn near. This pattern not only underlines the astounding nature of Bob's jump, but it also shows how the rate of progress accelerates once a new limit has been defined.

As with Paul Anderson's squats, Bob Beamon's long jump has confirmed our two hypotheses about performance: 1) our limits are far greater than we think, as superstars demonstrate every now and then, and 2) once someone blazes the trail, others will follow with previously unheard of performances. How does this apply to bodybuilders?

In the world of bodybuilding, given the subjective nature of evaluation, one can take issue with who is named as exemplifying the break with past standards of excellence, but here are four men who, each in his time, elevated the concept of physical excellence to grand new heights: Eugen Sandow, John C. Grimek, Sergio Oliva and Arnold Schwarzenegger. Of course, such a short list seems to ignore the contributions of a host of others—that's not the intent, so please bear with this example.

Before Eugen Sandow's appearance, the professional strongmen of the 1890s era were something less than shapely or svelte—men such as Apollon, Louis Cyr, Horace Barre and Henry Holtgrewe were impressive in their often-ponderous bulk and feats of raw power, but as showmen, they couldn't compare to Sandow. What was Sandow's advantage? A key was his "remarkable physique" and use of hitherto unseen "artistry and showmanship." Sandow defined new standards, melding previously unknown levels of both appearance and performance—setting the stage for such early Iron Game giants as Arthur Saxon, Lionel Strongfort and G.W. Rolandow.

After Sandow, there was a whole new idea about how strongmen should look, and people with good-looking bodies were expected to have remarkable capabilities and a flair for demonstrating them. Lest you think Sandow's influence is being exaggerated, note that the $250 commanded by a front-row seat at an 1899 Sandow show, in today's dollars, is more than double the $1,500 price tag hung on front-row Tyson-Spinks seats!

John C. Grimek hardly needs an introduction, but what other bodybuilder has the distinction of inspiring a limit on entering a physique contest because of his utter and complete domination? In 1940, the great John Grimek entered and won the AAU Mr. America title, a contest then in its third year and representing the pinnacle of physique competition. John's development far exceeded anything seen before. The next year, JCG showed up again, around forty pounds heavier and created such a stir that a rule was created forbidding any winner to re-enter the contest—John Grimek's supremacy on the posing dias seemed unassailable, and such a move appeared vital if the contest were to be preserved.

Like Sandow, Grimek was always known as an incredibly gifted showman (ask one of his contemporaries to describe what happened when John started to pose!), and also like Sandow, Grimek could *do* things with his muscles—not the least of his achievements was to represent the United States as a weightlifter in the 1936 Olympic Games. If you have any doubts about John's influence on bodybuilding, compare pictures of the top people before him to those who followed on his coattails: John Grimek opened the door to the world of modern bodybuilding.

Remember the first time you brought a muscle magazine home and showed it to, say, your mother and sister? Five will get you ten that, pointing to the bodybuilders, they said something like, "Their muscles are too big" and to add insult to injury, the next time they saw a relatively scrawny swimmer or gymnast on "Wide World of Sports," they said, "Now, that's a good physique!" When the physique competitors themselves say one of their colleagues is starting to look a little freaky, pay attention, because it won't happen often and when it does, a new era will follow.

Sergio Oliva wasn't dubbed "The Myth" for nothing—back in the sixties, people just could not believe his development and there was talk, even among competitive bodybuilders, that Sergio's muscles were too big! The Myth he was and The Myth he will always remain, but looking around today, there are a lot more guys who have some of that look than there were twenty years ago. If Sergio hadn't shown what could be done, a lot of genetic talent for bodybuilding might still be lying dormant today.

And of course, there's "The King of Bodybuilding," the one-time "Austrian Oak," Arnold Schwarzenegger, whose incredible body and exceptional personality became the catalyst for not only putting bodybuilding on the map, but also for showing that success on the posing dias could be transferred to other walks of life. Nobody had ever looked like Arnold before and nobody had acted like him either. And nobody—but nobody--can touch his success.

Ever since Arnold arrived, you didn't have to explain what a "pump" was. And now, if you're lucky, when you introduce yourself as a bodybuilder, others might assume you are en route to amassing a substantial personal fortune, becoming a leading box office draw, marrying into an eminent family and—demonstrating your total control—being able to tell a *Playboy* interviewer that her time would expire with your $25 cigar! Talk about coming a long way: Compare this scenario to even the recent pre-Arnold era, where the top gyms were nearly bankrupt and so were many of the top bodybuilders.

From Paul Anderson to Arnold Schwarzenegger, the world of weights has had its share of leaders, men and women who raised the ante a notch or two, and in so doing, created a new game, a game others would dare to play. The most important lesson to learned from these examples is not, really, the specifics of what each of these pioneers accomplished, but the fact that they opened up vast new frontiers.

For example, after Paul Anderson, 700-800 pound squats lost some of their cachet as others ventured into what had been an extremely exclusive zone. Likewise, after Sergio, the possibility of being too gifted genetically and too successful in tapping this potential in the gym seems to have receded. And after Arnold, well, maybe we're now ready for the concept of infinity.

Conspicuously absent from this discussion of breakthroughs, you might point out, are the leading women. "This is curious," you say, "because haven't modern female pioneers actually done some of the most revolutionary things in the sport? At least initially, didn't they face enormous social resistance?"

Absolutely, and it might even be argued that because their widespread involvement in each of the three competitive aspects of the Iron Game is only a recent event, women need to be especially attuned to underestimating their potential and particularly alert to the trail-blazing opportunities. The only reason for sticking with male examples above is because their longer history in the sport provides more data, and therefore, a stronger basis for making my points.

Keep your sights high, your training hard, your diet and rest on schedule, and next month we'll explore two of the key reasons we can get detoured along the way—reasons why we can have an undervalued sense of our limits. This will set the stage for describing some ways to break through the boundaries currently holding back your progress or aspirations.

3 Social Pressure as a Growth Inhibitor

Last month, IronMind® reviewed some of the trend setters in the world of weights, the people who set new standards, the leaders. This month's discussion will build on that framework: We will explore the psychological roots of why leadership is so difficult—to better prepare you for setting your own new standards and going on to achieve them. Get ready to jump over some of the common hurdles standing between you and greatness.

Let's take a breather from the weights for a minute, step out of the gym, and visit the research laboratories of two preeminent social psychologists whose experiments on conformity and obedience stunned the world. These studies provide a lot of food for thought for everyone, including bodybuilders and lifters seeking new heights of performance.

A few decades ago American social psychologists were interested in proving that someone like a Hitler could never rise to power in the United States. After all, our country was founded by people who broke away from a tyrannical monarchy and later, its tough pioneers pushed the frontier from the Atlantic, across the Great Plains, over the Rockies and the Sierras, and dumped it into the Pacific Ocean. So, the folklore has it that we're a nation of such rugged individualists that we could never be squeezed under the thumb of a ruthless dictator. To add a little scientific leverage to this idea, Drs. Stanley Milgram and Solomon Asch marched off to their laboratories to gather data and spin theories.

Asch tested the participants in his now-classic experiment by having them, one at a time, sit around a table with six other people and compare the length of a standard line to three other lines—one of which was an obvious replica of the standard line. The experimental task was to decide which line matched the standard. Unbeknownst to the participants, the other six people at the table were actually working for Dr. Asch and had been primed to give the wrong answer. Answers to the line-matching task were given out loud, going around the table.

What happened when several people answering before the real participant picked what was clearly the wrong line? Almost one-third of the people Asch tested ignored the information staring them in the face and conformed with the group—they also picked the wrong line! Who forgot to mention the story about rugged individualists to this group?

Milgram put a little added juice in his equally-classic study: Each participant was told to give an electric shock to another person, at the researcher's command. The experimental task was structured so that each participant was asked to give progressively higher shocks, and the other person was in another room. Again, the other person was actually working for the researcher, and the "shock" was fake, but conditions were extremely realistic and appeared to have fooled virtually everyone in Milgram's study.

Milgram was testing to see how many "normal" people would deliver a "lethal" shock to another person simply because an authority figure (the researcher) told them to. The real shock in the Milgram study lay in the results: About two-thirds of the people tested in Milgram's experiment followed all the experimenter's instructions to deliver shocks—past the point where the other person cried out, pounded on the walls, begged for mercy, and then stopped, apparently dead!

With two straight out fast ball strikes against the non-conformist, was science proving that we are just a bunch of weak-kneed conformists who were as cowardly as the people who carried out the orders of any past dictators?

Not exactly, although these experiments blasted the original hypothesis of unshakable American independence right out of the water. What was demonstrated by these studies, and all the follow-up research projects they inspired, is the formerly inconceivable power of social forces such as conformity and obedience. What we know now is that a lot, if not most, everyday people will follow the lead of their fellows—no matter how convincing the physical evidence to the contrary (think of the Asch study). We are also forced to face the frightening truth that most of us blindly obey "authorities," no matter how heinous their commands (think of the Milgram study).

Let's go back to the gym now and see what all this means for your next workout and the ones to follow.

Starting at the top, the monkey-see-monkey-do mentality captured by the Asch study demonstrates the incredible power of peer pressure to shape our attitudes and behaviors. If all your buddies at the gym are loading up on steroids, but you'd like to go clean, for example, you'll make life a lot easier for yourself if you make some new friends, people who are clean. If you want to train heavy, but everyone in your gym works out with 25-pound dumbbells, find a new training environment. If you aspire to win the Ms. O and your gym mates think a women's place is in the aerobics room, change gyms. The examples are endless, but the bottom line is to, "Avoid swimming against the social tide, whenever possible, by consciously picking when and where you swim." Save your energy for constructive outlets and the times when you simply can't avoid going against the tide.

Blind obedience, Milgram demonstrated, can lead to a lot of people getting hurt—and one of them could be you. The lesson here is to *think for yourself*, rather than just mimicking what goes on around you or dumbly following another's instructions, simply because they "know." You have a sore shoulder and the local top gun tells you that he always trains through injuries, with a sage comment like, "Look, Shorty, be a man: no pain—no gain." So you follow his advice and instead of laying off the bench presses for a few weeks to let your shoulder heal, you slop along, ignoring the pain signals—only to find yourself eight months later with the same sore shoulder and faltering bench you started off with.

Or, you go on a cadaver-derived growth hormone because an "expert" told you it was good for at least another inch on your arms. Your bones start to thicken and your skin coarsens. "This is pretty weird," you think, but you stick to the advice and stay on the stuff, because the expert said, "Don't worry, those side effects go away." He was right, but what he didn't tell you is that they go away because one day you might not wake up.

"O.K., but without all the drama, can this stuff about conformity and obedience gang up on me in the gym or hurt my training?" It sure can and here's the most common scenario. Let's say you have been training on a one-hour program comprising a few sets of moderate reps on a couple handfuls of basic exercises. You use heavy weights, eat good food, supplement wisely and get enough rest. Following this approach, you have been getting bigger and stronger, feeling better all the time.

Then, one-by-one, the folks down at the gym start following the advice of a master trainer who says, "Light weights, thirty sets per body part and two kilos of my marvelous 'Mega-Meta-Nutri-Anabo-Grow' a day." To reinforce his message, this messiah adds, "All the pros train like this." After facing some ribbing about your funky routine, you decide to get with it and hop on the bandwagon. In the first month, your muscles haven't gotten any bigger, although your bank account has shrunk. Being the optimist, you look at this pattern and think, "It must be like a long-term investment—the muscles will grow later, so I'll keep putting all my time and money into them, now." By the third month, your strength is down 30%, you have a bad cold, and two inches seem to have taken a vacation from your thighs. Two weeks later you get smart, evaluate your progress, or lack thereof, and return to your old program.

D on't let the shocking power of negative social forces send your dreams up in smoke: Keep your head up, your eyes and ears open, think for yourself and never—ever—forget to exercise your option on free will. Start letting your vision of yourself expand, because next month it's time to talk about shaping a very potent new you.

4 Remake

Up to 1983, the Honda Prelude was a, well, *nice* car—it looked a little sporty, handled O.K. and it even had all the legendary Honda quality, but it just didn't have any zip. In fact, it's nickname the "'Lude" was a reference not to it's full name, the Prelude, but rather to the drug Quaalude, which could put you sleep, if you weren't careful.

In 1983, Honda introduced a redesigned Prelude—the "new Prelude"— and it was a show stopper. It turned heads on the street, handled better than just about any Porsche, and its new three-valve-per-cylinder engine was more than an engineering breakthrough—it turned a one-time dog into a front runner. How did even Honda manage such an extraordinary break with the past? "The 1983 Honda began as a blank piece of paper," was the public response.

It makes good copy and it's certainly easier said than done, to be able to leave past limitations behind and to boldly march forward, but your first step toward achieving more for yourself is to toss out all the ideas you have about what you can and cannot do. "Genetics," I hear you grumble, "gave me these high calf insertions and I haven't seen you do anything to lower them, so how can I forget about what I have to work with?" "With my seven-inch wrists, how can I ever expect to gain weight, or any semblance of muscular bulk?" "I'm already 30-something—I'm too old to even pretend that I can accomplish great things... ."

Most of your concerns can probably be answered with the word "rubbish!" because laziness and ignorance so often pass for real limitations. Let's turn the table for a minute and assume everything is possible, and see what sort of self-image you can construct, but be forewarned, it could be awesome!

Within universities, it is widely believed that a disproportionate share of the major scientific contributions come from people who are relatively new to their fields—either by virtue of their youth, or because they recently switched areas. The prevailing explanation of this pattern is that such people are best-positioned to make major discoveries and theoretical advances because their thinking is unencumbered by conventional ideas in the field. In other words, they didn't "know" yet what isn't supposed to work, so they prove it does! This is truly a case where ignorance helps, so give yourself a break for a few minutes and play stupid. This might be harder for some than others, but the effort will be worth it.

Get comfortable, doing whatever it takes: Probably, loose clothes, no shoes, a quiet setting and pleasant temperature, lying on your back or reclining in comfortably chair. Use this exercise as an excuse to go to the beach or to the park to relax, if you'd like, but your bedroom or living room can work just was well. Wherever you go, bring along a pad for some notes.

Slowly draw in a deep breath and—this is important—fill your diaphragm, as well as your chest, hold it for a second and exhale. Remember, you're not posing right now, so it's not only O.K. to let your stomach stick way out with the deep breath you're taking, but it's crucial to this exercise. Take another slow, very deep breath and let your eyelids droop or even close, whichever seems more natural. Hold the breath for a second and exhale. We'll call this process "focused deep breathing" and refer back to it during this workout.

Slowly shrug and roll your shoulders to identify and release any tension there might be in your upper back. Gently roll your head around, lightly stretching your neck to, similarly, release any muscle tension in your neck. Next, arch your eyebrows as high as they go and release them, followed by making a yawning-type face—your facial muscles can store a lot of tension and we're trying to get rid of it. Relax and take a couple more focused deep breaths. If you feel any residual tension from your shoulders up, repeat the appropriate movement(s) described above. Don't worry if you don't get every last drop of tension to ooze out of your body right now—just try to get as relaxed as you reasonably can.

Now that you're relaxed, daydream. Go ahead and drift off into your own little fantasy. Let your thoughts flow through your mind, without worrying about hanging value labels on them (such as thinking your ideas are "good," "bad," "reasonable," "realistic," etc.). In fact, try to keep your daydream oriented toward images, rather than words. Why should you avoid evaluation at this stage and why does thinking in images help?

To be creative, by definition, you will be charting new territory, and in order to be most open to unconventional ways of thinking and to new solutions, it is useful to avoid jumping to conclusions which might restrict the possibilities. Being too quick to make value judgments will limit your ability to generate creative solutions, narrowing your perceptual range and creating a form of cognitive rigidity. Research psychologists have a lot of ways of illustrating how we miss solutions to problems by prematurely and incorrectly narrowing the realm of possibilities—and that's exactly the sort of error you want to avoid.

The reason for trying to think in imagery rather than words is tied to the structure and function of our brains. The lower portion of the human brain is often called the "old brain," because of its similarity to the brains of lower animals. This is the portion of your brain that handles simple, automatic functions, such as the reflex reaction of pulling back your hand if you touch a hot object, or dropping a weight if a muscle is tearing.

Unlike frogs, for example, humans can perform complex tasks such as learning, thinking and imagining—powers that are housed in the "new brain," the cerebral cortex, which surrounds the old brain. The cerebral cortex is minuscule in lower animals, but huge in humans and is divided into two halves, or hemispheres, each with specialized functions. Generally, the "left brain" controls verbal processes and is linear, logical and rational, while the "right brain" is visual, intuitive and the home of creative imagination.

Because the left brain might say "can't," "unrealistic," or "irrational" too early in the exploratory process, incorrectly narrowing your options, we'd like to emphasize the use of imagery, concentrating your mental activity in the right brain. Remember that you have two brains and the *right* one for this job is on the *right* side, the domain of images.

Back to your letting your mind wander, unfettered by words and "realistic" restrictions: Touch on the first time you remember encountering a set of weights, or someone who obviously used them. What was your reaction? How did you feel about what you saw? Did you feel inspired, intimidated, curious? Why? Can you form a mental picture of how you felt? The purpose of this exercise is to identify what initially attracted you to your iron-related activity: What felt positive the first time your paths crossed and what might have been a concern? To maintain productive form on this exercise (for which we'll borrow Freud's term, "free association"), stay relaxed, keep open to all the possibilities and let one image lead naturally to another. When you feel you have a good sense about this first meeting, write down some notes about what you recall.

Begin the second exercise just as you did the first, by getting relaxed, but this time, let your mind wander around the scene of your first workout and how it felt. What felt good and what didn't? Why were you there? Did you have an idea about what you might accomplish by training with weights? Again, conclude this exercise when you feel that you have reasonably tapped the storehouse of your brain and write down what you came up with, using another sheet of paper.

Shift gears now, remaining as tranquil as possible, and look at your notes from the two exercises you did. Can you see a pattern? For example, was your introduction to weights via seeing an impressive upper arm and was your first workout filled with images of building something similar for yourself? Did you see a defensive end make a tremendous sack, hear John Madden talk about his power ("Look at those legs go! Now that's power—BOOM!!—Hit him!—Watch him DRIVE off the line...) and then find yourself doing squats? Maybe you saw a Ms. Olympia contestant and got a whole new idea of female physique aesthetics and came away wanting that look for yourself. Note any patterns like this on a third sheet of paper. Also note any conclusions that leap out at you about why you pump iron, going back to your earliest encounters.

At this point, you can start to use your left brain again to analyze your reasons for training. To help warm up your left brain, stand up and stretch, taking a few minutes to let your system re-adapt itself. If you got deeply relaxed in the preceding exercises, you should be experiencing a change in consciousness something like waking up—having a sense of self-awareness that wasn't there before. If this feeling isn't clear, pay attention to how your awareness shifts when you wake up from a nap, the sense that "you went somewhere" and have "returned." Practice at structured breathing and some other exercises we will introduce later in this program will help you achieve deeper and deeper states of relaxation.

Once you have re-adapted to left-brain thinking, try arranging your reasons in terms of priority: What's the relative importance of each reason you train? Think about both your short- and long-term goals: Are they consistent? If not, try to adjust your goals so they support one another. Have you set short-term goals that you can reasonably be expected to attain, even if they are a stretch? If not, do so. What things are you willing to trade off or give up, either in terms of meeting your goals or in terms of your goals themselves? For example, are you willing to forego *all* sweets for several months to harden up for a physique contest, or spend years cycling through heavy squat programs to build a foundation for your lifting career? A trade-off might work like this: Perhaps you are willing to accept the rewards that follow from spending no more than five hours a week in the gym, even if that means paring back your contest goals. Throughout this exercise, really *think* about your training targets—the why, what, how and when of your training.

When you train with weights, you have to allow your muscles to recuperate to achieve the benefits of your exercise, right? That's why you are careful to rest adequately, eat soundly and supplement wisely between your workouts. There is an analogy in creative problem-solving (a form of *mental* training) which is usually called "incubation" and it is the period of quiet, following concentration, which usually produces the great insight or the solution to the problem with which you have been wrestling. We want to apply this same principle to your mental training program, so after you have completed the exercises described above, stop thinking about your motivation and goals for somewhere between two days and a week. That is, stop deliberately thinking about them, although *dreaming* about them would be very helpful. After you have rested, you are ready for the next exercise.

Once again, use a comfortable setting and structured breathing to free associate, but this time, let your daydreams concern the big picture—scenes and events that make you, or would make you, feel good about your life overall. Run through several scripts, as many as it takes, until you have a feeling that you have some clues about what kind of direction you would like in your life. Remember, this is a right-brain-exploratory-imaginative exercise so keep your evaluating left brain from spoiling the fun! As with the previous exercises, jot down some notes.

Then, and only then, invite your left brain to the party and do the same sort of analysis you did on the first two exercises, putting your rational mental powers to work arranging these desirable life goals in terms of their priority or relative importance to you. Once this is done, finish off by comparing this list with the one you developed based on what motivates your training and identify both how the two wish lists can overlap and areas in which there is conflict.

By reflecting on what got you into training and framing your training with the rest of your life, you'll get a sharper focus on your training goals and methods, as well as a deeper commitment to them. Following this routine also greatly increases your chances of succeeding because it will help you spot fundamental inconsistencies. For example, did you start training because you wanted to improve your health and find that dangerous, appearance-improving drugs crept into your life? Did you begin with the idea that you were going to make it to the pros, only to find that too many hours have been spent in bars or lying on the beach? Did you start off with the idea of winning an Olympic gold medal and let self-doubt and nay-saying "experts" chip away your will? Or, did you begin training with the idea of moderate involvement, only to find that your life has become one big superset? Use your new insights to adjust whatever got out of whack, or to reinforce the accuracy of your current trajectory.

This set of exercises isn't a one-shot deal any more than one trip to the calf machines finishes your lower legs, so be prepared to incorporate these techniques into your overall training program: Go back to your roots, using them as a starting point, and guided by your present experiences and future aspirations, paint fresh pictures of why you hit the gym.

Remember our warning, however, about awesome results, because just as good physical training helps you outgrow your clothes, good mental training helps you outgrow your self-image. Now go do it!

5

When Less is More and More is Less

Maybe you've seen all three and maybe you've been in all three situations:

1) The powerlifter, facing a PR final attempt deadlift for all the marbles, has his coach, eyeball-to-eyeball, screaming in his face and throwing in a slap across the chops for punctuation.

2) The bodybuilder, moments away from his debut in a national show, sits with a towel over his head, slowly drawing full breaths deep into his stomach while imagining the serenity of lying on a beach.

3) The Olympic-style weightlifter, having briskly paced twice up and down the platform, stands motionless over his third attempt snatch, the highest opener in the contest, but he's had two misses.

What are these people doing and why?

All three of these iron athletes are controlling their arousal levels, trying to home in on the level required for peak performance.

"If they're all shooting for top performance, why are they doing such different things?" you might ask. "The powerlifter seems to be trying to get as wired as he can—using every trick in the book to *boost* his arousal level. The bodybuilder seems to being doing *the opposite*—trying to help himself calm down—and the weightlifter seems to be in the middle. I don't get it."

The key to this apparent contradiction—that the most appropriate arousal level varies, depending upon the specific situation—can be explained by reviewing what research psychologists call the Yerkes-Dodson Law. Let's summarize how it has been tested in the athletic world, review its applications to the Iron Game and—most important—extract some principles to help you improve your performance.

First, what's arousal? As we use the term, it applies to the general state of physiological and psychological readiness, which has its roots in our prehistoric need, at times, to be prepared to stand and fight or to run for our lives!

Let's check your arousal level. Are you hunched over with sweaty palms, a racing heart, taking fast shallow breathes and your stomach in a knot because your reserves have been summoned, primed for the "flight or fight" response? Or, are you the picture of serenity, in a relaxed posture with a cool feeling on your forehead, a tranquil stomach, strong steady breathing and heart beat that's both slow and powerful? The former state describes common cues of high arousal and the second captures the common cues of low arousal. In the first condition, you are "wired" or "up tight" and in the second, "laid back" or "cool" (many-time world wrist-wrestling champion Johnny Walker is so cool that he's nicknamed "The Iceman").

How these different arousal levels interact with performance was first studied by psychologists in the context of a learning lab, where it was found that there is a curvilinear relationship between arousal and performance, and that the ideal arousal level declined as the task difficulty increased. Huh?

The curvilinear business just means that, at first, performance improves as arousal goes up, but at some point the pattern changes and increased arousal produces worse performance. The second point here is that the point of optimal arousal gets lower and lower as the task difficulty increases: Easy tasks seem to benefit from very high arousal, but extremely complex tasks require tranquility, the opposite of arousal!

Sports psychologists haven't missed the application of this to athletic environments, even if they generally fail to provide empirical support beyond the original Yerkes and Dodson data. In a far more scientifically rigorous work, based on the research evidence, scientific literature and empirical observation, Oxendine concluded that:

1) high arousal is essential for top performance involving strength, endurance or speed in the context of gross motor skills, but

2) high arousal interferes with performances tied to complex skills, fine muscle movements, great coordination, etc., and

3) slightly-above-average arousal is always preferable to so-called normal or sub-normal levels for *all motor tasks*.

Now you have a frame of reference for understanding why the powerlifter, the bodybuilder and the weightlifter described above were behaving so differently.

Powerlifting, with it's extremely elementary nature, benefits from good old arousal—the more the merrier, it seems. So the next time you are staring a heavy squat in the eyes, crank it up and you'll probably lift more: Pace rapidly and breath quickly, have someone scream at you or listen to carefully-selected, very loud music (several "Dire Straits" and "Led Zeppelin" songs have proven to be very effective for boosting straight line power in our clinical studies). Jerry Brainum and Dr. Fred Hatfield write regularly about ergogenic aids which can boost your performance—try them.

Executing a complex, highly-choreographed posing routine is a complicated task of the type easily disrupted by too much arousal. So while you don't want to get too laid back about it, for most people—beginners and intermediates, especially—performance will be enhanced if they work to reduce their arousal level a little before they hit the posing platform. Future columns will deal with arousal- and anxiety-reduction techniques in detail, but for now, stick with three basic tools:

1) breath slowly and deeply (use the focused deep breathing technique we discussed last month),

2) imagine peaceful scenes, and

3) say positive, soothing things to yourself ("I am calm and in control...").

Weightlifters stand on an interesting middle ground, because while their sport calls for tremendous gross muscle strength (the large thigh, hip and back muscles supply most of the power), it also requires precise coordination in a fairly complex pattern. Hence the need for weightlifters to be unusually attentive to both how aroused they are and what their optimal level is, before talking about instantly adjusting up or down. Get really relaxed, limp, and try to do a snatch with a broom stick—let alone hundreds of pounds—and see what under-arousal does to your performance. At the other end of the spectrum, I am reminded of two national class Olympic lifters I was training with twenty years ago. They were experimenting with amphetamines to improve their performance and while they felt great, they "overpulled" their snatches and had all their attempts land on the platform behind them!

It would be nice if research psychologists had some evidence demonstrating that these different strategies—knowing when to psyche up and when to psyche down—really worked for iron athletes. In fact, it has been reported that lifters employ adrenalizing (i.e., stimulating) images and self-statements on the powerlifts and a mixture of strategies on snatches. Additional evidence will be presented later, but this should be enough now to convince you that sometimes more (arousal) is less (productive) and sometimes less is more: Knowing the score depends on where you are.

Knowing when to psyche up and when to psyche down, you'll not only be able to lift more and pose better, but you'll also avoid grinding your teeth and beating yourself up when simply taking a deep breath and relaxing will work absolute miracles.

6 Inferior Interiors—Part I

Once upon a time there was a short little kid who got teased a lot by his playmates: "Hey, Napoleon—you little shrimp, you're a wimp!" A lot of that type of thing, or the French equivalent. Napoleon didn't need the world's widest shoulders to bear his king-sized grudge about such ego-bashing and, by golly, he'd show all those little *#@&'s from the playground—so off he went to conquer a very big chunk of the world before his luck ran out. A classic case of an inferiority complex and one way to deal with it.

Here's another. Delbert Garfinkle set out to prove he really wasn't the weenie everyone thought him to be, so he became a mountain climbing, hang gliding and motorcycle racing aficionado. Got all the gear—the latest and greatest everything, in such piles that he burned through four Visa cards and had to rent a garage to hold all the stuff he'd bought—read every book available and talked nothing but bivouacs, turbulence and leathers. Funny thing, though, was that whenever it was time to go climbing, gliding or canyon racing, Delbert—he just remembered—had promised to fix his ailing Uncle Ernie some chicken soup, or (what bad luck!) he came down with the flu. Inferiority complex, reaction type two.

The idea that bodybuilders are overcompensating for massive inferiority complexes has been around ever since the first person built some bigger biceps than the fellow in the next cave. After all, the common sense idea says, muscle mass and ego strength are inversely proportional, so anyone packing around that much muscle must be trying to make up for a 97-pound-weakling-of-a-psyche. Where do these inferiority complexes come from? How do most people deal with them? What can be done to overcome them? And, finally, is it true that Arnold only got big and strong and rich and famous because he had a foreign accent and a last name that was hard to pronounce?

The concept of the "inferiority complex" was developed by the psychoanalyst Alfred Adler, whose work starts with the idea that man is inherently a social animal—to the point of believing that man's most basic motivation is to belong to and participate in a group. The next step in Adler's theory is that we develop lifestyles which reflect our values. Feelings of inferiority arise when our lifestyles don't match our expectations, with feedback from others being a big source of our insecurities.

If you planned to go to Harvard Medical School, but flunked intro high school chemistry, *twice* no less, you might start to feel bad. You cruise along fancying yourself as Formula One material in search of a sponsor, but you still can't drive a stick, and hitting 60 on the freeway is a white knuckler for you. So you get glum. You'd banked on retiring, independently wealthy, by the time you were 25 and now, at 43, you're still getting passed over for the day shift at the McDonald's where you've been flipping burgers since high school. On and on.

And don't think you're the only one who has stubbed a toe along the way, either. Virtually everyone will run into something, sometime, that somebody else, at least, will label a failure. In fact, feelings of inferiority tend to be a natural by-product of our entry into the world. Ever watch a baby or a small child try to do what for you are the simplest things? Like walking or talking or eating with a spoon? We start our lives in a state of complete dependence upon those around us and it takes years before we fend for ourselves and this can upset our confidence if things aren't handled too well by those caring for us.

For example, if you were ridiculed every time you made a "mistake" as a child, or if you were ignored, or were overly-indulged and pampered, you would never have had a good chance to develop confidence. That's a wide spectrum of confidence crushers, so let's quickly review them. If you faced too much criticism, you were taught to believe that you had a history of failure—which wreaks havoc with your self-confidence because you'll simply expect to continue failing in the future. And if you were ignored, chances are good that you just never got your full share of challenges or rewards as you faced your expanding world—once again, your self-confidence got shut off at the level of a 12-inch arm. And if your parents did every single thing for you, you might have glided along fancy free until the first time you hit a challenge alone and then your psyche capsized because it had never been seaworthy in the first place—it lacked the ballast of personal success—others had always shielded you from the waves of the world.

So now that we know everyone's got one, probably, what do we do next? We could just ignore the little bugger and hope it will go away, or fall off, or mind its own business, but it never does. When you're talking inferiority complexes, you can run, but you can't hide.

You can be like Napoleon and do what psychologists call "over-compensate." The son of a pants presser builds an international publishing empire. The guy who lost some toes and nearly a leg or two becomes an Olympic-class runner. Sometimes these reactions are less predictable. The descendant of a Mayflower family becomes a madam. And the formerly-skinny coward becomes a 300-pound bully. The list is endless.

Even if these folks might go overboard, they're basically on the right track, because they have dared to look into the mouth of the tiger—they have had the gumption to become exactly what they didn't see in themselves. And that's the primary benefit of having these little twinges of inferiority from time to time: Insecurity can motivate improved performance, turning a onetime liability into a major asset. The lesson to learn here is that the absolute best way to overcome an inferiority complex is to attack the root of the problem. And the best way to do that is to change who you are, which is best done by changing what you do.

We've covered a lot of territory, so let's review where we've been for a moment, before continuing.

So far, we've seen that life presents lots of opportunities to be a little insecure about some things and there's really nothing unusual about that. We have also established that such feelings can be channeled into constructive activities which will eliminate the original source of these feelings. Finally, we also seen that people can get a little nutty (technical term) about their particular soft spots and overbuild in those areas. Armed with this knowledge, what's a game plan for turning our insecurities into our strengths?

The first step, as usual, is the most important: Be honest and identify your psychological soft spots. Don't think you have to go public with this self-appraisal by telling all on the "David Letterman" show, or leaking the story to the *National Enquirer*—do it privately, just admitting to yourself that this or that area of your psyche needs a little more mass. Second, reality test the reason for the friction. This is important, because people can get into trouble when their idealized self-images are set so high that disappointment, and ensuing feelings of failure and inferiority, are the natural consequence. Adjust your self-image if it seems to be a little out of whack, and you might solve your problems of inferiority immediately. Third, if the feelings of personal insecurity remain, identify a course of action and pursue it. Fourth, a couple of months after implementing your new action plan, reassess your position and adjust your program as necessary. Start chipping away at this process, and next month we'll build a detailed program for bulking up your psyche.

By the way, notice that this system of selectively training and developing your psyche is analogous to how you progress as a bodybuilder or lifter—you assess your strengths and weaknesses, specialize on weak points until they are eliminated, etc.

It might also be a good precaution to remember that as you become increasingly well-developed, you will stand apart from the crowd and it might be a good idea to cultivate a thick skin or have a sense of humor, as some people will assume things about you that just might not be true. Take what happened to Doug Hepburn, some years ago, as an example.

Doug Hepburn was a very massively-developed, incredibly-powerful product of the 1950s— Doug was so strong that even without drugs or wraps, he could have mopped the floor with most of the champion powerlifters emerging for years afterward. When you are that strong and have close to 300-pounds of muscle piled on a five foot nine inch frame, people might be prone to jump to conclusions, as when someone once asked Doug, "What's it like to be all brawn and no brains?"

"I don't know," Doug replied, "what's it like to be neither?" *Touche!*

Finally, just because someone is incredibly successful, don't assume he is merely compensating for a massive inferiority complex: Success is usually tied to achievement motivation, which is tied to self-confidence—the exact opposite of inferiority feelings. Don't get ahead of yourself, however, in reaching for the sky or you'll topple over like a high-rise without a solid foundation. Eliminate feelings of inferiority, then add a few stories of self-confidence, followed by new levels of achievement motivation and before you know it, you will have reached dizzying heights of success.

Keep training, between your ears as well as in the gym, and next month IronMind® will help you race toward the winner's circle by detailing a program for smashing through some psychological roadblocks. Start your engines.

7 Remodeling Inferior Interiors—Part II

L ast month we introduced those nasty little psychological gremlins, inferiority complexes, identified their origins, pointed out just how common they are, and briefly touched on the recommended strategy for squashing them. In fact, we made the bold claim that you can use your psychological soft spots to spur yourself to greater achievements. Let's quickly review our general strategy before we lay out a program for bulking up your psyche.

Last month we outlined the multi-stage strategy of direct confrontation. The four major stages in this process are:

1) Identify your soft spots,
2) Reality test to see if your expectations are reasonable,
3) Develop and implement an action plan, and
4) Reassess yourself to see whether your program needs adjustment.

This month, we're going to put this process under a magnifying glass, fill in the details and leave you with enough information to start a bulk and power routine for your psyche. Inferior interiors are about to be remodeled into show places.

If you're not honest when you identify your soft spots, you might as well bag the rest of the program, because it just won't work without a frank self-appraisal. Almost by definition, most people don't relish dwelling on their weak points, but if you can't acknowledge them, you can't eliminate them any more than you can build up your 14-inch arms if you keep thinking they already look like Mr. O material. How do you identify where you're too soft or small psychologically? Begin with social comparisons: When you compare yourself to others, what makes you the most envious?

For example, are you always saying, "If only I were as tall/rich/built/popular/etc. as..."? Your self-talk can reveal details of your psyche just as concretely as a photograph portrays your physique or as your training diary defines your lifting ability. Use the tool of self-talk analysis in exactly the same way visual data guides your bodybuilding programs and your performance log guides your lifting programs.

We're going to map the results of the self-talk analysis, so get out a piece of paper and write down something that you're sensitive about—general shyness, your height, the shape of your nose, or whatever else it might be. Put it in the middle of the page and circle it. As more ideas come out of your self-talk analysis, write them down, with a circle for each, on the same sheet of paper. Free associate, using each idea generated from your self-talk analysis, to possibly identify another, and use lines to connect the circled words that are related.

For example, you might first think of "money," which might make you think "Porsche," which might make you think "recognition." We'll call the last concept in the chain the "terminal point" and put a heavy circle around it. Don't be surprised if your paths cross, and more than one chain leads to the same terminal point. For example, you might start with "education," which leads to "college degree" which also leads to "recognition."

If you're not convinced that the self-talk analysis has pinpointed where your psyche could best use a little added beef or if you just want to get another perspective, try the same exercise, but use situation avoidance as your guide. For example, do you always duck out of parties/public-speaking/big contests/etc. We vote with our feet all the time, and where we don't walk is just as revealing as where we do. Complete your situation avoidance map just as described for the self-talk analysis, except that when you free associate after each word you circle, think about the why or how. For instance, suppose you start off with "parties" in your situation avoidance map and when you free associate, you realize that you avoid parties because you're trying to avoid having to "meet people," which makes you nervous because those situations make you "feel dumb."

Time now to move on to the second stage of our process, reality testing, so gather your maps. Look at everything you circled and pick the one item you'd most like to work on. It might be something that gives you twinges of insecurity from many different angles, which should show up in your maps as the end point of sever paths. Sometimes the most important item to you doesn't show up that frequently, but it's something that just really hits a nerve. Remember, this isn't a public exercise, so be honest with yourself and just pick what matters most to *you*.

Look at what you picked, and ask yourself whether it's realistic to focus on it. When you conduct this evaluation, be sure to consider all the angles. For example, if you are five-feet two-inches tall, it might not be realistic to concentrate on becoming an NBA center, but that's no reason why you shouldn't attack and destroy any qualms you might have about not having your head in nosebleed territory.

By the way, don't be too hasty about simply rejecting something that gnaws at your confidence, thinking that if you just label the concern as being an "unrealistic," all your anxiety will instantly disappear. It won't, so try to sift through the broad concept that's bugging you, tossing out the unrealistic portions, but keeping the portions you can attack.

Everything you've done so far in this exercise has been preparation for the third stage, developing your action plan. If it helps, think of stage one as being analogous to the stretching you do before you attack the weights and stage two as the warm-ups you do before you hit the heavy iron. Stage three is akin to your heavy sets—this is the home of all the reps that make you grow bigger and stronger. Begin this stage by free associating on your selected concept once again, but this time identify a range of examples of this confidence-killer.

For example, if you picked "social skills," you might list a variety of situations that make you feel insecure, all representing things you'd like to master: meeting new people at parties, negotiating for a raise, smiling at people you'd like to talk to, handling yourself with grace in a fancy restaurant, asking someone for a date, and so on. Generate at least a few of examples, and ten or so would be even better. Write them down on a piece of paper.

We're going to build a mastery-ladder now, taking the examples of your primary confidence-crusher and arranging them in order of their psychological clout. If you one of your examples absolutely turns your ego into jelly and leaves you hiding in the closet, put it on the top rung of your ladder. Put the example of the situation that kicks you in the psychological shins, slowing you down but not knocking you out, at the bottom of your ladder. Sort out your examples like this, filling in as many rungs of your ladder as you need. Now we're ready to climb the ladder, one rung at a time, mastering each situation and eliminating your self-doubt with each step.

"Thanks for helping me organize what makes my ego shake," you say, "but how about some tips for dealing with these situations? I need some help climbing this ladder!"

The good news is that if you go through the analyses we recommended, a few basic principles and tools will work wonders on the puniest psyche. Do your maps, run through the reality testing exercise and construct your mastery ladder. Next month IronMind® will give you some climbing tools which will help you fly up the ladder, adding muscle to your ego as surely as squats-plus-milk will pack it on your bones.

8 Building a Superior Interior

When Sir Edmund Hillary was asked why he had risked life and limb to climb Mount Everest, he gave his immortal reply, "Because it is there." You're going to climb the mastery ladder you built last month for an equally important reason: to make your inferiority complex disappear. Hillary had Sherpas, ice axes, ropes, oxygen and a lot of climbing expertise to help him on his assault of the world's highest peak. This month we're going to give you a few techniques and tools to help you reach the top of your world.

Reviewing for just a moment, we have learned that just about everyone has some psychological soft spots—inferiority complexes if you will. We established how these little demons get hatched, and asserted that the best way to wipe them out was to square off and face them head on. To help prepare you for battle, we had you develop a detailed map of the enemy territory by analyzing two things: what you say to yourself and what types of situations you tend to avoid. From these analyses you assembled a mastery ladder, ranking examples of your psychological bugaboos from the least vexing to the most vexing. Hang on now as we prepare for a quick trip to the top of your ladder.

The first tool we'd like to introduce is based on what clinical psychologists call "systematic desensitization," a lot of syllables for a straightforward, portable and powerful mind-shaping technique. In the classic clinical application, the therapist creates a hierarchy of fear-arousing situations ("You are standing on the couch to hang a picture" ... "You are dangling by your fingertips from the top edge of El Capitan"). Notice that the similarity of this structure to your mastery ladder is not coincidental.

Next, the therapist will teach the client deep relaxation techniques, along the lines of what IronMind® outlined in Chapter 4. Finally, the client gets deeply relaxed and the therapist asks him or her to imagine the first scene on the hierarchy (the least fearsome one), trying to stay very relaxed while imagining it.

The logic here is that a process called "counterconditioning" will take place: The relaxation response is incompatible with fear, so by linking the fear-inspiring images to the pleasant relaxation response—voila!—the fear will evaporate. The therapist gradually moves up the hierarchy, as long as the client can manage to hold both the feared image and the relaxation response. If fear wins out, the image is dropped and they will drop down a notch or two on the hierarchy and gradually work their way back up. Think of this approach as being akin to the way you cycle your way up to handling your maximum weights: You start with something manageable, gradually increase the load until you hit a local maximum, at which point you drop down and begin another cycle. Just as you can build your body with this approach, the same is true of your mind.

You are going to use the same process to conquer your mastery ladder—one by one, you are going to imagine the vexing steps on your ladder while maintaining a calm and confident feeling. Start by going through the structured relaxation exercise. Now imagine the first scene on your ladder—if you can do this without having your sense of calmness and confidence disturbed, go for the next step. If it knocks you a little off balance, don't worry: Drop the image and relax again. When you are feeling good, reintroduce the image, but start very gradually by nibbling around the edges first and gently easing your way toward the center. Keep at it in this way until you have mastered your whole ladder.

This approach is considered *cognitive*, because it is focused between your ears. Another way to conquer your ladder—and a more direct one—is through *behavioral* techniques, an action-oriented approach which is centered on actual experiences, not just mental imagery.

Behavioral approaches are steeped in *doing* and because we're talking about doing exactly what you are most terrified of, we'll show you some techniques for containing the fear factor to manageable levels.

The first technique is to stick closely to the order of events on your mastery ladder—don't think you will speed up your progress by skipping a step here or there. The idea of *gradually* boosting your stress levels in this exercise is exactly the same as the progressive resistance approach you take in the gym. Jumping to a 400-pound bench before you're ready won't build you up—it will just get you pinned to the bench. The same thing is true on your mastery ladder. And just as getting over-zealous in the gym can slow down your progress with aches, pains and injuries, getting ahead of yourself on your mastery ladder will only slow your ascent: You will probably be forced to retreat two steps for the one you tried to skip. So your watchword for the greatest progress is *steady* effort.

The second technique that can really add some zip to your progress up your mastery ladder is, as the Beatles sang, a little help from your friends. To be more specific, one of the absolutely most powerful attitudinal-behavioral change techniques available to clinical psychologists is called "participant modeling." As you guessed from its name, participant modeling proceeds by having another person walk through whatever you're scared to do while you watch, and then he or she helps you do it. Dramatically demonstrating the power of this technique, it's regularly used to cure snake phobias. You'd be amazed by the number of people who were absolutely terrified of snakes but could handle them with aplomb after a quick participant modeling treatment. Miracle cures, anyone?

And what if the reptiles you're fleeing are more social in nature? Like school-, work-, or party-situations? No matter. What gets you up to speed in handling one type of snake works just as well for another. Bring your best friend along to the party where you know you will be bumping into someone you're not quite confident enough to start talking to on your own. Guaranteed company isn't the only reason lots of people cruise the singles bars in pairs--it's a lot easier to make the tough moves by following someone else's lead. Scared to ask your boss for a raise, but don't think it'll work to bring your mother along to the meeting? Talk to some other people who have gone through the ordeal--get some pointers and use their experiences to script your own successful encounter.

This last example builds on the therapeutic technique called "symbolic modeling," wherein you don't get a live demonstration, but at least you can vicariously experience successful management of the difficult situation. Don't short-change vicarious exposure to successful modeling in feared situations, because it can be an extremely effective way to boost your psychological bulk and power—in fact, when you can't get a participant modeling session, nothing else is likely to be as potent a confidence builder as training with a good symbolic model. Even if you can manage to rely upon participant modeling throughout your conquest of your mastery ladder, you'll only aid your progress by throwing in a little symbolic modeling on the side.

Identify your fears, put them in order, and one by one you should be able to kick the stuffing out of them by using the techniques outlined above. In fact, you'll probably knock them off so fast that you'll wonder why you dragged around all that excess baggage of unnecessary fear for so many years.

Also, since confidence, like muscle, carries itself, don't be surprised to find yourself becoming a little lighter on your feet after you have trained on this program for a little while.

How long for some real progress? Remember what we said in an earlier column about not expecting these techniques to work in just one session any more than you'd expect to finish your calves in one trip to the gym. But the nice thing is that if you train on this program, you'll probably be able to march up a mastery ladder in much less time than it takes to pack another quarter inch on your lower legs. Since we're building your most important body part—your mind—that's particularly incredible. And if you need some added motivation to follow this routine, just think about how your progress could save you from an embarrassing moment or two down the road. Right Napoleon?

9 Shakin' the Gonna-Lose Blues

Billy Beaten remembers the first time he entered a contest—how he *KNEW* before he even signed in that he was going to end up in last place, and did—and how he's been bringing up the rear ever since. Living just down the hall from Billy and training at the same gym, Wanda Winner also remembers her first contest—how excited she was, and how she felt confident that even if she didn't capture top honors, she'd be in the hunt, which turned out to be exactly what happened. Funny thing is that Billy always expects the worst, usually doesn't try very hard to make the good things happen, and often ends up with just what he expected. Wanda, on the other hand, often enters the exact same situations as Billy, but she expects the best, and she usually gets it.

Billy Beaten has a bad case of what psychologists call "learned helplessness"—he's suffering from an affliction that has robbed him of his hope, and left him passive and awaiting the worst in just about any situation he encounters. Wanda Winner is just the opposite—she's brimming with confidence, always gives it her all, and carries her can-do optimism everywhere she goes.

How do some people learn helplessness? And if you're singing the "I'm Gonna Lose" blues today, how can you change to Wanda's "Winner's War Whoop" tomorrow?

"Learned helplessness" is the psychologist's label for quitting before you even start in a challenging situation: You throw in the towel at the bell for the first round. Sad to say, lots of people are afflicted with this reaction, and even sadder to say, it can be learned in just one situation, if it's sufficiently traumatic. The good news is that you can do some things that will decrease the chances of ever succumbing to the syndrome in the first place. And you also un-learn the reaction—with the help of a good psychological detoxification program. Let's get started by seeing how people learn helplessness.

In the laboratory, the classic experimental design for teaching helplessness involves putting the poor test subjects—dogs, rats and humans have all been used—in situations where they cannot escape from something unpleasant. As you can guess, the classic paradigm involves signalling that a shock is about to be delivered, but making it impossible for the test victims to escape from the shock. In later tests where these experimental subjects *can* escape from the shock, they don't even try—they've learned helplessness. If we could interview some of the dogs or rats used for these studies, they would probably tell us just what the humans say: Their early experience with the shocks taught them that all was futile—that what they did had no impact on their environment or their fate. Therefore, they "adapted" to their environment by not even bothering to try.

Randall J. Strossen, Ph.D./*IronMind*   **25**

People can be conditioned in the same way in the real world, and a popular explanation of why generation after generation of a family can remain stuck in a squalid ghetto hinges on the same logic: People can learn despair and come to accept their situations as futile, if disappointment and oppressive conditions are heaped upon them. In the same way, anyone who goes to a lot of bodybuilding or lifting contests can name at least one person who is beaten before the event even starts, and does the same thing contest after contest after contest. Fortunately, people can also learn to redirect their thinking, to become positive and purposeful, and this is how it's done.

The old line about an ounce of prevention being worth a pound of cure is applicable here, so let's begin by discussing how you can immunize yourself against learned helplessness. The key here is to learn mastery—in whatever small steps are required. Don't think you can start too small here because you can't: Begin wherever you can to prove to yourself that what you do does make a difference, that you can control your situation, that you are the master of your destiny. If you're bummed out about your bodybuilding progress, start by focussing on one small goal: Gaining or losing five pounds, not cheating on your ab work, putting half an inch on your chest, dropping refined sugar products, etc. If you're thinking about throwing in the towel on your lifting career, try the same approach of measured goal setting: Plan a cycle that will boost one of your assistance lifts by 15 pounds, improve your snatch with a period of technique work with light weights, make a small step toward the bodyweight class you'd like to compete in, etc.

Regardless of your endeavor, your goals should have four qualities. Each goal should be:
1) relevant—it should be clearly related to what you want to achieve,
2) objective—it should involve clearly observable, measurable events,
3) manageable—keep it modest and achievable, and
4) scheduled—set a time frame or deadline for accomplishing each.

If you really want to attack this program with gusto, get out a sheet of paper, and write down your goals with a brief explanation of how and why it satisfies each of these criteria. Hang on to the sheet of paper. Next, make sure you meet your goals, and then write down the completion dates. Now this piece of paper is your first diploma of proven success—earn some more!

It might sound suspiciously simple, but creating structured success experiences will arm you to defend your sense of self-control when the odds are against you. As you gain a little steam on this program, start to keep track of the things you have accomplished in your life that were challenges, maybe even things that you surprised yourself by accomplishing. These accomplishments need only to have personal meaning—don't worry if you haven't won public acclaim for your acts of historical significance and unvarnished valor. When the chips are down, and you're facing an impossible situation, give yourself pep talks, drawing from your past successes. Remember: Nothing succeeds like success, so go get some for yourself.

Another factor that can help you avoid learning helplessness is to fully acknowledge what's predictable, even if unpleasant and unavoidable, in your environment. For example, only one person wins any contest—that's not too pleasant for all the other competitors, but it's a predictable, unavoidable fact. You can weather possible psychological defeat in this type of situation by recognizing beforehand that only one person will win the contest, and planning to continue undaunted should that person not be you. This should also free you to go ahead and try your hardest to become that person. And be realistic in terms of predicting outcomes based on your relative performance level: Don't expect to beat Ed Coan if you're benching 275 pounds, and squatting and deadlifting 450 pounds—you can predict what will happen if he shows up at your next lifting meet. Just go ahead and lift, and try to pick your contests more carefully in the future if you're after first-place trophies.

Illusory control is better than no control, so superstitious rituals can help prevent or cure cases of learned helplessness. In fact, going back to our old friend the research studies with shocking results, if people only *believed* they could control the unpleasant events—even if they couldn't—it helped to inoculate them against learning helplessness. Maybe it's not time to throw away those lucky posing trunks, or to trade in your old lifting belt after all. On the other hand, if success has been a little scarce of late, it might be time to go out and get some lucky new training clothes—something that makes you feel like the winner you really are.

"Once burned, twice shy" describes the reaction of people who have thoroughly learned helplessness, but there is a way out of the trap. The objective here is to teach the victim that he or she really does have control over the environment, even if it means literally dragging them through some drills. For example, the laboratory animals that had learned to not even try to escape the shock had to be physically moved when the shock signal came on.

What happened next proves the symmetry of these adaptive links: Just as repeated failures created an expectation of future failure, the success experiences created the expectation of future success. Within a few trials of being dragged out of the "hopeless" situation, the test subjects relearned hope and began to escape when put back in the original situation. So too with people in more complex situations: Do whatever is necessary to show yourself that you control even the slightest portion of your destiny and you are well on your way to becoming free of fatalistic limitations.

Let's summarize the key points, so you can put this program to work for yourself:

• We all enter situations with expectations, some for success and others for failure.

• Histories of failure create expectations of failure and histories of success create expectations of success.

• Your expectations will shape your results: Expect success and you are likely to succeed. Expect failure and that's what you are likely to get.

• You can create expectations of success by engineering success and noticing your accomplishments.

• Accomplishments tend to snowball, so one small accomplishment can quickly roll into something awesome. The key is to just get going in the right direction and to keep going.

We all like to think of ourselves as active, capable agents who control our destinies, and many of our worst fears involve thoughts that we are being controlled by others, and are doomed to failure. What you expect—self-control or manipulation, success or failure—is largely what you will get. Go ahead, we dare you: Think big, act big, and *GET BIG RESULTS*!

10 Like Body, Like Mind: Become Some*body*

You know the story about the 97-pound weakling who used to hide in his bedroom, never had a date and would rarely appear in public because of all the sand he'd get kicked in his face. And you know how he sent away for a muscle building course, and emerged 90-days later with a physique that would inspire terror on the pro-bodybuilding circuit. Plus you know how he went on to win fame and fortune, and lived happily ever after since he was successful not just physically, but socially, economically and just about every other way you could think of. Nice story, but it never was clear just how changing one's body would change one's mind—how building or removing physical lumps could change the way you saw yourself and the way others saw you.

Can this happen? Does successful bodybuilding create a basis for success in the other parts of your life? Can the progress you make in the gym transfer itself to progress at school, work and getting along with others? You bet, and here's how it works.

You might not recognize the name William H. Sheldon, even if it was Dr. Sheldon who developed the theory of somatotypes you probably hear about all the time: endomorphs, mesomorphs, and ectomorphs (commonly known as fats, thicks and thins, respectively). Psychologists refer to Sheldon's approach as a "constitutional theory of personality" because Sheldon classified people on the basis of his three primary body types (or "somatotypes"), and further theorized that each of these body types had a dominant personality pattern.

The way Sheldon's theory worked, people could be rated from one to seven in terms of how much they resembled the perfect endomorph, the perfect mesomorph, and the perfect ectomorph: A score of one was very low, a score of four was average and a score of seven was very high. Thus, a 363 would be a husky individual, a 235 would be thin, and a 642 would be, well, round and smooth. As you'd guess, most top bodybuilders and lifters are primarily mesomorphs, but there's a lot of latitude for variations and with a little practice you can recognize how these different physical types appear.

For example, John Grimek is an essentially perfect mesomorph, Frank Zane is more of an ectomorph and Paul Anderson is more of an endomorph—so you can see that success comes in different shapes. And people can render amazing changes to their physiques: Compare photos of Dave Draper from the time of he was preparing for his 1963 Mr. A victory and to his present physique—where'd the endo go? If you really want to knock off your socks, dig up pictures of Bruce Randall, who bulked up to over 400 pounds in the late 1950s—in his quest to become the strongest man in the world—and then rapidly trimmed down to around 200 and picked up a Mr. Universe title. Naturally, you'll want to run to a mirror or to some photos and rate yourself.

What Sheldon did next isn't nearly as well-known as his basic body type research: He linked each somatotype to a personality pattern, or temperament. Endomorphs had a temperament called "viscerotonia," which included the traits of being sociable, relaxed, even-tempered and easy to get along with. Mesomorphs had a temperament called "somatotonia," which included being outgoing, adventurous, vigorous and assertive, if not outright aggressive. Ectomorphs had a temperament called "cerebrotonia," which included being inhibited, secretive and inclined toward solitude.

Bodybuilding, by definition, involves changing the appearance of your physique, so if Sheldon's theory holds up, it also means changing your personality at the same time—so all those old claims about fixing up your body and everything else good following could have some merit. Let's walk through an example with our friend, the 97-pound weakling, Steve Bean.

Steve Bean, or "Stevie," as his mother called him, weighed about 140 at five-feet eleven-inches tall. He wasn't that crazy about reading or watching TV, but that didn't mean that he spent much of his free-time outside of his bedroom. Stevie liked to dream about being popular, scoring winning touchdowns, hitting the top score on the big tests at school and going on to clean up in later years as a plastic surgeon, but for now, it was only fantasies in the safety of his bedroom. You might say that Stevie was a shy, insecure, retiring type, even if he'd like to think of himself as a junior James Bond.

One day Stevie's dad dragged home a set of weights, tossed them down in the basement and told Stevie to do four simple things: squat, bench, row and drink milk. In two months, none of Stevie's old clothes fit him any more, and guys who never talked to him before at school were asking him to come out for the football team, and more than one girl was openly asking how she could get a date with him. Stevie was starting to feel pretty good about himself and his future and now the real choices seemed pretty good. No doubt about it, Stevie was a new man—inside and out—and the whole world could see it. Even his dog quit growling at him—Stevie was finally getting a little respect.

Sounds pretty amazing, but that's really how it works: When you build your body, you look different, feel different, think different and act different. Other people, not being blind, notice the changes and so they act differently toward you. And don't think this is just a bunch of comic book hype either—you can go dig up fancy research studies about how physical appearance influences self-perceptions and social judgments on everything from intelligence to honesty, starting with little kids and working its way up to settings as diverse as courtrooms and the halls of corporate America.

Hardcore psych types will hasten to point out that Sheldon's research took some heavy heat in scientific circles as serious questions were raised about the details of his experimental procedures. That's fine, but even if you take the narrowest view and accept that his particular research program did not provide bombproof evidence supporting his theories, you can't conclude that his theory was necessarily off track. And you certainly can't conclude that one's body type is unrelated to one's self-image or to the way others will perceive you—the evidence for these links is substantial. And since you also can't quibble with the effectiveness of well-planned bodybuilding programs to render dramatic physical transformations, you are left with but one conclusion: Like body, like mind.

So the next time you're feeling a little lazy, not quite sure whether the bigger arms or smaller waist are worth the trouble, just remember what you're really doing: Becoming some*body*!

11 Outright Cures for Inner Conflicts

You want two more inches on your arm—no doubt about it—but in terms of sticking to your one-more-rep training and never missing a workout, there's been a little waffling. Like last week when you skipped the gym to go to the beach and the week before when you missed because you had a headache, even if it didn't keep you from going to a flick followed by a party, instead. And how about all those sets when you say to yourself, "It's okay if I save a little on this one, I'll make it up on the next set." Funny how the next set also sees you drop the bar with at least three reps left in your biceps. Sure would be nice to have another two inches up your sleeve, though.

An uncommon situation? No way. An incurable situation? Hardly.

What you're facing is the most basic inner conflict going—a fundamental "approach-avoidance conflict." Don't let the name throw you, because all this psychological label means is that you have a conflict between your interest in doing something (that's the approach part) and your reluctance to follow through as required (that's the avoidance part). The conflict is the natural result of simultaneously trying to run toward something (big arms, in our case), and running away from what's necessary to reach your goal (hard work, in our example). Let's develop a plan for defusing the conflict and putting you squarely back on the path to your goals.

One of your landmark bouts with the approach-avoidance conflict was the first time you went to the beach as a child. Chances are good that you were drawn to the water and ran toward it, only to gradually slow down as you got closer, and in all likelihood, you actually stopped short of jumping in—turning around instead and running back before you got your feet wet. Back and forth, back and forth, before you finally jumped in or left altogether—not realizing that you would repeat this performance pattern throughout your life!

In the case of dealing with the ocean as a small child, the avoidance portion of your conflict is easily attributed to fear—after all, not being dumb, you realized that a big bad ocean had plenty of scary things in store for a thirty-pounder who didn't even know how to swim yet. Fear is one of the most common causes of our approach-avoidance conflicts, so let's explore it a little.

In the gym, fear can come in many forms: pain and injury are the two most common, but more subtle things like entering unknown territory and facing your destiny can enter the equation. Let's concentrate on fear of pain and injury right now and leave some of the more esoteric causes of fear for another time. How often do you simply quit early on a set of, let's say, squats because your legs have failed you or because you realistically fear ripping some connective tissue from the bone? And how often just because you purely and simply are tired of gasping for breath while putting up with burning legs and a bar on your back that's trying to take two inches off your height? Pain's real, and the best way to begin coping with it is to recognize that you'll probably have to put up with a lot of the stuff to reach your body-building or lifting goals. Gee, maybe that's why someone said, " No pain..." But don't let this fear-of-pain thing get out of hand: If you are sufficiently motivated and take your workouts one rep at a time, you'll walk all over pain, leaving it limp and hanging onto the ropes for dear life. Honest. So get motivated, don't look beyond the next rep, and then you can probably kiss fear-as-a-workout-killer goodbye.

A second very large class of reasons underlying approach-avoidance conflicts results from "impulse versus reason" confrontations taking place in your head. Here's how that goes.

Impulse is what made you buy the hot pink shoes you've worn once and since left in your closet, over in the corner next to the guitar you bought two years ago and never learned to play. Impulse can get you everything from a social disease on Friday night to a winning lottery ticket on Monday morning. Reason, of course, gets you to floss your teeth, always say "yes" to your boss and to save your money instead of buying a new CD player. Whereas reason is controlled, practical, and realistic, impulse is spontaneous, uncensored, irrational and everything else a good Puritan would despise. Impulse can also trick you into lightening up on your workout this side of championship-level performance. That last one might be your biggest concern, so let's take a closer look at it.

Impulse will attack you in one of your softest spots psychologically speaking, by appealing to your interest in "immediate gratification"—the preference for getting your goodies right here and now, thank you. So when it's time to train, impulse distracts you with all sorts of tempting alternatives to gym toil. Of course, since nobody ever built a 19-inch arm or reached a 900-pound squat in one workout, you can see the bind you are in as a bodybuilder or a lifter if you always succumb to the temptations of immediate gratification. What we need to help us deal with this dilemma is a technique that will let us have our cake and eat it too—something that will give us a sense of immediate gratification, while keeping us on track to reach our ultimate objectives. The answer lies in restructuring our goals a little.

When you have a fairly lofty goal, like putting another two inches of muscle on your upper arm, you are set up for temptation by the muse of immediate gratification. After all, putting two inches on your arm will probably require an overall bodyweight gain of around 25 pounds, and we don't know of any system short of Dr. Frankenstein's that offers to add that much muscle in just one session. That means that realistically speaking, there are going to an awful lot of opportunities when you will be tempted to do something other than train on the schedule leading to your bigger arms. To minimize your susceptibility to distractions, you need to reduce the time when you must train without getting reinforced by your progress, and the best way to do that is to break your overall objective in smaller steps.

For example, if you're on an effective bulk-building routine, you can put a quarter of inch on your arms in an amazingly short period of time—the progress will come so fast that if you have any motivation whatsoever, you will hit the quarter inch gain before you even have a chance to consider getting distracted. Better still, hitting the quarter-inch milestone will reinforce your commitment to your overall goal of packing on another two inches, so you keep going and reach the next quarter inch, and the next one...That's the process in a nutshell: Neutralize the impulses that thwart your progress by breaking down your overall objectives into manageably-small subgoals. Take your lifting progress one rep or one kilo at a time and your bodybuilding progress in fractions of an inch—these small increments will add up to giant gains.

The third main type of inner conflicts that will hurt your training progress results from "desire versus guilt conflicts." This set of conflicts is a special case of "reason versus impulse" and comes in many forms, but here's a general example. You were raised with a basic sense of values which included an appreciation for getting a good education, entering a respected profession, making solid progress economically and living, overall, a pretty mainstream existence. For some time, you've had a burning desire to flex with the best or heave the heaviest iron around. Now the stage has been set for a classic "guilt versus desire" conflict because every time you hit the gym, you think about your Uncle Max, a prosperous dentist whose life is governed by the straightforward philosophy: drill, fill, bill. A big house with a pool and a new Cadillac every year are his badges of success.

Problem is that you're looking for more size here, less fat there, more power over there, and getting into the local Rotary Club might be less important to you than what brand of chalk they use in your gym. If you're like many middle-class Americans, a little voice (called your conscience) will probably keep telling you that championship-level bodybuilding or lifting is not a good idea—the chances of success are slim, the future is uncertain and the potential economic rewards don't merit the risks—and that you should be hitting the books, putting in a little OT at work or at least playing a round of golf, instead of moving metal in the gym.

Knock out the guilt with a little help from your old friend reason and a little cognitive coaching: Start talking to yourself about what you are doing and why: "I've chosen to reach (some bodybuilding/ lifting goal), and even though not everyone agrees with me, it's extremely important to me to reach it." That's it, keep going: "To reach (your goal), I'll have to make some sacrifices (remind yourself what they are), but they're worth it, because (remind yourself why you picked your goal in the first place)." And so forth. You might have been told that only crazy people talk to themselves, but the truth is that unless you want to be like your Uncle Max you'd be crazy not to remind yourself what you're all about, including the how and the why.

Let's recap the three main causes of the inner conflicts that might be interfering with your training progress and how you can neutralize each of them:

1) *fear* is most often going to arise from having to face pain and you can manage pain a) by staying motivated, and b) by taking your workouts one rep at a time,

2) *impulses* that distract from your goal can be minimized by breaking your overall goal into sub-goals, each quite easily achieved and each motivating you to reach the next one, and

3) *guilt* about maybe not following in your Uncle Max's footsteps can be reduced or eliminated by constantly reminding yourself what you want to do, why, and how you are going to do it.

Be sure to make room for these conflict-resolution tools the next time you pack your gym bag, and you'll gain more muscle and strength than you could from just about anything else you might bring along.

12 Mental Rehearsal: Mirage, Miracle Or Mediator?

Once upon a time there was a weight-nut named Frankie. Frankie liked being big and he liked being strong, so it was no surprise that he could usually be found doing one of three things: training, eating or sleeping. Frankie was no fool, though, and when his old way of doing things quit producing results, Frankie consulted an and older and wiser friend of his who turned him onto visualization, claiming that making better use of the space between his ears was the fastest way for Frankie to start gaining again.

So Frankie followed his friend's advice and began to incorporate formal mental rehearsal sessions into his hectic life: Twice a day, Frankie would kick off his Reeboks, shed his T-shirt and 501s, slip into his latest baggies and flop down on his back under the shade of his favorite poolside umbrella and imagine his success. Now Frankie never did things in a small way so when he got into this mental training thing, he also didn't slough off—two daily sessions of fifteen minutes apiece soon gave way to three, each breaking the 30-minute barrier, and then a fourth session was added daily. Figuring he was onto a good thing, Frankie built on his momentum.

Not that Frankie was just kicking back, mind you. He was really doing his mental rehearsal drill all right, staying positive and sharply focussing on his goals, which could never be accused of modesty: "And in the final posedown...Lee Haney and Frankie... ." And Frankie wasn't narrow in his goals either, as he took on and slew not just Mr. O, but a couple of world champion powerlifters and a great Soviet weightlifter whose name he couldn't even pronounce. And all this stuff was starting to make such a difference that Frankie had everyone in his gym talking.

"Where's Frankie?" was the gist of it.

The is truth is that Frankie was starting to skip some workouts and it was looking like a bad trend when he missed a week straight. To Frankie's way of thinking, he hadn't broken training, he was just, you know, putting a little more effort into the mental stuff, "And that's really the key, right?" was Frankie's reply.

Well, yes and no, but the simple and brutal truth is that the only reason for mental rehearsal is to facilitate action—and don't let anyone fool you into believing otherwise. So if you're spending all your time doing imaginary training and never actually hitting the weights, you will get great results all right, but the catch is that they will only be imaginary. This might be why Bob Hoffman once said, "If you lift imaginary weights and turn imaginary wheels, you'll get strong enough to lift imaginary weights and turn imaginary wheels."

Let's talk about this one a little because using mental rehearsal is such a popular topic these days that it's assuming the proportions of motherhood and apple pie.

Properly done, mental rehearsal won't grow hair on a barren scalp, but according to its fans, that's about the only thing it can't do: From Olympic champion downhill skiers, to PGA money leaders, to Mr. O winners, to the strongest men and women in the world—everyone will tell you that positive mental imagery is the key to success. Some people will even tell you that it can cure cancer. What you might not have heard, though, is that the mental stuff is just a precursor, or facilitator, for the results you want. Here's how it works, and how it doesn't.

Even a small sample of mental power is fairly astounding: Imagining a particular athletic movement produces the identical pattern of muscular responses as actually performing the movement; it takes seasoned race car drivers exactly the same time to imagine driving a race course as it does to really drive a lap; and the real pros at mental control can even perform such novel tricks as stopping their hearts (please don't try that one at home kids). Because mental rehearsal has such amazing real world correlates, it's easy to mistakenly conclude that the mental-physical link is direct and inter-changeable, but it's not.

What you think definitely affects what you do and vice versa. *Affects* is the key word here and so is the idea that the mind-body link works in both directions. Imagine yourself surrounded by a pile of gold coins and really get into it: Picture the shape of the mound, the exact hue of the gold, the inscription on the coins, etc. Did you make the coins appear? Then why would you expect the identical process to just pop an inch on your calves or add 50 kilos to your top deadlift?

What your imaginary journey will do is still pretty magical, though, and it will help you achieve your goals, but not just all by itself. Here are some the key things mental rehearsal will do:

1) Increase motivation—One of the biggest benefits of a good mental training program is to boost and maintain your motivation. Remember, real motivation is the difference between just being pumped while you're looking at Mike Neveux's latest photos of your hero today and actually going to the gym and doing what's necessary to get a pump tomorrow. Motivation is probably the single most important factor separating winners from everyone else, and successful mental rehearsal is one of the most effective tools around for putting motivation to work in your corner.

2) Accelerate learning—Suppose you're trying to learn a complex movement, whether it's your new posing routine, how to do a clean and jerk or maybe even ski a tough mountain: Mental rehearsal can be almost like a magic wand. Remember what we said about mental rehearsal producing a pattern of muscular responses identical to those produced by the actual act? That's right and that's how mental training can help you learn some pretty tough moves: It can add another dimension to your training and it gives you a way to get more mileage from your actual physical drills. For best results, alternate your physical and mental practice—use the mental training to improve your actual execution and use your physical practice to help form clearer images of even better execution...so go back and forth between real practice and imaginary practice.

3) Build confidence—Maybe the single biggest obstacle to breaking new ground for yourself—whether in terms of your physique, your strength, or even something like your career—is having the confidence to actually commit yourself to the hilt in pursuit of your goal. Without supreme self-confidence, you will never try as hard as will probably be required for success and with it, you'll probably jump right past people from a superior gene pool or with better social connections.

One of the real ironies of building self-confidence is that actual success experiences are the most potent way to build this positive belief in yourself, but mental training can help prepare you to go out and collect some success experiences for yourself. Mental rehearsal enters the picture because seeing yourself perform as desired in your mind's eye makes it easier to believe in yourself when the rubber hits the road. After you've done your 400-pound bench press in your head enough times, and trained in accordance with this goal, you are going to approach the actual weight fully expecting to lift it—you will be confident of your success.

Of course, these three things are nothing to sneeze at, and they set the stage for very impressive real gains in just about any endeavor you choose, so it's easy to mistakenly think that mental rehearsal directly produces the results you're after. But it won't—you have to go the next step and really go through the motions for yourself after you've dreamed about your greatness.

What all the mental rehearsal in the world will never do for you is actually set foot on the stage or the lifting platform, so, as Hoffman suggested, if you do nothing but imaginary training, all your victories will only be imaginary, as well. On the other hand, if you're really smart about it, you'll use mental rehearsal to 1) boost and maintain your motivation, 2) accelerate your learning, and 3) build self-confidence, and then you'll cash in these three chips for some really impressive results.

So don't neglect your mental training along the way, but always remember that the only reason you are doing all this mental rehearsal is to make it easier for you to achieve your real-world goals, and that will take something beyond lying on your back. Finally, remember what Frankie concluded: "To dream is cool/but without some sweat,/you can surely bet/you're just a fool!"

13 Outpacing Pain

When Roger Peterson looked in the mirror, he didn't like what he saw: a pencil neck gracing a flat and narrow torso which sprouted four stalks which passed for a pair of arms and legs. If he hadn't been spending most of his money on pricey super-supplements and most of his time on Mr. Blister's all-day arm routine, he might not have minded what he looked like, but the truth was obvious: Roger needed some muscle mass, so much that saying *more* muscle mass was giving him too much credit. Desperate for a solution, Roger decided to try the no-frills squat routine that had worked for his buddy, despite the warnings that he was going to have to run a painful gauntlet to reach his goal of piling an inch on his arms and several on his chest in a few short weeks. "Pain, ha!," he said, "I'm finally going to get bigger and stronger!"

Squats or not, anyone who is serious about making maximum progress in the iron world has to learn how to cope with some pain, so let's take a quick look at it and see how you can manage pain for better gains from your training. We're not promising to turn your next training session into a walk down Easy Street, but we can say that we have some proven pain-management techniques that could help you make the big gains you're after.

First, let's establish that pain serves a biological function that is no less important than ensuring that the species is preserved: Were it not for pain signals, we might walk around mutilating and killing ourselves without giving it a second thought. That's not the type of pain we're interesting in controlling. We want to help you manage the type of pain that is—almost by definition—a necessary by-product of championship level training. Remember what your junior high school PE teacher used to scream at you when you wanted to quit in the middle of his push-up drill? "If you stop just because you're tired, you'll never get any stronger." He was right, and his idea that you could just grit your teeth and squeeze past the pain barrier is part of the story, but how about a little added help from our friends, the research psychologists?

Given the role of pain in preserving life and limb, and the fact that pain signals are messages from nerve endings to the brain, you might think that pain is just a biological phenomenon. Then you would just say that the more intense the sensory input, the worse the pain and that would be the end of the story. Fortunately, pain has a very large psychological component; fortunately, that is, because that gives us an opportunity to put our minds to work on pain management. In fact, the "gate-control" theory of pain integrates the physiological and psychological factors, stating that the pain message sent up from the nerve endings is potentially modified by the brain's messages that are sent back down the system. What influences these messages from the brain?

As a small child, you got help learning to identify pain because when you did something potentially injurious, you got reassuring hugs for your effort. This is why children will sometimes look at their mothers after a fall to see whether or not they are supposed to cry. This is also why you can unlearn pain to some extent by simply relabelling your experience and trying to convince yourself that it really doesn't hurt. And that's a good start, but there are some other tools you'll want to bring to the gym, as well.

Our old pal motivation is a real big one, and something the hypnotism junkies might not know or be willing to tell you is that research has shown that basic, garden-variety motivation can help you withstand pain just as well as hypnosis, and the ability of hypnosis to help people withstand pain has long been one of its real selling points. So don't think you require hypnotherapy to crank out the growing reps: You can crash through the pain barrier and reach the growth stage by getting motivated. Keep your goals and rewards in mind at all times and your motivation will stay high.

Practice can also work absolute wonders in the pain control arena, and it's not restricted to exotic feats like walking barefoot across hot coals. You can adapt to pain just as you get used to any stimulus. If you want a very simple example of this process, consider the first time you ate Mexican hot sauce and how quickly you acclimated to the taste if you kept at it. It's the same process with other forms of pain, and don't neglect to complement your real world practice with a little mental rehearsal: Imagine yourself conquering the pain barrier for some good reason.

The standard approach to pain-control techniques in sports takes the tack of using either *associative* or *dissociative* techniques. Associative techniques openly embrace the painful phenomenon, recognizing for example that you are breathing hard, that your muscles burn, etc. Dissociative techniques avoid the painful cues by using distraction techniques, which boil down to thinking about anything but the task at hand.

Early research on these two distinct pain control techniques focused on long distance runners, and it was learned that the better runners emphasized associative techniques. These runners didn't stop at the fact that they hurt, but rather, they used their bodily messages to regulate their pace, stay within themselves, and so forth. Thus, associating with the pain gave the runner excellent cues for how to enhance their performance. The dissociative approach had originally provoked interest because the Tibetan monks who run 300 miles in 30 hours(!) were adept at these methods, but dissociation was also originally linked to the less-successful competitive runners. Later research straightened things out by concluding that *generally* associative techniques are superior, but there are *always* times when dissociative techniques are called for.

Let's put this theory into practice with one of the most painful—and productive—things you can do with a barbell: the classic 20-rep squat routine for fabulous gains in muscle mass. For the uninitiated, the guts of this routine is one set of 20 squats with your normal 10-rep poundage, with several deep breaths in between each rep. If that's not enough, you add five pounds to the bar every single workout. Don't be too quick to dismiss this program, because it's a safe bet that you will never work as hard on anything else in your life, and it's also a safe bet that you will pack on so much muscle a month that even the pharmaceutical folks will be envious. But first you have to get through the squats, and that means you have to stare down the tiger of pain. Let's use the techniques we discussed, focusing on association and dissociation, to grind out the set of squats.

Reps one through five might be a little uncomfortable because you're not fully warmed up yet, but they don't really hurt, so you can associate with what's going on in your body: your legs starting to pump up, your chest lifting and stretching out with each deep breath, and your pulse quickening as the breaths and the reps climb. You *associate* with these feelings, reminding yourself that what you have here is "growing cues"—the precursors to size and strength. Reps five to ten can still be handled with associative techniques, but you must be motivated to keep reminding yourself that the intensifying cues really just signal exactly what you want most: You are about to grow.

Reps ten to fifteen are pretty much where you will either win or lose the battle to complete the set, and this is when dissociative techniques can be very helpful. That's because by now, the pain could be getting so acute that you need a cognitive strategy that focuses on *shutting out* the negative messages ("I'm getting crushed...my lungs are on fire"), rather than one that focuses on the positive messages ("I'm growing," etc.). If you're really good at cognitive control, you might mentally leave the gym many miles behind and simply plow ahead at this point, but most people, Roger Peterson among them, need a little help in the form of *dissociative* techniques.

Effective dissociative techniques range from chanting a mantra to picturing a favorite spot in great detail, but when Roger asked his mental training consultant for some help, he didn't want to fool around with anything that was complicated, expensive or difficult to learn. His friend reminded Roger of the basics: 1) staying motivated by focusing on why he was following this routine, 2) using the mental rehearsal technique he had showed him a few months ago, and 3) remaining confident that his pain-control ability would improve with practice. Then he said two magic words to Roger: "Led Zeppelin." He recommended the song "When the Levee Breaks" played as loud as Roger's Walkman would go without distorting or producing ear damage—whichever came first. Alternatively, he said that he'd also had great results with Dire Straits' "Money for Nothing," but there was plenty of room for personal preferences.

So Roger followed his advice, pushed the pain barrier back long enough to stick with the squat program for 6 weeks and then he went out to buy some new clothes, because after having packed inches of muscle all over his body, it was time for a new wardrobe.

14 Top Gainers Observe: The Learning Curve

Remember how much progress you made in your early days of training? How you got bigger and stronger with just about every workout? It sure was easy to stay motivated then, wasn't it? Now things aren't so straightforward and if you actually plotted your "progress" lately, the line sure wouldn't be going straight up. Instead it might be pretty flat or maybe it would look like the ragged edge of a saw blade, with all its up-and-down spikes. It's as if your body has suddenly forgotten everything it once knew about how to make gains. What gives? How can you get back on the upward track?

For some solid insights into the process of making gains, let's turn to our friends the research psychologists and their good buddy, the learning curve. As you would guess, learning curves graphically show how competence or skill increases with practice. Since we're interested in knowing all we can about how to make progress, let's take a look at the classic learning curve and see what it tells us about your gains in the gym. We'll keep using the word "learning," but substitute or "progress" or "gains" if you would like.

In the make-believe world where theory and practice match, it's very easy to describe how learning takes place, and the whole process can be described in three neat stages: 1) after a warm-up period with little visible progress, 2) learning starts to really zoom, before 3) finally levelling off. This pattern is the classic S-shaped learning curve, so-named because it looks like a stretched-out S lying on its side. Let's take a closer look at this pattern and see how it relates to your work in the gym and your performance on the platform.

The flat initial period of the learning curve corresponds to the skill-acquisition phase. This is when you are learning how to execute a particular movement. As you would guess, learning complex movements, such as a squat snatch, or learning to get the right feel for somewhat subtle exercises, such as the Rader chest pull, takes longer than learning something as straightforward as a standard barbell curl. In this first stage, it might seem as if not too much is going on, since visible signs of progress might be absent.

Because you generally carry extra enthusiasm into a new endeavor, however, you march forward, brimming with confidence and eagerness, despite what the tape, mirror and scale tell you. And for good reason, because all of a sudden things click one day and you start progressing by leaps and bounds, ratcheting up a notch or two every time you train. It's as if you had to lay an invisible foundation to support your progress and once it was in place, the structure of your dreams grew before your eyes.

Then one day you felt a little off, but it didn't really seem to be anything to worry about in the wake of your recent gains. Not until you were a little off again, and again, and—bad news—yet again. And now you understood why

Richard Farina said, "Been down so long it looks like up to me." This is the dreaded flat portion of the classic learning curve, the vexing third stage which could well be the biggest bugaboo in your training today. What's going on and how can you super-charge yourself for progress once again?

The prevailing explanation for these annoying plateaus in learning curves is that you have reached the limit of your performance, given your current skill set. For example, when your power clean has been stalled out at 90 kilos for longer than you care to admit, it could easily be because your present level of skill just won't budge another kilo: Suppose you've learned to squeeze the bar off the floor with a flat back and straight arms, but you still swing the bar out from your body, and your second pull is more of a whimper than an explosion. Until you improve your form another notch, your power clean might stay just exactly where it is.

For the bodybuilder, "skill" involves not only executing your training movements correctly, but also knowing just how to hit the precise balance in your stress-recuperation equation for maximum growth. Sometimes you need to learn new ways to boost your productive stress and other times you need to learn new ways to boost your recuperation. We know of a fellow who asserts that there is no such things as overwork, just undernutrition, so let's concentrate on the idea of learning to boost your productive stress. The most direct way to increase the work load is to knock off more reps, slap on more weight, and/or decrease your rest periods. It's when your body can't adjust to these options that your progress stagnates: You have tapped out your ability to overload your muscles and as a result, have quit gaining. Help!

The standard advice at this stage is to take a short break from training, and it's a good way to go, as the rest can help you renew your enthusiasm, give your body a chance to catch up on its much-needed rest and might give your brain enough time to quietly boost key motor skills. It's also a good time to change your routine, as is also commonly advised, with the sage comment that "A change is as good as a rest." Let's get a little more specific about each of these approaches.

The idea behind the rest option is that, in effect, if you pause long enough to catch your breath, you'll be able to gird your loins for a really herculean effort, which will lead to legendary gains once again. Sounds simple, but it really works. Remember that you are resting with the objective of coming back to your training ready to melt iron with your renewed intensity; you are not just slowing down the overall pace of your training routine. Unless you are severely overtrained, about a week off should work miracles for you, so if it doesn't, keep reading.

Changing your routine is another potent way to restimulate your progress up the growth curve, and here's how you do it for best results: Find something that is different enough from your current routine to be refreshing, but close enough to jar yourself into the same sort of progress you were seeking in your old routine. For example, let's say your bench press is stalled out, and you're still 25-odd pounds this side of your objective. Our principle would suggest switching to something like heavy incline presses or dips, not high-rep cable crossovers. Think of the change in your routine as another path to the same goal you've always held, not a new route to a new goal, and you'll be on the right track.

Suppose you've rested and suppose you've changed programs and you still aren't getting anywhere? How can you get back on the steep part of the curve.

If you're injury-free, basically rested and feeling fresh psychologically, you need a way to regain the enthusiasm you had when you were gaining smoothly, and the best way to do that is to spark some gains. If that sounds like a circular process, that's because it is, but you can break the vicious circle by turning to your most important body part: your brain.

First, you've got to understand that learning curves are idealized, or stylized, representations of the path of progress, usually based on the average of many cases. This averaging process smooths out all the spikes that are sure to appear if any one person's progress were tracked, and makes everything look more orderly than it generally is. This is a vital insight, because once you realize that everyone progresses primarily in fits and starts, you'll be better prepared psychologically to cope with your flat periods or outright reversals. Sometimes just being armed with this knowledge gives trainees enough added zest to push on into the next growth zone, so keep reminding yourself that it's normal to hit periods of little progress, but if you persist, the gains will follow.

Second, when you get stuck in a third-stage plateau, think back to your days in stage one. What happened? That's right: Nothing at first and then, bang, explosive gains. Instead of looking at your present position as being the top of one learning curve, think of it as the bottom of the next one. That's because your progress as a bodybuilder or lifter isn't just one self-contained learning curve. Instead, your passage to mastery is like a staircase of one learning curve leading to the next one; some steps are short, some are steep, and some might even sag a bit, but their general direction is up. In this perspective, what you had viewed as periods of stagnation can now be appreciated as the forerunners of your next steps forward. This is a case where the half-empty glass proves to really be half-full.

It's easy to be enthusiastic when your arms are practically growing before your eyes and each time you max out on the bench you hoist more than the time before. But no matter how great and frequent they are, these glory days will fade into the night. This is the juncture where the champions are separated from everyone else, because the champions persevere even without any immediate outward sign of progress, while everyone else throws in the towel as soon as the guarantees of immediate gains disappear. Because you understand how the process works, you keep the faith in the tough times and gain, Gain, GAIN for your efforts.

15 The Two Sides Of Three-Point Shots—Part I

The first side of the three-point shot story comes from motivational psychologist Dr. Robert Kreigel and goes like this: Already possessing some of the deadliest skills in basketball, Magic Johnson sat down one day and asked himself a tough question, "What's the weakest aspect of my game." Next, he did something still tougher; he gave an honest answer. Finally, he did the toughest thing of all: He attacked his weak point head-on, and as they say, the rest is geometry. What we'd like is to have you apply the same process to your training, whether you are a competitive bodybuilder or lifter, or are just working out for your own satisfaction. Let's talk about it.

Most of us have a quick and well-trained response to our weak points: We run from them. Most of the running takes place in our heads, by simply denying the existence of our weak points, although sometimes our feet actually do the shuffling, but either way, we routinely fail to confront our weaknesses.

It happens all the time in your training. Let's say that you have rotten legs, but instead of ever working on them, you make sure that they are always covered. And if anyone ever asks you about them, you give your arm a menacing flex and say, "Later days, pal" and head over to the preacher bench. Lifters do the same thing, and sometimes they really get carried away, some to the point that they become pure one-lift specialists ("Hey, look at Mort, he's doing 25 pounds on the Weaver stick!"). Without getting personal, you can probably name bodybuilders and lifters who come in with the same weaknesses contest after contest, year after year.

And the same thing happens even more often outside the gym, where your weakness might be, for example, following through on ideas: One month you're going to import Arabian horses, the next you're restoring classic American cars and this month all you talk about is your concept for a fast-food chain. Mentally, you cope with your lack of follow through by rationalizing why each of your preceding ideas suffered a fatal flaw ("The horse market is out to pasture," "Exotics are the only real play in cars," and so forth), and if someone starts asking embarrassing questions ("Say Bob, how's that pony-deal coming along?"), you can suddenly notice the gleeb who has been making eyes at you from across the room and quickly excuse yourself.

The reasons for our persistent denial of our imperfections are deeply psychological, and are worth examining because in the safety of talking about people in general, we might learn some things we can apply to improve ourselves, in the gym and out.

Sigmund Freud and his followers would have it that we do not confront our weaknesses because to do so would threaten our egos, or our self-concepts. Freud gave this matter a great deal of thought and generated a long list of so-called "defense mechanisms" used to protect ourselves from painful thoughts.

For example, with *projection* we blame others for our difficulties, or attribute our own undesirable impulses to others. The person who always says, "Those judges hate me...it was all political" might be projecting his failures on others. Similarly, if you see the world as filled with nothing but people trying to hit on you or rip you off, you might be covering up your own impure motives by projecting them on others.

Compensation involves masking weaknesses by emphasizing a desirable trait or making up for shortcomings in one area via overgratification in another. For example, the folklore has it, of course, that bodybuilders compensate for frail brains and frailer egos by building up their bodies. Similarly, rags-to-riches stories of grand economic success are apparent cases of compensation.

Reaction formation involves blocking dangerous impulses by endorsing the opposite point of view. For example, people who are threatened by unacceptable sexual impulses become anti-pornography crusaders. Or, big-time steroid users take every opportunity to publicly condemn the use of drugs.

Freud's list of defense mechanisms goes on, but these three should give you an idea of how you might be covering up your weaknesses.

Without engaging in serious ego-bashing, consider yourself, now. This can be a little scary, and after years of practice, your psyche will be pretty good at defending itself, so a few tricks will help you get inside for a close look. Let's put together a training program.

The Training Program
First, keep this exercise private, as there's nothing like public exposure to throw up another layer of defenses. You don't even have to describe any weaknesses you uncover out loud; just acknowledge them silently, or if even that is too scary, admit the *possibility* that such-and-such might be a little weak for you.

1) Top of Mind Impressions: How many times have you been told that if you didn't know the correct answer, that you should just stick with your first guess. There's some undeniable power in top-of-mind impressions, so we recommend that your first exercise in your self-assessment program be just that. Quick: What are your weak points? Remember, you don't have to go public with this, so go ahead, admit that your 14-inch calves don't look so hot under your 27 inch thighs, or that your 250-pound bench press is somewhat less spectacular than your 700-pound deadlift.

2) The Audit Trail: Even if your every move hasn't been recorded on film, tape or a disk, you have left a surprising number of footprints as you have been here, there and everywhere else. Take a look at your training log, photos, contest results, and any other documentation you might have available. How do you stack up? Where do you need a little more work? If you need a little perspective for this exercise, examine your audit trail in light of your goals, how other people performed in the same time, and most important, by comparing one aspect of your performance to another. This last measure is the key because what we're striving for is relative perfection—conquer yourself first and the world will follow.

3) The Enemy's Eyes: Sometimes your worst enemies can be your biggest allies, if you just manage them correctly. Here, for example, try thinking about what your harshest critics might say about you, painful as it might be. Go on, show them how tough you are, just like a boxer daring his opponent to lay his best shot on him, but because you're imagining this shot in the privacy of your home, you're carrying a lot of insurance into the deal. Well, what'd they say?

The Analysis
If running through these three exercises didn't leave you with a crystal-clear idea of where you can stand a little improvement, take your program another step or two. The next levels of intensity involve some of the most powerful tools available to mankind: a pen or pencil and a piece of paper. Begin by just making a list of the ideas that surfaced in each of your three exercises. Sometimes, the

mere act of writing down your thoughts sharpens them enough for a critical new idea—the answer—to break through. If you are really looking for evidence of an undeniable pattern, draw a circle and write down everything in it that you came up with in your first exercise.

Now draw a second circle, overlapping with the first one and put everything in it that your second exercise produced. Anything that showed up in both exercises goes in the overlapping area and is something you should really consider attacking in a serious way. Draw the third circle so that it overlaps the first two and repeat the analysis you just performed. Anything that shows up in all three circles is probably your best starting point.

The Action Plan

You've made it through your honest self-analysis, looking for your soft spots, and have identified one or more. The final step is to eliminate them. "Easy for you to say," you mutter, "you don't have a one-foot neck on a four-foot chest." Here comes a surprise: When you specialize on one of your weak points, be prepared for awesome progress. It might sound unbelievable, but most people have weak spots because they never concentrate on improving in those areas, not because they tried to make progress and failed.

Don't fall into the trap of thinking just because you're MVP-material you have no room to improve, or conversely, that no matter what you do, that you are doomed to a lifetime of warming the bench. Give yourself an honest self-appraisal, noting a key area for improvement, and then set out to conquer it. Next month we'll take a look at the other side of the three point shot, by exploring the idea of identifying your strong suit.

16 The Two Sides Of Three-Point Shots—Part II

Last month IronMind® presented the idea that even when you are at the top of your game, it's beneficial to honestly evaluate where you can improve yourself. We also laid out a program to help you identify these areas for yourself, and hopefully got you launched on a self-enhancement program. This month we'd like to continue our self-enrichment program by examining how you can zero in on your unique strengths. This is the other side of the three-point shot.

"Why focus on my strong points?" you might ask, "it makes sense to concentrate on my weak points, but isn't it just a waste of time to put a lot of work into the things I already do well?" You might also be thinking that this advice contradicts what we said last month, even if you're too polite to say that out loud. Let's see how these two pieces fit together.

Weak points often lose a cause for you: Crummy calves can keep a physique title out of your reach, and a lousy deadlift may block you from winning the powerlifting contest of your dreams. And your weak points, when you address them directly, often improve much more rapidly than your strong points will. But, it's your strong points, buffed to the limit, that will usually win for you, even if they ultimately gain more slowly than your weak points. That's a lot of ideas to digest, so let's take them one at a time.

First, the idea of weak points losing things for you means that there is often an underlying reason why your weak points are a real long shot for ever becoming your strongest point: If you have high calve insertions, your lower legs will never look like Steve Reeves's and if you have long thin arms, a shallow chest and long legs, your bench press is unlikely to ever be at the same level as your deadlift. So, the object here is not to become the best bencher in the world, for example, but to get to the point where your bench isn't killing your overall placement in contests. The irony is that because you have probably been neglecting your weak points for some time, they will gain very quickly when you concentrate on them. The catch is that while putting an inch on your calves is a great step forward, if they began at 14 inches, they're still puny compared to your 27-inch thighs. That's why you're trying to eliminate the ability of your weak points to kill you in contests, rather than thinking of them as your pathway to victory.

Your strengths, however, are your meal ticket, because you win by being 110% and your strengths are the areas most likely to hit 110%. The irony here is that your additional progress on your strongest points might be somewhat slow, but that's just because the final steps to perfection are usually very demanding. Suppose you cleaned and jerked 300 pounds the first time you tried the lift and got over the 400-pound mark amazingly fast. Now, as you draw closer and closer to record-level performances, it's natural for your progress to slow down a bit—even though you are still firmly on track to becoming the greatest ever on the lift.

So you decide it makes sense, this idea of going from good to excellent, but where to start?

Did you ever wish someone could simply look at you and immediately say, for example, "You are virtually guaranteed to win the Mr./Ms. O if you train intelligently," or even, "You can certainly become an outstanding mechanical engineer if you put your mind to it." Sometimes a little omni-science would be a welcome relief from the staggering set of uncertain options you face every day. Even if we can't offer you a crystal ball, we can help you with this search for personal excellence.

As with your program last month, we are focusing on your areas of *relative* excellence—everyone is stronger at some things and weaker at others. What we could like to do is identify those areas of greatest strength, with the goal of taking what's good and making it spectacular. Economists might describe this as playing off your *comparative advantage*—leveraging those talents or resources where you hold the upper hand—and that's a handy phrase to keep in mind during this program. Strange as it might sound, it's sometimes very hard to see where you really excel.

Take Larry Scott, for example, the proud possessor of a pair of arms that still look amazing almost 25 years after he won the first Mr. O title. Larry tells the story about how he first began training by just doing one exercise, standing triceps extensions (which he performed with a tractor axle, by the way). This narrow focus carried over to one of Larry's early days in Vince's Gym when somebody asked him to flex his arms and he automatically hit a triceps pose. Larry says he never even consid-ered hitting a biceps pose until this person asked him to and then calmly told Larry to concentrate on his biceps because they were his best body part. You know the rest of the story.

If those incredible Scott biceps could escape self-detection, chances are good that you too have some latent talents that might put you on the map if you could just identify and cultivate them. Let's get started so you can produce an A-1 personal harvest, taking a look at how this process works in your overall life before we specifically turn to muscles and strength.

Probably the single most common reason for people missing their areas of greatest strength is because their perceptual focus is too narrow. For example, perhaps you were raised with the idea that there are but three paths to success and happiness in life—becoming a doctor, a dentist, or a lawyer—and you have always had your attention limited to those three options. Then you are unlikely to realize that your design skills are peerless, or that virtually nobody in the world can beat you through hairpins on a motorcycle. When you're focusing on nothing but your biochemistry test scores, you can miss an awful lot of excellence in other areas—it's just that simple.

In the weight world, this type of limiting thinking commonly takes the form of making you feel that unless you are successful in high-level competition, you're nothing and so you quit training altogether. Another twist is that you immediately get pushed into one of the three major weight disciplines, based on what other people value, rather than which one suits you. Thus, regardless of your abilities and interests, you might become a bodybuilder, a powerlifter or an Olympic lifter, and you view the people in the other areas as being a bunch of rejects.

These preconceptions result in some outstanding talent getting wasted: People get disgusted and quit far short of their potential because they're not pro-card candidates; Olympic gold medal weightlifting potential gets wasted on bench presses, curls and deadlifts; naturally thick-skinned people with tremendous latent strength never tap it as they seek definition by starving themselves and toying with baby weights.

To get a handle on your strongest suit you really need an outside perspective, where "outside" specifically means beyond the sources that originally defined your appropriate interests. For example, one of the greatest benefits of traveling to new areas and meeting new people is that you get exposed to fresh ideas and you see some different ways to skin the same old cats. But you don't have to go on a

Himalayan trek to find a new way to see things: You can do it your own backyard and you can use the same tools you used in last month's self-enrichment program, so let's summarize them.

Once again, top-of-mind impressions are important, so, quick (!), what do you do best? What do you like doing the most? Don't limit yourself by only thinking about what you *should* be good at or what you think you *should* like. In fact, the only "should" in this program is self-honesty: You should tell yourself the truth about what you like and where you excel.

Use the audit-trail exercise again to see what your past performances can tell you about the areas that produced your best performance and the most personal satisfaction. Don't limit yourself to just the immediate past either, as it's sometimes easiest to get a clear perspective by looking way back, identifying a pattern, zooming in a couple of years later and trying the same thing, and so on. Chances are good that you will see the same pattern for the entire period you examine—you've always been great at ___ and always really enjoyed it too.

Last month we used the enemy's eyes to help form our view of where we could use a little added shine. Let's do the same thing in this program to see what those foes might, even if begrudgingly, admit you're good at doing. You might have to listen carefully to find anything complimentary in their criticism, but it will often come in the form of, "...is good at ___, but..." and they wind up with fifteen minutes on what they view as your weak points. Dump everything they say except for the one piece of praise.

Wrap up this stage by analyzing the data just as you did last month, by looking for consistent patterns: For example, which strengths would your top-of-mind impressions, your audit trail and your enemies all agree on? That's the seat of your strength.

At the end of this exercise, you should have at least one area that makes you say, "Man, I'm good" and after a little concentration in that area, you should be saying, "Man, I'm incredible." Chances are it will be true.

17 Take Charge

Pat and Lee had both been training for several years before they entered their first contests, small regional events in their respective home towns. As things turned out, they both had identical results on that first day out, as both landed in fifth place instead of winning it all as they had hoped. At this point, the similarity ended, though, because Pat persisted and went on to wipe out the competition at the same contest the following year, while Lee, although still training and competing, felt luckless and accepted whatever hand fate would deal.

Why is Pat persistent and why is Lee luckless? Do patterns like these really exist? If you're stuck in Lee's rut, what can you do to become more like Pat? For some answers, let's briefly visit a little psychological theory, and then put together a training package to help *you* be more like Pat. Our goal is to create people who take charge of their lives and make their own good luck.

One of the most powerful psychological theories for explaining how people behave involves what is called "locus-of-control," a label describing whether someone believes that he or she largely controls what happens (internal locus of control) or that he or she is largely the victim or beneficiary of outside forces (external locus of control). If you believe that your destiny is largely the result of what you think and do, you probably have an "internal personality." If you believe that your destiny is largely the result of chance, unpredictable events or what influential people do to you, you probably have an "external personality." Psychologists test individuals for their locus-of-control orientation by giving them a forced-choice questionnaire which presents pairs of statements and for each pair, one of the statements must be picked. Called the "I-E" scale for short, this test quickly sorts the internal locus-of-control types from the external locus-of-control types.

Adapting the I-E scale to fit the iron world, here's a short test to give you an idea of how internals and externals might differ on their world views. Read each pair of statements and choose the one that sounds more like what you think and believe. Don't worry about choosing the "right" answer; just be honest.

1. (a) I can't understand how the judges make their decisions *versus* (b) There is a direct connection between how I look and my contest results.

2. (a) Bad luck often is the result of the mistakes people make *versus* (b) Much of the unhappiness in people's lives is caused by bad luck.

3. (a) With enough effort, drugs can be controlled in sports *versus* (b) Athletes will always find ways to use drugs, even if they are prohibited.

4. (a) Genetics account for most of the progress people make *versus* (b) Training, diet, rest and attitude determine how much progress people make.

5. (a) Champions are made *versus* (b) Champions are born.

6. (a) Winners get all the breaks *versus* (b) Winners know how to pick up the pieces when they crash.

7. (a) Big contests are primarily political *versus* (b) The best person usually wins the big contests.

To interpret your responses, compare them to the choices of an internal personality: 1) b, 2) a, 3) a, 4) b, 5) a, 6) b, 7) b. External personalities would have picked the opposite answer for each pair of statements. How'd you do? Do you think along the lines suggesting an internal personality or along the lines of an external personality?

Getting a handle on whether you're more of an internal or more of an external is important because it gives you a guide to such things as how long you will persist in the face of adversity. And since everyone who does anything seriously is bound to face adversity, this is an abstract way of estimating how much you will succeed. Let's take charge now.

Remember a lifting goal that had you stymied for a long time? Just how many times did you miss that 300-pound bench press before you finally made it? Did you notice that after you had missed it more than a few times that you started to *expect* to miss it, which, sure enough, is just what you did. You had gotten to the point where you no longer viewed making the lift as being within your control, so you actually eased up when you should have been redoubling your efforts. Somewhere along the way you had lost the faith and you no longer believed that anything you did would have an impact on whether you made that bench press.

Then one day something funny happened: For whatever reason, when it came time to hit the big three on the bench, you forgot to think about it. You just went blank mentally. No big internal pep talk ("Come on Louie, you can do it") and no little persistent needler either ("You're gonna blow it, Louie, just like the other 59 times"). Just quiet. The funny thing was that you flashed the 300 like a warm-up. In fact, it went so easily that you had to go back and do it three more times over the next week before you believed that you had finally crashed through that barrier.

Then came the funniest thing of all: Now you *believed* that you could do 325 pretty soon, and within two weeks, after really put out on heavy doubles and triples, that's exactly what you did. What happened is that you snapped out of the rut that had trapped you in a pattern of believing that you had no choice but to fail if that's the way the wind was blowing.

When you quit telling yourself that you'd miss, you didn't, and when you *proved* to yourself that you could succeed, being a rational person, you *knew* you could succeed some more. So you tried harder and you succeeded way beyond anything you would have bet was possible a few short weeks earlier.

This is how the system works:

1) Nothing builds confidence like success, and the harder you try, the more you will succeed. Most people don't fail because their goal really was unattainable; they fail because they didn't really believe they could reach their goal, so they only put out a 75% effort.

2) You need to believe that what you do influences what you will gain, and if you are having trouble with this idea, scale down your goals, or temporarily focus on a different goal. For example, if you're having trouble cracking the top ten, plan to break into the top five before thinking about taking home first place. Or, if your back squat isn't moving up no matter how hard you try, switch to closely-related exercise, such as front squats, to win back your confidence by carving out a history of progress and success for yourself.

3) If you're really stuck in the rut of believing that you don't control your destiny, just tell yourself that you're going to *pretend* what you do matters. For a few weeks, pretend that if you try hard—going for that last rep, and then doing yet another; sticking with your diet, etc.—you'll get results. Remember, you're only pretending, so there's no danger of embarrassing yourself by trying hard for nothing. What you will get is real results and a new belief that what you do matters a whole lot.

4) Get a training partner who will keep encouraging and—if necessary—goading you into making continual progress through relentless effort. It's no accident that many of the bodybuilders and

lifters who make the fastest progress train with people who scream encouragement like there's no tomorrow. Did you think cheerleaders were just for the fans?

Talent is great, but it's also greatly overrated. Determination, which comes from a belief in your own ability to succeed, is what usually sorts the winners from the losers. Determine that you are going to succeed, and start running your life the way you'd like. Accept some personal responsibility: It's time to take charge.

18 Forging Through Frustration

Several years and as many titles into his bodybuilding career, John Day announced his goal of winning the Mr. Olympia to a few of the guys at his gym. They nodded respectfully and then, one by one, reminded him of four fatal little facts: 1) calves are still considered an essential body part, 2) John had no calves, 3) even if he did, with his muscle insertions, they'd look a lot more like lollipops than diamonds, and 4) nobody is likely to win the Mr. O with such an obvious genetic flaw. Naturally, in the face of such *privation* John was frustrated.

Across town, *deprivation* was producing its own case of frustration when Billy Bomber blew out his squat suit while warming up for the State Championships. Squatting without his super suit would be nearly un-American and patriotism aside, Billy just couldn't afford to give up those big, free kilos, so this year's title hopes were fading fast. It was an especially cruel twist of fate because Billy really had what it took to be competitive that day—with his suit, that is.

And then there was you: A week after you finally found it—the magic chest routine that was guaranteed to pack inches on your chest—you were already wondering if your favorite shirts came in 3XL. Never mind that the routine had giant sets that would make Hercules crumble, you were going to follow it faithfully and come what might, nothing would interfere with your training. Trouble was that just when you needed the incline bench and the 85s, a real mean-looking guy commandeered both, and was knocking off super strict incline curls with such ferocity that you decide to just wait politely while he rested, curled, rested, curled, rested, curled...on into the night. Being *blocked* like that, it's no wonder that you were frustrated.

Frustration is no more or no less than being kept from reaching an important goal. You might be frustrated by not having something required to meet your goal, such as John faces with his genetically-crummy calves. You can also be frustrated when something you need is no longer available, as in the case of Billy's blown squat suit. Or you can just plain get blocked—by someone taking *your* bench just when you want it, for example.

Just like our friends above, you're likely to encounter some form of frustration from time to time as you pursue your goals. So what do you do about it?

Aggression has long been tied to frustration: Following a poor shot, an otherwise mild-mannered accountant wraps his golf club around a tree with such bad intentions that even Iron Mike might be impressed. Ever seen somebody miss a bench press and then punch a hole in the gym wall? Or, how about the runner-up in a major physique contest who smashed his trophy on stage because he thought he should have won? These are examples of the frustration-aggression link, but we all know that even if it might feel great at the moment, violence isn't a constructive response unless you're in the ring or on the gridiron.

The Persistence Factors

Your primary objective when frustrated should be to figure out a way to stay on track, a way to persist in moving toward a rewarding goal. This is the acid test, because a lot of people quit at the first sign of opposition. Whether or not you work through frustration depends upon several variables, so let's review some of the key factors influencing your willingness to persevere, and see what we can learn from them.

Self-Confidence

Foremost among these factors is your self-confidence, which will often determine whether you will even undertake and pursue a task in the face of obstacles. And because confidence is acquired through previous successes, it's easy to see that continual frustration or outright withdrawal can easily be self-perpetuating. Alternatively, the ability to forge through frustration to reach your goals can also become your natural pattern. Illustrating this sequence of responses, Arnold's willingness to embark on an acting career was undoubtedly bolstered by his bodybuilding success, and when he ran into frustrations in his new career, he used the self-confidence built by his previous successes to surmount them. On the other side of the coin, habitual losers weren't born that way, they just practiced the pattern so much that it became automatic. The moral here is to practice succeeding, at everything you do.

Desire

The strength of your motive and your desire to reach your goal, naturally enough, are key influences on your persistence, so if your heart isn't really into what you're doing, your mind and body probably aren't either. Get really pumped and you'll wade through a lot of obstacles without even giving them a second thought. That's why the people who are intent on gaining can really crank out the growing reps, and barely consider their self-imposed torture. If your desire is wishy-washy, you'll probably never make it past your warmup sets.

Proximity

The closer you are to your goal, the more you will fight to reach it, and that's why you always need subgoals. Take your arms a quarter of an inch at a time, your bodyweight five pounds at a crack and your PR deadlift in measly little kilos. This way you will do more than keep reaching your milestones, you will program yourself for continued success, and hit your intermediate and longer-term goals before you know it.

Magnitude

The magnitude of the obstacles frustrating your progress is tied to your perceptions of your ability to overcome them in much the same way as their proximity: Big obstacles open the door to detours just as surely as do distant goals. Also, your expectations about your ability to overcome obstacles depends largely upon your previous experiences with the same or similar obstacles, and a person might not even begin a task if he feels his chance of success is poor. Once again, you can see the importance of subgoals: Break your five-course serving of frustration into bite-sized bits.

Ability and Options

Your estimated ability to overcome an obstacle can determine whether to persevere, wallow in frustration, or change goals. For example, John Day's calves really might preclude a victory in the Mr. Olympia, but since he's so genetically gifted otherwise, that might be about the only title he can't clinch, so he only needed to alter his goals very slightly to end his frustration. As things turned out, he soon added many more titles to his collection, and then there were videos, the clothing line and a host of other ventures he suddenly had time to pursue, so it's doubtful that he ever really missed the one title that eluded his grasp anyway.

And Billy Bomber realized that he could borrow a squat suit from someone in the previous weight class, and being even tighter, it helped him post a PR squat en route to his victory—never mind that it took four guys to stuff him into it and moved his voice up an octave and a half. And while you considered staying frustrated in the face of the bruiser taking your equipment, you opted instead to do a little extra decline work with the 100s, instead, and got so sore for your effort, growth seemed inevitable.

19 For Love Or Money?

When it's really getting tough to stick to your pre-contest diet because you work in a restaurant with greasy-but-great-smelling food, don't you lust for the life of the full-time athlete, free from any distractions? When your full schedule forces you to train on clean and jerks at six in the morning—a full four hours before your joints are willing to suffer such torture—don't you fantasize about being a pampered Eastern Bloc athlete, who opens the training day with a forty-five minute massage? And when your temples are threatening to burst as you eke out the last couple centimeters of a PR pull, don't you think about how nice it would be if powerlifters made bucks as heavy as their totals?

When the going gets tough and you start to look for the escape hatches, it's always tempting to inflate the demands of school, work, family, friends, and everything else that might be competing for your time and attention. And because the vast majority of people who hit iron in the United States are amateurs, it's always tempting to say, "Well, if only I were a pro... ." Would you really be cruising down Easy Street, then?

Let's see what some relevant psychological research suggests, and what we can learn to help you fine-tune your psychological suspension system to absorb any bumps and jolts that might lurk on the road ahead.

Imagine a psychology experiment that aroused hunger, thirst, pain, frustration and aggression in its subjects (if only fatigue had also been included, we might have had a perfect simulation of a workout!). And since this was an experiment, the researchers not only tracked how the subjects said they felt, but also measured their actual physiological responses. This was great because it told the researchers how much the experimental subjects thought they were suffering, as well as how much they actually were suffering.

After establishing a baseline, the experimental subjects were divided into two groups. The subjects in one group had a good reason to continue their torment, as they were given money, a good explanation or a strong dose of social pressure. The subjects in the other group didn't have a good reason to continue; they just agreed to continue with the experiment after being given a choice. Which group do you think was able to cope better with continued frustration?

Most people guess that the first group would do better: After all, they had even been *paid* to endure their frustration. Truth is, the second group did much better, even though the physiological measures indicated that they actually suffered as much as the first group.

What happened, though, is that the second group evidently was able to exert cognitive control over the negative experiences: It was as if the members of the second group had persuaded themselves that the experiences weren't going to be that bad, and so they weren't. Remember that this is purely a between-the-ears phenomenon, because their bodies were in just as much torment as the first group. And it really worked.

This means that anyone who trains purely for the money, the glory of winning and all the other trappings of success, is actually *less* likely to persist in the face of training adversity than the average trainer whose only reward is looking, feeling and being better for his or her efforts. This is why some pros fall apart extremely quickly once they're knocked off their pedestals, and why some amateurs just keep plugging away, rain or shine, year in and year out.

Now that you know the theory, how do you put this idea into practice? Just how can you manage the "disadvantages" of amateur-level training and turn them into "advantages" that will help you forge ahead?

1) *When you think you are in control, you are.* Piles and piles of psychological research demonstrates that if you merely believe you can control a painful stimulus, such as an electric shock, it doesn't hurt as much. Hapless victims, on the other hand, always bleed more.

You chose to walk the path toward improved strength, health and development—nobody forced you to. You were the one who realized that hard work on the basic exercises, although strenuous, would help you meet your bulk and power goals. You were the one who signed up for a stint of 20-rep squats to blast your body to new levels of size. You were the one who decided to diet for razor sharp cuts and a real shot at the state title. Just don't ever forget who is responsible for the discomfort of training—you are, and for very good reasons, too. Your reasons.

2) *Savor your training from the inside out.* Remember that guy who used to always make a big deal about his 400-pound bench and how he—being so big and bad—was going to the NFL soon, with an annual tax bill likely to dwarf your five-year earnings? And remember how when he didn't make the cut, he started to get scarce around the gym, and the last time you saw him down there, someone had to haul two and a quarter off his chest before he suffocated?

You never had NFL aspirations, being realistic about things like your 5'5" stature, but you kept pounding away, at both your benches and your career, enjoying both for what they offered. Funny how on the same day you benched 405, guess who came around to clean your pool?

3) *The tougher you are, the tougher you'll get.* Ever notice how when you quit at the eighth rep on what's supposed to be a 12-rep set, on the next set you're down to five, and then you just kiss off the last two sets altogether? And it also works in the other direction: When you get really fired up and crash through a pain barrier, the next pain barrier folds a little easier, and then you pick up momentum and get a sense of being nearly indestructible. You can build up scorn for training pain, and you can also build up some functional psychological callous for other challenges as well.

Even though you had to put in a lot of overtime this past month, you never missed a workout, and by virtue of having stuck with your training through some tough times, you don't even think about breaking training, now or ever. We know an Olympic speed skater who used to shovel sidewalks to earn money when he was growing up. Instead of complaining about this later, he always pointed out how that work helped him become a better skater, by making him tougher. Play tough and you'll get tough.

4) *Self-discipline creates time and energy.* How many times are you tempted to say, "I can never stick with my contest training and diet while holding down my job and going to school"? If that's what you believe, that's what you'll get. But what you might find instead is that you can use the challenge to develop added self-discipline that sweeps you to new levels of achievement. In fact, you can use self-discipline to tap into a new physics, one in which you can create both time and energy.

That's why it's not uncommon for college students who feel overburdened to find that their grades go up and they suddenly have more free time when they take on a part-time job. It's as if the added pressure creates energy by burning up the fat stored in the old system. So instead of making you crumble, the added demands just made you a leaner, meaner machine.

Use these four principles to help manage your daily demands and to integrate your training into the rest of your life. And just in case you're still in doubt about anything amateur having any advantage over anything professional, just remember that the word "amateur" comes from the Latin root for "love." And you know what conquers all.

20 Believing Is Seeing

Even before Harry Hapless hit his first pose, the judges had him scored down in the cellar—after all, wasn't Harry the guy who always came in fifteen pounds too heavy and had thighs barely bigger than his arms? Trouble for Harry is that this time he was ripped to the bone and after months of intense specialization, his legs were set for some serious walking—as in over the competition. Too bad the judges couldn't see it, though.

Willie Wunderkind, on the other hand, could enter a contest on a whim, coming in way off his best and a good bit off the top two or three in the contest, but no matter, because seeing Willie's name on the entry list made it a foregone conclusion who would win the contest. After all, Wunderkind didn't get his name for nothing.

And the same thing goes in lifting: Steve Shallow probably would get red-lighted for lack of depth on his squats even if his rear end brushed the platform, so bad was his reputation for always trying to squeak by with his shallow dunks. And yet another lifter might pause, buck and never quite finish his pull but still see nothing but three whites for his attempted deadlift and get a gold for the contest. What less does a contest promoter and self-proclaimed champion deserve when he lifts?

What we've got here isn't the usual case, where seeing is believing. Instead, what we have is a case of believing is seeing. Stick around if you want to see and believe how this works, for you and against you.

What we're dealing with is how *expectations* shape *perceptions*, or a case of what you think is what you see. And don't assume this doesn't happen, because even if the process is purely psychological, it's about as real as a three-foot thick slab of concrete. We all "see" things that don't exist, just because we expected them to be there, and the phenomenon isn't limited to bodybuilding and lifting contests, either.

Cognitive psychologists, who use computer analogies to study human thought processes, are the leading experts on how and when people make errors like this, and they have clearly demonstrated that humans are imperfect information processors: What goes in isn't necessarily what comes out. In fact, what research has repeatedly underlined is that our wishes, expectations and fears makes us particularly alert to information supporting our impressions, and more or less oblivious to all else. And if we need it, our memories help out by filling in a few blanks with the type of information we need to keep our belief systems comfortably intact.

That's why after months of debating your purchase, when you finally buy a Porsche 944, you suddenly begin to notice 944s all over the place, always filled with the type of people you'd like to associate with, and so forth. Funny thing, though, is that when your repair bills exceed your rent, *that* never really registers. Since you decided against a Corvette, you never notice them much at all—except when you pass bowling alleys, or hear about how much they rattle—and surely not at all when they blow you away at stoplights. We all tend to seek out information that confirms our beliefs, values and actions, and ignore or discredit everything else.

"But all that's very abstract," you say, "and judging a physique contest or the depth of a squat, for example, is such a simple, visual act, so how could people make gross judgmental errors based on what they see. After all, eyes don't lie." Or do they?

A very potent demonstration of how even something as straightforward as your visual perception can be manipulated involves psychological research with a drawing that can either be seen as a beautiful young woman, or an ugly old woman—the choice depends on slight changes in orientation. What has been repeatedly proven in psychology laboratories is that by first showing subjects a picture of a young woman, they become much more likely to "see" a beautiful young woman when looking at the drawing. Show them pictures of an ugly old woman first, and that's what they'll "see" when they look at the test drawing. So what you see is what you were prepared to see, and one person's ugly old woman is another's young beauty.

Psychologists call this phenomenon *psychological set*, and it's similar to the way you start a race: "ready, *set*, go." Think of "getting set" as putting yourself in a position ready to react in a predictable way, trying to anticipate the final command without registering a false start. Psychologists often show how much one's set influences perceptions and, in turn, how easily one's set can be influenced by doing experiments with nonsense words.

The nonsense words are flashed on a screen and the people in the experiment are ask to identify them. The power of one's psychological set is tested by giving the people in the experiment different directions about what kinds of words to expect. For example, one group of people might be told to expect words related to animals and another group might be told to expect words about travel. Flash the letters "pasrort" and the first group will say they saw "parrot," while the second will say they say "passport."

The moral here is that you had better try to use other people's expectations to your advantage, and the way to do that is to cultivate the type of image you want to have. In a word, *condition* your judges, your competitors, and your audience to see you as you would like to be seen.

For example, walk into your contest, or your gym for that matter, as if you're on top of your game, and that's probably how you'll be perceived. Slouch in, slink around the corners, and you'll probably be categorized as only being on the edge of things, rather than as a central player. Come into the Olympic trials looking and acting like someone Ahmad Rashad should be interviewing, and you won't hurt your chances of making the team.

Try to use advance publicity to reinforce the image you want, so that before the judges and audience even lay eyes on you for the first time, they are preconditioned to see just what you want. Have you ever talked to someone on the phone about the car they were selling, and had them do such a convincing job of pushing it, that you were ready to sign your check the moment you laid your eyes on it? It's the same thing in terms of managing your public image.

And don't forget to pack the audience with your friends, so that when you first step on stage they can yell things like, "They should have just mailed you the trophy, Ed, and saved us the plane fare." At lifting contests, when your buddy is getting ready to come out for his opening squat with 240 kilos, work your way up close to the judges and say to the person next to you, "I saw this guy double 320 last week without even pulling up his straps." Make those judges think they're the oddballs if they don't realize your buddy is the winner, or is taking a weight that should go like a warm-up.

Don't forget to help out yourself in the final moments, either. If you are a weightlifter, for example, who has genetically poor arm lock, don't forget to show the judges how your arms clearly don't hyperextend, *before* they mistakenly turn you down for incomplete extension. Make sure their frame of reference on your lifts is you, and not some ideal you don't fit.

This brings up a point about candor, because it's not always the wisest thing to openly discuss your weaknesses with the people who will be evaluating you—whether it's the public you want to please or the judges you want to woo. In a perfect world, you might be perfectly open, but in an imperfect world, you are better off emphasizing your strong points rather than giving everyone a running start at cutting your down. There's no point about lying about being in great shape when you're not, but there's also no mileage in it for you to emphasize your weak points. Just concentrate on your strong points instead.

A lways set the stage for the impression you want to make, because believing is seeing, and it's what's in the brain, not what hits the eye, that counts. Where the mind goes, the eyes will surely follow.

21 Hypnotism: Hotbed Of Hype

"Psst, hey buddy. Afraid of the dark, want to quit smoking, or maybe you need to lose weight? Look at what I've got for you: A little bit of magic. Guaranteed to work, and only $49.95 a pop. Hypnotism."

It's been said that hypnotism is the most widely known but least understood means of altering consciousness. And because a lot of people will try to sell you on hypnotism in various forms, take a few minutes to become better-informed consumers. Let's see what we know and what we don't about hypnotism.

Hypnotism got its first day in the sun when an 18th century Viennese physician named Anton Mesmer mixed faith healing, mysticism and astrology, dressed them up in scientific terminology and sold the resulting brew to the public as *mesmerism*, a miracle cure for pain. Mesmer's underlying theory rested on magnetic animal fluids, but this was later replaced in the mid-19th century with the term *hypnosis*, from the Greek word *Hypnos*, the god of sleep.

Shortly afterward, hundreds of operations, including amputations and cataract removals, were performed with hypnosis as the only anesthetic. Hypnotism continued to gain scientific respectability as it was studied with increasing precision, and in the 1930s Clark Hull initiated true psychological research in the field at Yale University. Unfortunately, this research program made history for another reason: One of the experimental subjects successfully sued Yale for damage as a result of her hypnotic experience, and Hull's program was terminated.

Hull then turned his energies to learning theory, which conveniently relied on rats, rather than people, as the experimental subjects. In recent years, Ernest Hilgard of Stanford University and Martin Orne of the University of Pennsylvania have set the standard for scientific research in the field of hypnosis.

To hypnotize someone, the hypnotist must first create conditions that will deeply relax his subject, exercise his imagination, and thus guide him toward a) giving up some control to the hypnotist, and b) accepting some distortion of reality. While media presentations of this process commonly involve the hypnotist whipping out a magically-imbued mandala which is seductively swung back and forth, while the powerless subject is inexorably drawn into a deep hypnotic state, that's not what really happens.

In fact, the hypnotist might just ask his subject to concentrate on a thumbtack stuck in the wall and to gradually become relaxed or sleepy. (Sleep is used a convenient metaphor, but the subject does not actually go to sleep.) If everything goes according to plan, the subject finds it easy to follow the hypnotist's suggestions in terms of behavior and experience.

Ernest Hilgard has characterized the deeply hypnotized state as follows:

1) The planning functions decrease, and the subject waits for the hypnotist to tell him to do something.

2) Attention is redistributed, and the subject will focus on only what the hypnotist tells him to focus on.

3) Reality testing is reduced, and distortions of reality are accepted without question.

4) Suggestibility is increased, although there is less of this than is commonly supposed.

5) Acceptable roles are readily enacted, even when they involve complex activities.

6) Post-hypnotic amnesia is often present, so subjects won't remember what took place while they were hypnotized, until a prearranged signal is given.

With all these unusual qualities, it's surprising to find that brain activity patterns (EEG) and all other physiological measurements (e.g., respiration and heart rate) of hypnotized people are characteristic of the waking state. So, by all bodily appearances, hypnosis is a variation of the normal waking state, and about the most definitive statement top scientists are willing to make is something like, "Hypnosis is an altered state of consciousness."

To gain a better understanding of what hypnosis is and is not, let's briefly review some of the most common myths surrounding the subject.

1) You can be hypnotized against your will. False. Even if this is the basic stuff of many fictional accounts involving hypnotism, that's just what it is: fiction. The first rule of becoming hypnotized is that you must be willing.

2) Everyone is equally susceptible to hypnotism. False. Although many unethical or ignorant practitioners of hypnotism would have you believe that anyone can be deeply hypnotized (by themselves, at least), nothing could be further from the truth. (See below.)

3) Only a hypnotist can hypnotize you. Once again, this might be bad for business, but it's false. With practice you can learn to hypnotize yourself, just as a hypnotist would, and teaching self-hypnosis is a goal of hypnotic training. In fact, if you keep reading, you'll see that you might not even need to get hypnotized at all, in order to meet your goals.

4) Hypnotism allows you to do all kinds of things you cannot do otherwise. False. Still another bad break for the hypnotherapy business, and quite a shocker, but there is a high correlation between responsiveness in the wakeful state and responsiveness in the hypnotized state. In other words, there is only a relatively small increase in suggestibility, and most of the things people can do after hypnotic induction, they can do anyway.

5) Hypnotism is pure bunk—the province of carnival showmen and insecure people who like to lord power over others. False. Even if incompletely understood by modern science and over-hyped by many of its practitioners, hypnotism has obvious potential value not only for helping us understand basic psychological processes, but also for dealing with applied situations such as managing pain or retrieving material from memory.

Finally, should hypnosis have a place in your repertoire of mental training tools? As explained above, hypnosis doesn't necessarily have unique abilities in terms of altering your behavior, and most people can't even become deeply hypnotized, anyway.

But don't assume that it's useless, because anything that can help people go through surgical procedures as traumatic as amputating an arm without anesthesia must have something going for it. In fact, the area of pain control has seen some of the most impressive applications of hypnosis, and properly used, anything that can help you sit on top of pain might also help you make big gains.

If you've tried other methods, or are just curious, and especially if you sense that you are highly hypnotizable, you might find a good hypnotherapist or perhaps a self-hypnosis guide, and give it a try for things like pain management, or breaking a mental barrier blocking a PR lift.

"The Shadow," made famous in a 1940s radio serial, used hypnotism to "cloud men's minds" and to discover "the secrets that lurk in the hearts of men." Less dramatic, but closer to the truth, you might use hypnosis to simply "relax your mind" and "learn new responses." Maybe this is a case of shrinking a shadow by throwing more light on a subject.

*****

Who's susceptible to hypnotism?

Contrary to popular opinion, the ability to become deeply hypnotized varies widely across different people, and most people are only slightly or moderately susceptible to hypnotism.

Generally, a person's ability to become hypnotized can be determined from the first attempt, and although some people who are initially difficult to hypnotize might later become hypnotizable, hypnotic susceptibility has been shown to be quite a stable characteristic.

A convenient way to measure one's hypnotic susceptibility involves a standardized test (the "Stanford Hypnotic Susceptibility Scale") which is administered in the waking state. This test contains twelve items, graduated in difficulty, and your score comes from the number of items you pass. The first item tests whether or not you fall over in response to the suggestion that you are swaying backward; the second item tests whether your eyes close while you stare at a target and are told that you are getting sleepy; and so forth. The final item on the list is passed if you can recall no more than three of the previous eleven items.

Nearly half the people tested only scored from 0 to 4 on this test, although scores from 5 to 12 indicate the ability to achieve deeper levels of hypnotism. Based on his research, Ernest Hilgard has estimated that roughly one out of four university students (the population he tested extensively) can achieve satisfactory levels of hypnotism and perhaps 5-10% can reach more advanced levels.

Even though hypnotism is a measurable, stable characteristic, predicting who is susceptible based on personality characteristics is no easy matter. Broadly speaking, however, the people who are most hypnotizable have the ability to become deeply involved in subjective experiences, and can relax easily and not be afraid to relinquish reality testing for a period of time.

Early childhood experiences seem to be a key determinant of one's hypnotic susceptibility, as the capacity to become deeply absorbed in imaginative experiences appears to come from parents who were deeply involved in such things as religion, music, reading or an appreciation of nature.

Also, severe childhood punishment appears to be a contributing factor, with the conjecture being that this teaches children blind obedience and/or to escape to the realm of imagination.

22 Stress Inoculation

Marty Muscles had a big date coming up: On the first Saturday of next month, Marty would strip down to practically nothing more than a little posing suit, step on a well-lighted stage, and then countless strange and critical eyes would dance over, well, Marty's muscles. Was Marty scared? You bet. Was Marty stressed-out? Right off the scale, and potentially right out of the contest.

Regardless of whether you are about to make your debut as a competitive bodybuilder, chances are nearly certain that you have a lot of stress in your life. Perhaps you're a powerlifter who has lost a title on your last two outings because you missed your final deadlift, and guess what's staring you in the eyes yet again? Maybe you're an Olympic lifter trying to qualify for an international team and just missed your first two attempts in the snatch. Or maybe you're facing a big test in school, a tough presentation at work, or perhaps a thorny heart-to-heart with a significant other. All of these situations, plus a lot more, spell stress.

Stress begins its work at the physiological level, triggering the famous "fight or flight" reaction in the sympathetic division of the autonomic nervous system: Your heart rate increases, your breathing becomes deeper, blood is shunted away from your internal organs and into your muscles, glucose is released into the bloodstream, and you begin to sweat. If you're facing a sabre-toothed tiger, you want your body to be primed this way, so stress of this type has a constructive evolutionary purpose: It prepares you to save your life.

And of course training is a stress, but that too is constructive because you regulate the stress and keep it within the bounds of your recovery rate, growing bigger and stronger for your efforts. What we are concerned with controlling is stress that would otherwise run out of control, or at least hurt your performance. We want to whittle away at the type of stress that leaves you with a harried, grim look or ties your stomach into a bombproof knot. What we want to chop down to size is the type of stress that either eats you up or makes you want to run and hide.

If you live in this state, or visit it too often, bad things happen. You develop high blood pressure, your cholesterol level rises, you grind your teeth, and maybe you develop ulcers or have a stroke along the way. It's virtually certain that you will at least be uncomfortable and that your performance will suffer, so what, if anything, can you do to combat stress?

In fact, you can do an amazing job controlling your reactions to a specific stressful event, and you can learn to do it yourself, applying the general principles again and again, as you face stressful events throughout your life. We'll attack stress with a training program called "stress inoculation."

Our Program

Situation

You are facing a specific stress-filled event, maybe training-related, maybe not. Just thinking about this event (an upcoming contest, for example) gives you a queasy feeling, and rather than feeling yourself getting stronger and conquering it, you feel threatened by the event.

There are at least four different ways to respond to the stressor: 1) ignore it, hoping that it will either go away or that you will just walk over the frightening event, 2) fold in the face of the event and hide in your closet, 3) employ a general relaxation/coping strategy, or 4) use stress inoculation to approach the threatening event cautiously, nibbling away at it around the edges rather than trying to just swallow it in one gulp.

Option #1 will probably hang you out to dry as the problem will likely remain a problem even if you ignore it. Option #2 is fine if you are content to wimp out in the face of challenges. Option #3 is better than nothing, but decidedly less effective than #4, the stress inoculation approach.

The Theory

Psychological inoculation is based on the same principle as biological inoculation: If you are exposed to a weak form of a negative stimulus, you can build up antibodies, as it were, to cope with the main event. Think of stress inoculation as following a training program to build up your mind the same way you build your body with gradually increasing workloads.

Let's say that you have verbally committed yourself to climb El Capitan with a couple of your friends by the end of the summer, and even though you are technically capable of it, the idea of dangling by your fingertips with nothing but thousands of feet of air under your heels makes you jelly-kneed. Our theory says that you prepare for your assault by taking El Cap in small steps, digesting one vertical foot of granite at a time, until you master the whole thing.

C onveniently for us, this preparation can take place purely in the mind, and more good news, such cognitive preparation strategies have proven to be remarkably effective.

Research

Psychological research has borne out the wisdom and effectiveness of cognitive stress inoculation strategies. For example, a sample of patients facing surgery was randomly divided into two groups: The patients in one group received standard (minimal) information on the surgical operation they were facing, and the patients in the other group received an enhanced description, which allowed them to anticipate and come to grips with the operation. Following surgery, the patients in the second group not only complained less, but also consumed about half the morphine of the first group and was released, on average, three days earlier than the first group!

In another psychology experiment, subjects watched a film showing dramatic accidents occurring in a woodshop (cozy little things like a man being impaled by a wooden plank). One group of subjects had no forewarning of the accident. The second group practiced general relaxation. The third group cognitively rehearsed the scene before seeing it on film. Physiological arousal measures indicated that general relaxation helped the subjects cope with the stressful film compared to no preparation, but it wasn't nearly as effective as the cognitive rehearsal strategy.

Your Routine

At least once a day every day before your BIG EVENT, get relaxed physically. Lying down on your back is best. Make sure that your clothing is comfortable (no tight belts, neckties or size 6 jeans on size 10 bodies), and that you are comfortably warm. Take about five slow, deep breaths. As you inhale, concentrate on drawing in pure energy and as you exhale concentrate on expelling tension. Next run through five counts for your right leg, and five for your left leg. Do the same thing for both arms and then five more for your whole body. For each of these counts breathe slowly and deeply while saying something like, "I breathe deeply and slowly. I am relaxed."

After you have gone through the full twenty-five counts you should be pretty relaxed, even the first time you train on this routine. If you really hit this right, you will be aware of thinking but unaware of your body, the surroundings, etc. With practice, you will be able to hit the relaxed state more easily and more completely, so keep at it.

Once in this deeply relaxed state, you will be tempted to fall asleep, but don't, as you have work to do.

You want to confront your stressor now, gradually, taking advantage of your relaxed state and your ability to exit any time your stress level gets too high. Your goal is to stay relaxed as you master your stressor in small steps. Begin imagining the details of your target situation, taking your time and thinking about how you could cope with the attendant stress at each step, and then master it.

When you hit a stage that jacks your stress level up too high, back off, get relaxed and try again. Keep at it and you will be able to work through the entire problematic situation, learning to keep your stress at a tolerable level throughout the exercise. As a result you will develop coping strategies that will help you respond effectively to the otherwise stress-laden situation when you face it in real life.

You can't always avoid stress-filled situations, but you can learn to use stress inoculation techniques to stay below redline and avoid burning out or blowing up along the way. Good luck!

23 Faith & Desire: The Breakfast Of Champions

"*If a man wants to be something so bad and he's young, I believe that his body and his mind will change...to adapt to what the desire is. He literally can alter everything in his system—mind and body—if the desire is true. It will not work if the man is untrue to himself and untrue to his belief in all of the things in his existence. He has to have an absolute faith in some force that is helping him; you can call it what you want: 'God,' 'The Supreme Being.' He feels that he is in contact with this force. He is true to that force. If he is arrogant, if he is untrue, if he lies, if he is dishonest, in this one aspect, it won't work, which means that the antenna to his force has been severed, and he can never realize his dream. That is the penalty that the man pays." —Douglas I. Hepburn*

In 1953 a lone Canadian representative to the World Weightlifting Championships was seeking to do something most unlikely: With a shriveled lower right limb, no teammates and only last minute contest help borrowed from the British coach, Al Murray, Douglas Ivan Hepburn was taking on the legendary John Davis, the man who had swept the heavyweight class in every world championship and Olympics since 1946. Hepburn was also taking on the dominant American national team, backed by Bob Hoffman's York Barbell Company, and in those days, the American lifting team was a full-fledged international powerhouse.

Hepburn got off to a strong start, setting a new world record in the press with 371 pounds, and maintained his lead of approximately 30 pounds going into the clean and jerk. Today, Hepburn recalls how he had a premonition the night before the contest that he was going to win. But Davis was threatening the dream, and the contest was coming down to the final clean and jerk.

Three earlier operations to correct a mild case of clubfoot had resulted in fused bones in Hepburn's right ankle, leaving him with a stiff and essentially muscleless lower right leg. This made it tough to get low enough on his cleans and contributed to the missed clean on his second attempt. Now on his third attempt, facing the do-or-die situation and without knowing how or why—never having done it before and never to repeat it—Hepburn hit a low position and cleaned the weight. He stood, jerked it and was the new heavyweight world champion—the strongest man in the world!

As a youth, Doug was involved in a lot of sports, from gymnastics to cycling—his clubfoot and an eye ailment only served to spur him on to greater success—and in the back of his mind he always carried the desire to become a great strongman. When he was 16, Doug was introduced to weights, and he began using a typical bodybuilding routine. Not surprisingly, the great John C. Grimek was Doug's hero and to this day when he mentions Grimek, his respect is obvious. Within a few years, Doug had added about fifty pounds of bodyweight to his 5'8-1/2" frame, and was starting to attract attention with his pressing ability—whether he was pressing barbells or dumbbells, standing up or lying on his back, lifting people over his head or doing handstand press-ups with his massive body, Hepburn's ability to press truly ponderous weights was never in doubt.

By the summer of 1950, weighing about 240, Hepburn was already pressing over 300 pounds, and doing a perfect curls with almost 200—just the kind of power you'd expect from his *bona fide* 20-inch arms. By this time he was getting famous on the popular Vancouver beaches where he was a lifeguard, and he was about to be introduced to the rest of the world as he visited, first, New York's biggest names in the Iron Game, and then stopped by the very heart of the American lifting scene, York, Pennsylvania. Each time he lifted, Doug dropped jaws.

Over the next several years, Doug got really big—usually weighing around 280 pounds—and really strong, becoming not only the world champion in the Olympic lifts, but also becoming even better on what would later be recognized as the powerlifts. Not that Hepburn was even limited to just those six lifts: Doug feels, quite reasonably, that in his prime he could have walked into a room and broken the record in any or all of about two dozen lifts—from squats to one arm presses to two arm curls, he was supreme.

With all the chemical enhancers and support gear used by most of the top powerlifters from the 1960s forward, it's easy for the raw numbers posted by the lifters of earlier days to take an unfair pounding. Easy, that is, unless you are talking about the truly elite strongmen, such as Hepburn. Take a look at the authentic, unassisted lifts of Hepburn, as recorded by David Willoughby, and your eyes should widen:

Press off the rack	440
Two Hands Press with Dumbbells	350
Press Behind the Neck	350
Two Hands Military Curl	260
Bench Press (wide grip)	580
Jerk Press (off rack)	500
Crucifix	200
Squat	760
Deadlift	705

Absence of drugs and support gear aside, remember that Hepburn did these lifts in the mid-1950s—in the days of James Dean, black and white TVs, "phonographs" for playing records, and cars with big fins and enough chrome to sink the Queen Elizabeth. Bodybuilders back then lusted after 17-inch arms, and lifters were awed by 500-pound squats. Performing against that backdrop, you can see why Hepburn was something more than a superstar: He was a bloody legend.

Just as you would guess, Doug trained hard on the heavy exercises, but the key to his training progress was "the principle of one-repetition gains"—the idea that you need to make small, but continual improvements to reach soaring heights, and the smallest unit of advancement was an additional repetition. Doug feels that in order to succeed, making this extra repetition has to assume absolutely primary importance in one's training, and he used to consciously conserve both his physical and mental resources until he made his extra rep, getting up to it as quickly and as effortlessly as possible. As you would guess, prodigious feats at the table followed, as he had to stoke his energy system: "The atomic furnace of the muscle is the ability to burn the blood sugar and have it explode in the muscle."

Mustering intense desire is the other force that must trigger an explosive reaction according to Doug's philosophy, and to make a maximum lift, he feels that it must assume an importance second to none: "You want it more than anything in the world—your whole life is this one lift because you have a building block if you can make that and you can go to the stars."

Surveying the lifting scene today, Doug is deeply disappointed by the drugs and the support gear which have defiled what can otherwise be an art form, and he is puzzled by the decline of Olympic lifting in the United States, compared to powerlifting: "I think frankly that some of these powerlifters should get into Olympic lifting. Any American who could beat the Russian superheavyweight would be highly-publicized, he would be a very important figure in the United States—he would probably make the cover of *Time* magazine."

And just in case you aspire to be that man, Hepburn has some advice which harkens back to the idea of believing in and being true to something larger than yourself: "You cannot be arrogant and be a great man or a world champion; you have to be humble. A man has to learn humility and he has to learn that his masters came before him." A man who perhaps should have learned this lesson was the top American superheavyweight of a few years back who, after making a record lift, sauntered up to Doug and said, "Light my cigarette." In keeping with Doug's philosophy, this man never amounted to anything on the international level.

The incomparable Alexeev, on the other hand, is the example Doug uses to illustrate the other side of how this works: After his final clean and jerk at the 1976 Olympics—a staggering 562 pounds—Alexeev had the fans at Montreal absolutely beside themselves. Apparently oblivious to the pandemonium he caused, Alexeev ambled back toward the dressing area without so much as glancing at anyone, but he stopped along the way to bend down and shake the hand of a little boy seated by the aisle. "That's the kind of man that makes a champion," concludes Doug.

24 KISS And Grow

When James "Buster" Douglas stunned the world by knocking out Mike Tyson, the first interviewer into the ring with the new champ was quick to try to explain to the world just how and why this mighty upset had occurred. His analysis went something like this: "Buster, you kept him at bay with double left jabs, you leveraged your height advantage and kept tagging him with stiff rights, you tied him up, you maintained that delicate balance of constant pressure....*blah, blah, blah*...Was that your *strategy*? Is that what you *planned* to do tonight?"

"I planned to whip his ass," Buster replied, and you know what? That's just what he did.

There always comes a time when the simple truth emerges for exactly what it is: The simple truth. Let's talk about that idea and see how it can help you get bigger and stronger. This is more important than you might guess, because we all tend to be biased against simplicity and somewhat awed by complexity.

One of the most common categories of letters we receive at IronMind® Enterprises is also one of our favorites. This is how they run:

Dear Dr. Strossen:

I've been training for years and had barely made any progress in gaining size. I enjoyed reading your book [SUPER SQUATS: How to Gain 30 Pounds of Muscle in 6 Weeks], but didn't see how anything that sounded so simple could work for me. I started the program anyway, but was a little skeptical. After a couple of weeks, I could tell something was happening, so then I really attacked the program the way you recommended. In two months I gained 25 pounds, my squat went up 110 pounds, my bench press went up 65 pounds and just as you said, I outgrew all my clothes. Everybody at my gym is amazed and wants to know how I did it.

How could something so simple work? Many thanks.

Sincerely,

Greg Moore

Yes, we are conditioned to believe that complexity is the advanced stuff, and simplicity is for beginners or dolts.

Simplicity is deceiving because it's often mistaken for lack of understanding or lack of depth. That's what you mean when you say someone has a "simple" understanding of something. Because a lot of "simple" explanations are actually "simple-minded," there's a reason for our bias against simplicity. Actually, simple-mindedness is just a case of partial understanding. Truly simple explanations, however, understand the situation so thoroughly that they immediately zero in on what is important, and toss out all the window dressing.

For example, let's say that we want to teach you the basics of visualization to improve your self-confidence, boost your motor skills in a particular sport, or mentally condition you to deadlift 500 pounds for the first time. If we really wanted to go Madison Avenue, we'd would recognize that what we are selling is 99% sizzle and 1% steak; that is, we would recognize that we need to wrap up our basic concept in a pretty package so it seems more attractive to you, and also so that it seems unique in the marketplace.

So what we do is dump the idea of calling our process anything as simple as "mental rehearsal" or "visualization." How about if we say instead that we are going to use "auto-psychogenic response activation to predispose you to success." Chances are you will be confused by the latter phrase, but you are also likely to give us the benefit of the doubt and be impressed. Who knows, maybe you'll send us a check for $49.95 so you can buy one of these things for the dashboard of your car. You can guess how things snowball from there.

Adventures in complexity are not all borne of simple greed, and they're sometimes necessary. But if you want to boost your hit rate in whatever you do, why not use the same principle they love to death in the military: KISS, which stands for "Keep It Simple, Stupid." When in doubt, cut things down to the bone. Chances are that you will find it a refreshing and very rewarding approach to whatever has been thwarting you.

Suppose you have been having trouble layering another inch on your somewhat massive arms. You already tried the routine that just about sank your PC when you logged it in. This was the routine that cut your rent because you had to move into your gym to stay on schedule, and it also had you setting your alarm at three different times during the night to take various combinations of amino acids. Then you called on all the experts you could think of to analyze the situation: Each gave you a program and charged you before you left the premises, but guess what? Your arms still didn't grow.

After consulting everyone this side of Dear Abby and running up a food supplement bill that looked like a phone number, you decided to chill out for the day and just reflect on matters yourself. Sorry, you actually decided to "engage in some non-judgmental brainstorming, followed by bottom-line oriented game plan formation." As a result, you got smart and decided, "Why not KISS and maybe make out like a bandit." Here's how your brainstorming session went...

"Let's see, to get bigger arms I need to make the muscles do more work than they are used to, so I have to boost my training poundage and/or reps and/or sets or cut my rest periods. Since I've been on this 30-sets-per-bodypart routine, my poundage are starting to look like they belong in the aerobics room so maybe the smartest thing to do is cut way back on the number of sets, but make a real effort to max out in terms of reps per set. Maybe I can really crank up my training weights too.

Next, since I want my arms to get bigger, that means more muscle mass and since I'm already rock-hard or just-about, I have to gain weight, in the simplest terms. That means hard work on a handful of basic exercises and then some serious work in terms of nutrition. Maybe I should just go back to consuming more high-quality protein, with a balanced and abundant intake of vitamins and minerals. This is starting to sound too SIMPLE."

Suspicions of simplicity pushed aside, you followed your game plan: Heavy work on a handful of basic exercises, with constant attention to making just one more rep and then putting another five pounds on the bar. Out of the gym, it's been a generous and balanced diet laced with protein supplements plus vitamin and mineral supplements. To help keep your motivation high, you regularly relaxed and visualized both the means and the ends of your success.

A month later, you're ten pounds heavier and your arms—honest—have moved up a big 3/4 inch.

Just about anyone can make something simple appear very complex; it takes a smart person to make something very complicated appear to be simple. So be smart: KISS and grow.

25 Inner Qualities, Outer Results

Even if they weren't explosive, Carl's gains were rock-steady. In fact, in the three years he had been training, he had truly transformed himself: He had added 45 pounds of solid muscle to his frame, which helped explain why his arms had gone up about four inches and his chest had gone up more than ten. Probably because he always trained hard on basic exercises, his strength had also increased enormously, and while he had been benching a mighty 60 pounds when he started training, now he was doing reps with over 300. And he wasn't just a one-lift specialist, either, as from power cleans to curls, Carl could move some decent iron.

Carl wasn't likely to be mistaken for Shawn Ray, and his lifts weren't keeping Ed Coan or Alexander Kurlovich awake at night, but Carl was living, breathing proof of just what sorts of miraculous changes resulted from sound training. And the way Carl was going, the best was yet to come: He might not win the *IRONMAN* Invitational next year, or break any world records at the Goodwill Games, but based on all the evidence, next year would find him an even better man than he was now. Carl wasn't getting celebrity endorsement contracts for his progress, but the truth is that Carl was a 100% real success story. So what was Carl's secret weapon?

It wasn't banned substances, because Carl was a lifetime natural. It sure didn't seem to be a mystery supplement, either, because even though Carl used a fair amount of food supplements, his core products had been around for decades. And his routine, well, it wasn't exactly the stuff that made publishers or equipment manufacturers smell money: You could usually write it on the back of an envelope and it relied on the most basic of equipment. So what was it that allowed Carl to keep making progress?

If a secret observer were to follow Carl around the gym, what he would notice was that Carl always seemed focused on his workouts, and while just about everyone in the gym was at least going through the motions of training, watching Carl left no doubt that he was a man on a mission. For starters, Carl was sweating heavily while a lot of the others were dry as a bone. And the sweat was the natural result of the fact that Carl's sets were intense and his rest periods were brief.

So the sweat told a story: Carl was knocking off sets with a 2:1 advantage over most of the people in the gym, and each of his sets represented real quality work. Since Carl was doing many times the work in the same amount of time, his industrial-strength intensity was making him sweat like crazy compared to most. And, funny thing, his gains were coming at about the same rate as he sweated.

The next thing the secret observer would notice was that when he was in the gym, Carl's mouth had but one primary purpose: To suck in air. So while others talked about the Raiders's latest plans to move, Carl was just pumping and breathing, breathing and pumping. Not that Carl couldn't talk the sports page as well as the next guy, but while training, he rarely uttered more than a sentence to anyone, and sometimes made it through his whole workout saying no more than, "Could I get a spot on this set?" Carl might not have known that some Eastern mystics use days of silence to boost their spiritual powers, but what he did know was that talking leaked energy and broke his concentration. On the flip side, Carl knew that the less his mouth worked in the gym, the more his muscles did and the better he gained.

This thing about psychic energy really seemed to be a factor, because more than one person in the gym noticed that when Carl was around, *they* had better workouts. Part of it, they understood, was that they couldn't help but get a little inspired when Carl was in the gym, because when he was toasting his muscles set after set, it awakened a sense of self-pride that made you push a little harder on your own training.

But it even went a little deeper, because when Carl moved over next to you, you could almost feel a force field in that part of the gym. It was as if Carl was using his energy to create more energy, and some of it was spilling over for you to soak up. There was a lesson in here about how hard training could fuel even harder training, and how intensity could be more than learned by observation; it could be absorbed from the environment.

Stepping back a little from Carl's actual sets and reps, the secret observer noticed something else about Carl: He had an attitude about him. It wasn't that Carl was a rose-colored-glasses kind of person, because he saw the cracks in the sidewalk as well as the next guy. But instead of dwelling on them, tripping over them, or even falling in, Carl focused on using the sidewalk to reach goals that were important to him, his goals.

And it wasn't as if Carl was a trust fund baby with nothing to do but train: Carl's day began at 4:00 A.M., with his extra job, but he was in the gym by 8:00 every morning, and even though the next thing on his schedule was his full-time job, he always seemed more energetic and more cheerful than the guys who were unemployed and just spent most of the day hanging around the gym, working crossword puzzles in between desultory sets of benches and curls. Carl did have an attitude about him, and it was pretty simple: Carl believed that if he tried hard and tried smart, he'd get what he wanted. And history was proving Carl right.

What Carl might not have consciously realized was that he had a few inner qualities that made this whole process tick, and what you might not realize is that you can cultivate these same things in yourself—so you can make progress like Carl's. Here are the secret ingredients:

1) Goal-orientation: At every moment, Carl knew where he wanted to go, and that's what not only put him on track, but also helped him arrive. For example, while Carl began his training with the general goal of getting bigger and stronger, the process of goal-setting became increasingly specific as it later included a target date for winning the state title, etc. Carl was so goal-oriented, that he didn't just go to the gym for "a good workout;" he was there to hit 180 kilos for five reps in the squat that day, and so forth. Every time Carl picked up the bar for a set, he knew what he was shooting for.

2) Self-discipline: Thinking great thoughts is nice, but there's a world of difference between concept and reality. Because the bridge between these two is usually an awful lot of hard work, having the self-discipline to do the required work is what separates the dreamers from the achievers. Having self-discipline is what got Carl to the gym and through his high quality workouts. Having first set important goals, which required these workouts, is what gave Carl the motivation to maintain his self-discipline. Actually, Carl had already learned this trick about maintaining a high level of self-discipline: Because he largely did things that were truly important and valuable to him, the required self-discipline came pretty naturally.

3) Basic satisfaction: Sure there will always be ups and downs, good days and bad, but you need to hit a rhythm that is right most of the time. And you need to spend your time doing things that you think are worthwhile, things that leave you with a sense of satisfaction. Dissatisfaction creates the restlessness that destroys the focus needed for championships results, and dissatisfaction also creates the type of constant stress that erodes your energy. A quick test of your basic satisfaction level is to see whether you are primarily running away from something, or toward something. Our friend Carl had paid some dues along the way, but after some work, he had put his house in pretty good order and was satisfied with his basic life and his future plans; so when he hit the gym, he was armed with the fully committed feeling necessary to grind through the painful reps.

If you're not getting the results you want from your training, maybe it's time to look beyond the externals, and peer inside. Maybe it's time to do a little mental housecleaning. Maybe it's time to bring out the inner qualities required for outer results.

26 Concentration: Cognitive Cool

Things had come down to the last lift: With the Olympic gold medal in balance, it was going to be either you or Boris Lifterupski on the winner's podium. Visions of hearing the "Star Spangled Banner" dance inside your head, and there's even a glimpse of you signing a lucrative contract with Coca-Cola... .

Events had unfolded quickly up to this dramatic moment: Despite getting off to a shaky start by missing your opening snatch, you settled down and made your next two attempts, plus your first two clean and jerks. Boris had lived up to his billing as a fabled, well-oiled Eastern Bloc athletic machine, and had gone six-for-six, emerging with a total five kilos ahead of you. Even better for Boris and worse for you, each and every one of those five kilos between you and him represented a new PR for you.

But you are the lighter lifter and have one lift left, so who knows, those five kilos—and the gold medal—just might be within your reach, if only you can really get focused. You are understandably nervous, and from deep inside of you a little voice is screaming, "Concentrate! Concentrate! Concentrate!..."

Even after you wake up and find yourself late for school in Des Moines, Iowa rather than dueling for Olympic gold in Barcelona, Spain, the message for success lingers: "Concentrate! Concentrate! Concentrate!"

And the story is pretty much the same for bodybuilders: No less an authority than Arnold Schwarzenegger has repeatedly said that bodybuilding is a matter of training the mind as well as the body, and since the mind leads the body, beginners especially need to learn how to develop their mental abilities to the max. Concentration is one of those critical mental skills for the bodybuilder, and Arnold says that with practice you can eventually learn to concentrate so well that you will be able to send blood to a particular muscle just by thinking about it. (Incidentally, this isn't just gym hocus-pocus: Well-trained subjects can demonstrate this ability under the strictest laboratory conditions.)

So firm is Arnold's belief in this need to focus precisely on the muscle you are training, that he has suggested that you carefully note the exact site of muscle soreness when you begin a new exercise, so that you know just where to concentrate each time you do the movement.

The net result then is that whether you are a weightlifter who has to concentrate in order to produce increasingly powerful explosions of muscular force, or whether you are a bodybuilder who needs continual concentration in order to coax your muscles to grow, concentration is a key to your continued progress. Let's take a look at what concentration is—and is not—in order to develop some training guidelines and routines that will help you boost the size and strength of this crucial cognitive skill.

Concentration is selective attention, and the best way to understand this idea is to look at what psychologists call "the cocktail party phenomenon." This label describes how even when you are involved in a primary conversation (such as talking to someone at a party), you can end up paying more attention to a secondary conversation (such as what someone else is saying about you) even if it has less physical presence (e.g., it's quieter and coming from across the room, etc.).

Research psychologists have done a lot of work in this area by playing one message in the subject's right ear and another in the subject's left ear, and without getting bogged down in technical nuances, the consistent basic finding is that people overwhelmingly pay attention to just one of the messages (often being so oblivious to the "other" message that they don't even know whether it was in a foreign language).

Think of each set as being your primary message, and the rest of the world as being your secondary message. Ever wonder about the people who could "train" while keeping up a conversation, or the people who can make eye contact with and say "hi" to everyone who walks by while they are doing concentration curls? Both of these are cases of the mouth taking precedence over the muscles, and that's just the way the results will line up, too.

Another way to look at this idea is to say that concentration is a scarce resource, one that you should conserve and use wisely. Ace motorcycle racing instructor Keith Code likens your attention to a ten-dollar bill—spend too much on trivial things and there won't be enough left over for the important ones, so he constantly urges his students to "save" their attention for the things that count most. Sherlock Holmes put a little different English on the same idea by explaining to Dr. Watson that he (Holmes) always tried to avoid cluttering his mind with unnecessary facts, lest the important ones get squeezed out.

At least for lifters, the stereotype for concentrating is to pace back and forth, while exhorting oneself to attack the barbell. And when all else fails, some modern-day powerlifting coaches have taken a lesson from the cornermen in boxing who haul off and slap their charges, "To get their attention and make them concentrate harder." The problem with all these approaches is that they are really "adrenalizing," i.e., they coax the release of epinephrine ("adrenaline"), which fuels the "fight or flight reaction," and getting a little more jazzed is the opposite of what most people need for better concentration. Most people, most of the time, can boost their concentration by *relaxing*. Here's how it goes.

To get a little mystical about it for a minute, think of ultimate concentration as merging with your chosen activity—there's no more you versus it, and certainly no more of you standing on the outside of your task looking in at it. You just melt into it. Don't think that this means you have to trade in your jeans for a white tunic, and your baseball cap for a turban; even if we go ahead and say that full concentration involves "ego transcendence," the feeling is no different than what you have when you are fully absorbed in a book, or while daydreaming. To increase your ability to really concentrate, then, you need to boost your skills in blanking out everything around you—especially your own thoughts. Do the opposite—by letting your mind race around—and your performance will fall. That's why baseball players say, "Full mind, empty bat."

Physiologically, our goal is to reduce efferent activity; that is, we want to reduce the number of messages your central nervous system is sending to your muscles. One of the most effective ways to lull your brain into a relaxed state is to focus your attention on a repetitive event: You can repeat a sound or a phrase over and over (that's what chanting a mantra does), or even simpler, you can just focus on your breathing pattern. Let's try the breathing approach.

Sit upright in a chair, or on a stool or bench, with your feet flat on the ground and your forearms and hands resting comfortably on your thighs. Try to sense the rhythm of your heartbeat, or you can actually monitor your pulse if you would like by putting a finger from one hand on the opposite wrist. Inhale for three or four heartbeats, and then exhale over the next three or four heartbeats. Do about a dozen reps, ideally at least once in the morning and again in the evening, every day while you are developing the basic skill of focusing on your breathing as a way to quiet your mind.

When you hit the gym, try to do all the little things that will aid your concentration: Leave your problems outside; don't talk any more than necessary while training; train in a compatible physical environment, and so forth. If your mind starts to wander, or as a prelude to hitting the Big Set or making the Big Lift try this routine: 1) Use the breathing exercise to re-center your attention, 2) visualize the exact movement(s) you want to make, and 3) return to an empty mind and then attack the weight.

Meanwhile, the next night you are back in Barcelona. You sit quietly breathing in a rhythmic pattern, first using a little verbal self-coaching, then just an image of the lift you want to make, and then nothing but a sea of white light. When you start your pull, you might be anywhere for all you know. And even when the crowd goes wild as you get set for the jerk of your life, you still keep things on brain-detached autopilot. After all, when you have rammed the bar overhead, and won the whole thing, there is still plenty of time to invite your brain back to the party. It might even come in handy negotiating that Coke contract.

27 Creating Competence

Whether you are training at World Championship levels, or just for the personal satisfaction of hitting the best shape of your life, you are travelling a long road. And more than once along the way, you are likely to get discouraged—so discouraged that you might either consider quitting, or you might simply ease up a little on the pressure required to take you to the top. To help you stay on track, we are going to take a look at a psychological factor that either helps you in your quest for progress, or pretty much puts on the brakes for the whole thing. What we'll end up with is a head start package to keep you keeping on.

Self-perceived competence is the main factor that keeps people striving and achieving: If you see yourself as competent, you will keep stretching and growing. Conversely, if you see yourself as incompetent, you will withdraw from challenges and as a result be virtually guaranteed of being shut out when it comes to success.

It has been said that one of our greatest joys is seeing ourselves as active agents who control our own destinies, and that seeing ourselves as helpless creatures plunges us into the depths of despair. So much for the view from the mountain top. Let's do a little bottom-fishing first, and then tie the whole process into training—getting built and getting strong.

To really illustrate how this process works, let's first reverse things and lay out some keys not for creating the self-impression of competence, but for *in*competence. That way, if you are interested in building your competence you'll know what behaviors to avoid. Sometimes this approach has a little more punch, and it can also be easier to explain. Think of this as something like the psychological counterpart to being told which snakes are poisonous before you hike through the jungle.

Engineering Incompetence

Want to see yourself as incompetent? Just follow these four rules:

1) Surround yourself with authority figures who constantly put you down. The best way to start down this path is at birth, with your parents, but since you have little control over this now-distant event, pick the rest of your shots especially carefully. For example, if you can land a job where your boss scowls and grunts at you, publicly-ridiculing and privately-terrorizing you, this can go a long way toward making up for a good childhood. And if you had a bad childhood, it will be a natural extension. The result should be a steady decrease in how you perceive your competence and if you stick with the ogre long enough, you will eventually come to believe the worst things he has ever uttered about you.

The same thing goes in school: If it's an incompetent self-image that you want, try to find the most pompous, insecure teachers in the most intimidating subjects, and then let them have at your ego. Keep at this ego-bashing for at least a year under intense conditions if you are serious about thinking of yourself as being truly worthless.

And if you can swing it, try to stay under the thumb of some authority figures who are fully aware of your training goals and never miss an opportunity to ridicule them. For example, if your boss snickers as you walk by and says something like, "Here he comes, Mr. Pounds & Inches," then you have it made.

2) Always set yourself up for failure. For example, if your best deadlift is 490 pounds, and you have bombed out in your last three contests, don't even think about opening with anything less than 525. And when you miss it, be sure to go up at least 20 pounds for your second attempt.

Similarly, if you are a beginning bodybuilder, seek out the most hard-core gym in your area, find out when the heavies train, and make sure to be there and use your 14-inch arms to elbow your way into as much humiliation and embarrassment as the big guns will dish out. If you want to tri-blast on this program, also enter a physique contest before your chest measurement gets ahead of your waist, and be sure to go in as pasty-white as you can, wearing an oversized posing suit. Remember: Nothing fails like failure, so fail, fail, fail!

3) Rehearse your failures to keep the bad feelings about yourself fresh. Since you are equipped with a higher-order brain, you can create all sorts of symbolic and imaginal stimuli to remind yourself that you are just a worthless bleep. Remember that time you tried to change the oil in your new Jeep, but you put the oil in the radiator by mistake? Or the time you got stuck benching 85 pounds in your basement, while pretending you were Ken Lain going after 710, and your eleven year old sister and her friend had to pull the bar off your chest?

That's the sort of stuff that can buckle the knees of grown men and women, so revel in it if you want to shrink your sense of competence. Remember the mental training motto for incompetence: "If something hurt your pride, take the memory for another ride!" Again and again.

4) Establish unrealistic goals. For example, Paul Anderson once got a letter from a fellow who not only had his heart set on winning an Olympic gold medal in weightlifting, but he even wanted to win the superheavyweight title the following year. This fellow was wise in seeking the advice of the world's strongest man, especially because our aspiring Olympic hero weighed all of 124 pounds at the time of his letter! This sort of thing can do wonders for creating the self-image of incompetence: If you set unrealistic goals, you set yourself up for repeated failure. And you know what we said about nothing failing like failure.

Engineering Competence

So there you have it: Four powerful principles to launch you on the road to incompetence, with the fringe benefit of probably never accomplishing much, in the gym or out. Of course, you might elect to go the other direction—to engineer competence—and see just what sorts of things you can accomplish. Let's try reversing our fundamentals-for-blundering and see what we end up with. For example, suppose we take our first rule for engineering incompetence and make a few changes, what do we end up with?

1) "Surround yourself with authority figures who constantly build you up. The best way to start down this path is at birth, with your parents, but since you have little control over this now-distant event, pick the rest of your shots especially carefully..." You work through the rest of the translation, ending up with something like, "If you can swing it, try to surround yourself with authority figures who are fully aware of your training goals and never miss an opportunity to support them."

Let's summarize and illustrate how the remaining three principles are transformed for crating a self-image of competence.

2) Always set yourself up for success. One of the true heroes at the Seoul Olympics was Naim Suleymanoglu, a 132-pound weightlifter who not only made all six of his lifts, and won the Olympic

gold medal, but who also broke six (!) world records in the process. How can a 132-pound guy clean and jerk well over 400 pounds?

Well for one thing, we are told that Suleymanoglu literally misses but a handful of lifts each *year*—counting training and competition! Talk about conditioning oneself for success. Think about that the next time you have missed a 198-pound snatch nine times in one workout and are considering going for your tenth attempt. Just remember: Success breeds success.

3) Rehearse your successes to keep the good feelings about yourself fresh. Don't think this stuff doesn't work, and don't think that success in one area doesn't transfer to another. Take pride in your past accomplishments and remind yourself of them—especially when you face a new challenge or just experienced a setback.

We get a lot of mail from people who have taken themselves to new heights on the 20-rep squat program, and besides transforming their bodies, they have developed a new level of self-confidence: They can succeed, and they know it because they just proved it under the squat bar.

4) Establish realistic goals. This should be self-evident, but a lot people don't distinguish between what we might call "aggressive planning" and, frankly, "delusions of grandeur." Remember that realistic goals are in no way self-limiting: Once you meet them, just reset them a little higher. On the other hand, don't use the guise of realistic goals as an excuse to lower your standards. No matter where you are, your goal should be to improve; just make sure that you plan achievable forward progress.

If your training has been in a slump lately, see what you can do to strengthen your belief in your own abilities: Recreate yourself in the image of competence, and break through to new standards.

28 The ABCs & Feeling Good

Things were looking good for aspiring pro-bodybuilder Bert Stover: After winning his class in a for-real regional contest, he was off to the Nationals in his lifetime-best shape. Would he crack the top five? Maybe the top three? The possibilities were dizzying. Unfortunately, Bert barely squeaked into the top ten, and to add insult to injury, a few of the guys he had slain at his regional event jumped ahead of him at the Nationals. Bert started looking for his crying towel.

Let's face it, Bert saw this as more than just a slap in the face; he saw it as a step backwards that involved both current cash and future prosperity, not to mention more than a dash of ego. Don't you feel lousy when something bad happens to you? It's really as simple as ABC. Or is it?

The Anatomy of Negative Feelings

When you feel bad about yourself, the first thing you usually think of is the critical event that started everything: In Bert's case the critical event was his poor placing at the Nationals. Let's call this event A, since it was the first in the chain of events. Most people don't notice it, but the next step in the misery-chain is something really bad they say about themselves based on the critical event; this is event B. For example, Bert might say something like, "I'm a failure because of my poor showing...All of my plans are shot...What will I do now?" Event C is the final stop: It's feeling lousy about yourself. Really lousy.

What we are going to do is examine this pattern a little, and by adapting the work of Dr. Albert Ellis, we are going to attack this standard process. What we will end up with is a system that will allow you to take an unpleasant event (A), handle it rationally (B), and end up feeling okay (C), even if things didn't begin according to plan.

Thoughts and Feelings

How many times have you heard someone (maybe yourself) say something like: "I understand that intellectually, but not emotionally." Or, "I know I shouldn't get upset, but I am!" Intensive clinical research has often shown that, in fact, most of the time even if we claim to disbelieve an idea that could make us feel bad, we actually believe it.

For example, we might publicly declare that, "Winning isn't everything," but deep in our heads, we say things like, "If you're not winning, you are losing...Second place is no better than fifth...If you're not going forward, you are going backward...Nobody loves a loser..." What psychologists have learned is that not only do thoughts and feelings go together, but it's what we think about something that determines how we feel about it.

That statement might not impress you until you realize that you can learn to change the way you think about things, which means that you can also change the way you feel about them. The great promise is that you can reshape your thinking to eliminate a lot of unnecessary negative feelings about yourself. Let's see how this works and then apply it to a couple of situations you might encounter.

The underlying idea is that when something happens to us, the reaction isn't just an automatic, pre-programmed response. Instead, we can influence our reaction by what we tell ourselves about it. So when you didn't hit your PR attempt 275-pound clean and jerk, you can criticize yourself for your miss ("You wimp...You jumped back...) and make yourself feel bad. Or you can just let it go, reinforce your effort ("Good try...You really attacked it...You will probably make it next time...) and leave feeling good about the whole thing.

Notice that in both of these options, we start off with the same initial event (A: the miss), but depending upon how we handle the second stage (B: encouragement or criticism), we end up with wildly different outcomes (C: confidence and optimism, or discouragement and depression). As they say, the choice is yours.

"Cute theory," you say, "but isn't this a little unrealistic? Do you want Bert to do back flips about his lousy showing at the Nationals?" Actually, this approach is very realistic—much more so than most of the grief that masquerades as "realism." Let's talk about that.

Is it realistic for Bert to start thinking about drinking Drano just because he was down a few places in his big contest? Come on, would the sky have really opened for him even if he had hit his goal? Do you really think that fifth place would have won all sorts of big endorsements and cover opportunities, and that tenth just left him out in the cold. And even if placing a few places higher would have been nice, why act as if you just lost an arm, a leg and maybe an eye to boot? And can't you think of any recent pro contests where the runner-up, or worse, netted more publicity than the winner?

Save your grief and misery for when you will really need them. When you accidentally break a dish, do you let it ruin your life or do you pick up the pieces and march forward? Think about this process and decide whether you are actually being unrealistic about getting so upset about something that recently didn't go your way.

Certainly, when something undesirable happens, it's perfectly reasonable to be sad about it. What we are trying to eliminate, however, is the tendency to take an unfortunate event, become deeply depressed by it, and end up slapping a label like "worthless" on ourselves. If you are having difficulty separating these two types of reactions, try the following exercise the next time you are extremely upset (depressed, anxious or angry, for example). Following our friends in clinical psychology, let's call this approach *rational imagery*.

Rational Imagery

1) When you are upset, run through what has happened to you, and how you reacted to the event.

2) Imagine yourself confronting a group of your friends with this question: "What do you think would be a reasonable response under these conditions?"

3) One by one, work through your reactions to the situation, testing the rationality of your response(s) with your friends' reactions.

4) When your friends think your reaction is not reasonable, work together to identify one that is.

For example, if you get fired, you might be tempted to drink yourself into a stupor, or look for an external agent to blame for your dilemma. Although both approaches might bring momentary relief, neither is a reasonable reaction; if nothing else, both fail the test of being reasonable because they do absolutely nothing to solve the problem of being unemployed.

Reasonable reactions under these circumstances would be a) looking for another job, b) trying to determine what factors might have led to your being fired, and c) attempting to manage these factors to avoid a repeat of the undesirable outcome.

Remember that the essence of this approach is that *what* happens to you is less important that *how* you react to it, and that when bad things happen to us, we tend to greatly exaggerate just how bad they really are. To compound the problem, we then get caught up in a tangle of irrational beliefs, negative self-labels and actions that not only don't solve the problem, but also are even more likely to exacerbate it. Instead, stay level-headed when something bad happens, and guard against magnifying the size of the problem. Simultaneously develop a reasonable action plan that solves the problem and forestalls a repeat incident.

Apply this process the next time you are down, and see if it doesn't help clear the air and immediately put you on track to feeling better. After all, feeling better is really just as simple as ABC.

29 Four Ways To Woe

Last month we talked about some ways to take the edge off disappointments. This month, let's take things a step further and explore how certain common thought patterns can set you up for feeling bad. Specifically, we'll try to give you a little insight into four basic patterns of thinking that often lead to unnecessary conflicts, stall purposeful action, create overall tension and produce destructive levels of anxiety. After all, even if you have a system for taking the edge off negative outcomes, wouldn't it be even better if you could avoid a lot of problem situations in the first place?

Dichotomous Reasoning

"Dichotomous reasoning" is the psychologist's label for dividing everything into the world into two opposite groups: good versus evil, right versus wrong, and so forth. The opposite approach is to recognize shades of gray, or some sort of middle group in between the two extreme positions.

In sports, one of the most striking examples of the fallacy of dichotomous reasoning takes the form of winning versus losing: Witness the standard interview with an Olympic silver medalist that opens with the stock line, "You must really feel bad... ." Suppose instead that you took a relative point of view. Then the interview would begin something like, "Man, you faced the best in the world today and beat 73 of them—all but one competitor, and even that was close. You must feel great... ."

Walk through some of the situations that have gotten you down lately and see whether or not some dichotomous reasoning has given your emotions a bum ride. For example, have you been telling yourself that you are "soft" when you wish you were "hard," or maybe calling yourself "small" when "big" is what you want, or maybe saying that you are "weak" when "strong" is your goal.

Get away from these potentially destructive two-box approaches by stepping back and putting yourself on a continuum—in all likelihood, someplace between the two endpoints. Maybe you want to get "harder," "bigger," or "stronger," but at least give yourself credit for what you have already accomplished.

Overgeneralization

Overgeneralization creates problems that are closely related to those of dichotomous reasoning: Overgeneralization tells you, for example, that all shrinks are crazy, all lawyers are liars, or closer to home, that all contests are won by drug fiends. As in these examples, overgeneralization usually takes the form of negative stereotypes, but what are called "false positives" can be just as dangerous. For example, you might believe that all food supplement companies are honest, just as easily as you might believe that all food supplement companies are dishonest.

As with dichotomous thinking, the way out of the trap of overgeneralization is to learn to recognize shades of gray. Now you realize that while one company might dump starch into a can and label it "100% Egg Protein," another might offer a product that specs out exactly as advertised.

Because this approach puts the burden on you to make judgments on a case basis, at first glance it's tougher on you, but your longer term reward is that you will be spared the unhappiness of rampant paranoia and broad distrust on the one hand, and the risk of being sucker-punched at every turn, on the other. Keeping an open mind pretty much sums up your way out of the trap of overgeneralization.

Overreliance on What Others Think

"What will your mother think?" is about all the ammo a Nurse Ratched needs to drive some people to suicide, but even if you're a little tougher than Billy Bibbit on this score, just how much misery enters your life because you overrely on the judgments of others? In therapeutic settings, insecure patients are chronically plagued by their inability (real or perceived) to please everybody. If you are caught in this bind, you simply have to realize that not everyone is going to be liked by everyone else, and if it makes you feel any better, a lousy reason might underlie someone's dislike of you.

People who train with weights are especially vulnerable to psychological—and physical—fallout due to this thought pattern. For example, a competitive bodybuilder might risk his health to satisfy a small group of judges and fans ("Even if I kill myself, at least I'll look good"), or she might put up with some pretty strange and undesirable side effects to gain the muscle mass her peer group admires.

Or a naturally athletic and strong woman might be afraid to excel in strength sports because most people would think it was an odd pursuit for a woman. And many ordinary bodies will stay ordinary because their owners have been told by too many others that "all those muscles are ugly" or "what good is all that strength anyway."

Arms that measure over a foot and a half around, 800-pound squats and 500-pound clean and jerks are not the stuff of the average person, so if you have serious iron aspirations, you will automatically set yourself apart from most people; and this sort of social distance can make you the source of envy and admiration, or ridicule and scorn. The bottom line for all who would be uncommonly built or uncommonly strong is that you are absolutely going to have to make peace with the idea of having at least one foot out of the social mainstream. Try to enjoy your celebrity status, or you will never survive out there.

Enculturation

"Enculturation" is the process of learning the values of your culture: It's the idea that "when in Rome, do as the Romans do," and problems in this area are closely related to those stemming from overrelying on what other people think. Unlike averse reactions from a specific person, problems of enculturation center around being at odds with the whole culture. Sometimes successful enculturation is a matter of life and death, as in the case of obeying traffic signals, but often it's simply a matter of marching to the same standard as everyone else.

The most important thing about this socialization process is the rarely discussed fact that almost no cultural belief is absolute: Consider cannibalism and you will realize that even the things we are most likely to take as absolute and given, are not universally shared. So what does this have to do with bigger biceps and heavier totals?

For starters, think about those hearty souls who dared to publicly present a view of the female physique dramatically different from any standard previously established or openly admired? What of 5' 9" Paul Anderson weighing well over 350 pounds to be the world's strongest man, when he could have cut down to 275 and merely been huge?

And don't forget that once upon a time, Sergio Oliva was viewed as simply too big, as in having muscles that were too well developed. Notably, Paul Anderson and Sergio Oliva had crossed the line not only with the general public, but even with their peer groups: Other lifters and bodybuilders were in shock over these men.

Recognizing that we all are social animals to some extent, when people don't fit into the social mainstream, they often end up in a subcultural group of some type. That way lifters can support lifters because when everyone else in the group has 30-inch thighs, you don't have to think of your legs as being enormous—the other guys' are just small. And bodybuilders don't spend all their time with pencil neck CPAs—they are often in the company of their well-developed peers. The idea here isn't to support your weirdest fantasies by seeking out the company of a wacko cult, but simply that it will help you stay on track toward your goals if you associate with people who share your goals.

Next time you start coming down on yourself, stop early in the process of self-criticism and check what you are thinking: Don't let the four ways to woe steal your show.

30 Backing Off To Bag The Big Ones

Years ago my friend Peter Johnson revealed his secret formula for winning bicycle races: *"Lots of guys train at 95% all the time, and when they race, they also ride at about 95%. I train at about 80% a lot of the time, but when I race, I ride at 110%. And that's why I win races and they don't."* This is a critical concept, and it applies whether you are a bodybuilder or a lifter, regardless of whether you compete or simply train for fun. If you ignore this principle you may win some battles, but chances are that you'll lose the war.

The challenge here is to know when and how to back off the gas a little, so that when it really counts, you can put the pedal to the metal. Let's walk through a few examples, using a lifter, a competitive bodybuilder, and Mr. Average iron-tosser. Let's take a look at the representative walls each bangs his head against day after day, and lay out a quick alternative for each.

At the heart of many problems of trying too hard at the wrong times is a popular myth: the idea that if we somehow just keep trying hard enough, our progress will be straight up. We'd all like to believe this is true, so our first reaction when we run into an obstacle is to fight back and try again with another frontal assault. So when a lifter misses a weight, he might take it again, and again.... There's a fellow around here who likes to tell people about the time it took him 23 attempts in one training session before he made the 120-kilo snatch he had been chasing.

That makes for colorful stories, but such training tactics are actually counterproductive in the long run. "Why?" you ask. "Didn't that just prove he could conquer the weight?"

Sure he conquered the weight, but it took 22 misses to do it. That means he not only risked injury time and again, but he also practiced missing the weight 22 times for the one time he made it. That's a 4% hit rate—not exactly the type of odds that build confidence for the next time he faces the bar. And what of the physical and mental fatigue from that effort? So for two days he'll be too sore to even comb his hair, and when's the next time you think his brain will be ready to hit a big one? A week? Two weeks? A month?

What if he had backed off after even his first miss, if an honest self-appraisal indicated that it was just too much for him that day? What if he had dropped back and hit some nice crisp doubles with 100—doubles that not only etched the pattern of good form deep into his brain, but that also built his base strength and bolstered his confidence. In fact, so many good things might have happened from following Plan B, that he might have been able to outright drill the 120 on his first try the following week, and even put another 2-1/2 kilos on top of that the week after.

Not that this concept is just for lifters, either, because bodybuilders have their own ways to ease up in between for better long-term results. For example, have you ever seen the guys who are so concerned about always being within a couple percent of their hardest possible shape, so they never get any bigger? Month after month at the same muscle mass level soon turns into a perennial affair because they are so intent on never letting themselves float above contest condition.

In the same time period, other bodybuilders had taken their off-season seriously and allowed themselves to get a little smooth as they packed on some serious gains in size, then they hardened up for a contest, got a little bigger after, a little harder next...and so forth. So while the first group would surely have racked up more points for being "in shape" day in and day out, the second group was really making progress. And guess which group walks away with all the hardware at the contests one year out?

And then there's the average guy training with weights—pining away for an honest 17-inch arm on top of his 7-inch wrist and thinking that if he could ever bench 315, he'd feel like Pat Casey and Ted Arcidi rolled into one. Let's face it, the average person—fighting for progress—has the continual challenge of staying motivated in the face of gains that are less than world class. For this guy, the main challenge isn't from the fellow next to him in the line-up: It's to stay focused on his training when his gains aren't herculean in size or dizzying in speed. His competition is all the distractions that have sucked other people out of the gym and landed a lot of them on the couch. For this guy, it's keeping himself in the gym, and away from "Miami Vice" reruns.

This is the fellow who needs to follow all the tricks used by those at the top. He needs to avoid burning out on maximum singles while keeping an eye on moving ever heavier poundages, just like the champion lifter, and he needs to know how to boost his overall size, symmetry and cuts, just like the top bodybuilders. Because his progress is likely to be slower than the top guys enjoy, our hero needs to be especially alert to avoid burning out en route to his goals. In fact, a major key to an effective strategy for him is to cycle intelligently.

Let's say he's trying to push up his bench by 35 pounds in the coming year. He might just go for broke in the first month or two, and maybe get halfway to his goal. And then he'll probably break down mentally, physically, or both, and spend the rest of the year wallowing around his starting weights, or even below.

Conversely, he might plan out a few cycles of training that allow for some natural sawtoothing—the little ups and downs that normally accompany training—but in a way that paves the way for *generally* upward progress. Not only is he going to vary his plan of attack before he gets stale, but each time he switches to a new program he drops back to moderate weights and gradually increases them over the life of the cycle.

For example, he might start off with a cycle that doesn't even include any benches: just fairly high reps on seated dumbbell militaries, inclines and dips. About two months out, he's on moderate reps, and now it's presses behind the neck and benches. Then it's a cycle of fives on the bench, and he's suddenly halfway to his year-end goal and guess what? He's not only at a PR on the bench, but also in terms of his enthusiasm and his confidence.

Back to the seated dumbbell militaries—lower reps now—and some close-grip benches, followed by some moderate inclines. And then another cycle of fives on the bench, followed by a final cycle of triples and doubles, with the gameplan calling for max singles a couple of times in the last three weeks. Funny thing is that he actually hits his year-end goal a month early, and for a triple no less. Sometimes the fastest way to reach your goals is to slow down a little on the way.

Consistent, hard training, we all know, is the one of the key ingredients to big gains, so it probably sounds like heresy to suggest that sub-maximal efforts have a definite place in the big-gainer's training plan. But knowing when to go all out and when to back off is as important in the Iron Game as "knowing when to hold them and when to fold them" is to the gambler.

31 Delay Of Gratification

The ability to voluntarily refuse immediate gratification—to give up a small pleasure today for a larger one tomorrow—is at the heart of will power. Psychologists refer to this process as "delay of gratification," and while it's true that civilization could not exist without this ability, let's not ignore its role in the realm of really important things, like getting bigger and stronger. Very simply: If you don't learn to delay gratification, even the most genetically-gifted athlete will barely leave the starting blocks, and the average person will remain just that: average.

Let's begin by taking a look at how the overall process works, and then apply it to your training, both short-term and long-term.

A funny thing happens to a lot of guys when they turn 16: They get their driver's license and guess what, they want a car. In the no-delay-of-gratification scenario, our victim succumbs to his immediate pleasure and drops out of high school to fry burgers and buy a car. True, all he landed was a rusted-out Pinto, but it is a *car*. And he got it *now*.

Our hero, on the other hand, delays gratification, and makes do with double-dates and occasionally wrangling the keys for the family car, even saving his summer job money for college. By the time both guys are twenty, our victim has a brand new Camaro, while our hero is wheezing around in an older Volkswagen. In another few years, the victim still has his Camaro (sporting a few door dings by now) and our hero has just driven a BMW 325 off the showroom floor. In another few years, our victim still has his Camaro, but our hero traded his Bimmer for a Porsche 911. You get the picture.

The so-called "Protestant Ethic," with its puritanical demands that impulses be delayed and pleasure be avoided, clearly portrays an ultimate form of delay of gratification. Puritans were not what you'd call a fun group: One of my graduate school professors, Dr. Lee Ross, once said something like, "Puritans were driven by the deep-seated fear that somewhere, somehow, somebody was having a good time." And they wanted to put a stop to such foolishness.

Such extremes are not what we are talking about. What we want you to achieve is the ability to trade the little tweak of pleasure today, for a big-O level blast tomorrow.

Let's see what the psychology research laboratory has taught us about delay of gratification, and then apply it to your training.

Many of the classic studies in delay of gratification involve young children as the experimental subjects. After all, children are notoriously poor at delaying gratification (demand something right now and you are likely to hear, "Quit acting like a 3-year old..."). So research on whatever can boost children's "will power" surely should yield principles that can be effectively applied to adults. Let's focus on two primary findings.

Monkey See, Monkey Do

Avoiding scientific niceties, we call the first principle "Monkey see, monkey do" because laboratory research has clearly demonstrated that you will be influenced by what you see others do, including whether or not they delay gratification. In one study, children were tested for their ability to delay gratification after they had been in one of three experimental conditions: 1) live adult models who delayed gratification, 2) written statements about delaying gratification, or 3) no exposure to any modeling (live or via written statements). The children were tested immediately after the experimental procedure, and again one month later.

It wasn't just that the exposure to the delay of gratification models boosted the kids' ability to delay their own gratification, but even more impressive was that the effect was still strongly present one month later! So one exposure to a model could reverse the child's initial tendency to delay gratification or not, and that one exposure had a lasting impact.

Now you know why your parents were always trying to keep an eye on who your friends were, and you can see the importance of spending your time with people who share your goals. If you hang around with the party-hearty crowd, you might score your victories, but they won't be in the gym or on the platform. On the other hand, if you spend your time with people who share your goals of getting bigger and stronger, and are willing to make the sacrifices it takes to reach these goals, you will be surrounded by constructive role models, and it will be easier for you to keep your training on track.

The Blind Eye

The second principle we want to review is whether or not you should focus your attention on your distant goal. For example, let's say you want to have an honest 17-1/2-inch arm and be able to do a strict 220-pound press behind the neck. Right now, your arm tapes 14-1/4 inches (with a little slant to the tape) and you can do a 45-pound press behind the neck (if someone puts the bar on your shoulders first). With everyone fully intoxicated on the miracles of visualization and mental rehearsal, the smart money probably says that you should keep your mind's eye focused on your distant goals. But should you?

Research with children faced with getting a preferred reward after a long wait, or a less-desirable reward after a short wait were presented with one of four conditions while they waited: 1) the preferred reward in front of them, 2) the less preferred reward in front of them, 3) both rewards in front of them, or 4) neither reward in front of them.

The both-rewards group barely waited at all, the two groups faced with one reward (preferred or less-preferred) waited a moderate amount of time, but the no-reward group had by far the longest waiting time. The lesson is clear: Sometimes it's best to turn a blind eye to a distant goal, or you will be distracted from your immediate task.

The best way to manage this in a training environment is to only look at your long-term goal out of the corner of your eye, while you keep your vision focused on the what it takes to make the next small step forward. Namely, think about the next 1/4 inch on your arm and the next five pounds on the bar, but don't focus on the whole territory you need to cover to reach your goals, or you will probably never make it.

Cognitive Transformation

The final twist in the blind eye approach is to use a technique psychologists call "cognitive transformation," and while we don't have time this month to get into this in detail, here's the essence of how it works. The trick is to transform the difficult into the easy, the boring into the interesting, and so forth, by relabelling your experience so you can stick to your task.

Let's say that you are trying to whittle through the lard around your waist and as part of your program, you have to do a pretty fair amount of ab work. On each rep, instead of thinking about your burning abs hurting, for example, you think about the washboard abs that are forcing their way to the surface. And instead of just counting out the reps in a straightforward sequence, try counting "1,2,3...10" and then "10,9,8...1," alternating up and down the scale until you're done. The technique of cognitive transformation can take you pretty far if you push it, so give it an honest try.

Remember that if you have worthy goals, they will probably take time to achieve, and conversely, anything that can be achieved in a flash will probably last about as long. So don't cheat yourself by always folding for instant gratification: Be willing to hang tough until you get what you really wanted all along.

32 Giant Steps To Glory

Charlie Moore might not have put it in so many words, but his philosophy could be summed up thusly: By steps to the stars. And not that anyone could find fault with such sage thinking, because don't we all know that it's those hairline increases that add up to extra inches in the biceps and it's those 2-1/2-pound PRs that move you to the stratosphere in your lifts. And if that's not enough proof, don't we all know that most of time you really can't gain much faster than at a snail's pace anyway, so making steady micro-steps actually looks pretty good after all.

Charlie had stuck with the program, adding a quarter of an inch here, a pound there, and three years into his training, his results were most noteworthy. The problem was that three years into Charlie's training was two years ago, and after a pair of years with gains that could only be measured on the wrong side of the decimal point, Charlie was getting discouraged.

Even more dangerous from a gaining point of view, Charlie was coming to see himself as a guy who looked and performed exactly the way he was right now. Not that this was sheer stupidity on his part because, remember, Charlie had been staring at himself—unmoving—for roughly 730 days, which was more than enough time for such a bright young man to get used to what he saw.

The real problem here wasn't just Charlie's being stuck physically. The real problem was that Charlie was getting stuck mentally. Charlie had come to accept his present condition as his predictable future condition. And if you want to bring your future gains to a rubber-burning halt, just start thinking that tomorrow and the next day will see you just as you are today. As we have said before, "Where the mind ventures, the body can surely follow." So when your mind heads for the couch, your future lands in the garbage can.

Whether motivated by true belief or sheer desperation, one day Charlie decided that it was finally time to get a fresh opinion on his dilemma so he went over to talk to a guy he'd heard about, a guy who applied research psychology to matters of might and muscle. This is approximately how their conversation went.

"I've been stuck for about two years, and no matter what I do, I don't make any progress." Thinking it appropriate to add insight and confession to a conversation with someone trained in psychology, Charlie added, "Maybe my genetic potential is like my Visa card—tapped out."

"I see," said the good doctor, trying his hardest to sound like the clinical psychologist he wasn't, but instead of moving into Charlie's love life or questions about early childhood relationships, he asked Charlie a few questions about how he was training, and then they talked a little about Charlie's original goals, as well as his current short-term, intermediate and long-term goals.

From his questions, two things were obvious to the good doctor: 1) Charlie was stuck somewhere between his original short-term and intermediate goals, and 2) the way things were (not) going, Charlie was ready to whittle down his long-term goals to just about where he was right now. That was the red flag the good doctor was looking for.

"Charlie," he said, "I'd like to tell you about a psychological phenomenon called *self-fulfilling prophecy*—three words that spell trouble if you're on the wrong side of them, or give you the keys to controlling your destiny if you are on the right side of them. Right now, Charlie, you're on the wrong side of this beast, so let's talk about it and then turn things around for you."

"Cool," said Charlie, because if nothing else, the good doctor had planted him on a comfortable couch with a dynamite view of a mountain out the window.

"*Self-fulfilling prophecy* means that what you expect is what you get," began the good doctor. "It helps explain everything from academic performance to racial prejudice to sex-role stereotypes, all of which are interesting and worthy phenomena for social psychologists to study.

"But," he continued, "I'm not going to dwell on things like when teachers think their classes have stupid kids, the kids do poorly, or that when the kids are told that they are stupid, they seem to become stupid. Just take my word for the fact that tons of psychological research has shown that people can unconsciously influence their own behavior and that of other people, to shape the results they expect. Expect stupid, get stupid. Expect lazy, get lazy. And so on."

The good doctor glanced over at Charlie to see if he was impressed with this recitation of scientific fact, but Charlie seemed to be concentrating on following the path of a hang glider that had just launched from the nearby mountain top. The good doctor knew it was time to speed up his spiel.

"Charlie, you have come to expect virtually no progress, and that's exactly what you have gotten. Worse, until you change your expectations, you will continue to get no progress."

"O.K. big time," Charlie was thinking to himself, but being well-mannered, he just asked, "What's your recommendation?"

"**9**0-some percent of the time it's right to train according to the principle of taking baby steps toward your goals. But every now and then, it's time to take giant steps—to just try to break away from the clutches of gravity, if you will, and soar to new heights." The good doctor wasn't sure whether he had come up with a nice literary description or just made a monkey of himself, but he kept going.

"When you get in a deep rut, sometimes it's useless to try to crawl out—you need to think about exploding out. What you need to do is demolish the very obstacle that has been blocking your progress. Let's say you have been stuck at a certain level of muscle mass for a *long* time and it's less than what you want. Then it's time to throw the conventional wisdom to the wind and forget about putting on a few pounds of muscle a year—start thinking about putting on that much a week for a short period of time. Radical, Charlie; you've got to get radical."

The good doctor studied Charlie's face and could see that his words were having an impact, so he continued.

"The idea here is to completely remake your concept of what to expect of yourself—you are going to make such major progress toward your long-term goals that we call this type of training 'giant steps.' This is the type of training that will retool your body so rapidly and so dramatically that your mind will be forced to construct a new image of what you are and what you can be. And this new self-image will help you continue to make even more progress after you have completed your giant-step training.

To make these giant steps, your training will most likely be characterized by three features:

1) Specialization: It won't be an all-purpose routine. It will have very specific goals (gaining/ losing a certain amount of weight, pushing a certain lift way above your present PR, etc.). This is really the time to pick your shots very carefully, beginning with your top priority. If you don't have your training priorities lined up, that's the place to start.

2) Intensity: Effective giant-step programs aren't for the weak-hearted, so if you aren't prepared to bust a gut, you probably won't be able to cut it on a giant-step program. Louis Abele used to say that he worked so hard on his leg and back specialization programs that his teeth hurt from the breathing! Think about that sort of effort when you consider training intensity.

3) Unconventional: The giant-step programs are off to the side of the mainstream, so expect to do some unexpected things when you are in this type of training. Let's face it, conventional programs produce conventional gains. Since you are looking for extraordinary results, expect to have to do some extraordinary training.

By now Charlie had gotten the message and the bug had bitten, so he bounded off the couch, thanked the good doctor and raced home to map out his next cycle of training, because now he knew that in about six weeks the old Charlie Moore was going to be just that. Charlie was taking a giant step to glory.

33 Becoming The Best

Billy Ray Jones had something on his mind. Things were getting so bad, in fact, that he had literally been losing sleep over it. Billy Ray had been in hard training for several years, with more than a little to show for his efforts. What was getting under Billy Ray's skin, though, was that he not only wanted to be better, he wanted to be the best.

Now Billy Ray was no fool when it came to something as serious as this, so he had already checked out the competition and made some notes on their strengths and weaknesses. From this analysis, Billy went the next step and created an image of a new champion who would slay all the current top guns—first he used paper and pencil (with a lot of eraser thrown in), and then he transformed his rough sketch into a sharp mental image that he waved before his inner eye day and night. Too much of it at night, in fact, because there was something about this whole process that was getting under Billy Ray's skin and kept waking him up around 3:00 A.M.

It wasn't that his goals were lofty, to say the least. And it wasn't even that the realist in Billy Ray was already gasping just thinking about all the hard work that lay between Billy Ray, current incarnation, and Billy Ray, King of the World. What it was went beyond the mere mechanics of what it would take to be the best.

The problem was that Billy Ray wanted the formula for success—he wanted to know what were the key ingredients he would have to mix to end up at the level he wanted: the best. What Billy Ray needed was a game plan for getting great, a high level strategy that he could use to guide his daily action plans.

Billy Ray decided to call a guy he had heard about, a guy who was reputed to possess a rare ability to diagnose and cure many of the ills that lodged in the heads of his fellow trainers. In actuality, what Billy Ray got was a guy who was still fuming that Alain Prost lost his Formula One World Championship after a dubious crash, and was busy fantasizing about all the hate mail he'd like to send to a certain Brazilian race car driver. Being a professional, though, the guy managed to push his frustration aside, as he tilted back his Ferrari cap, and listened to Billy Ray's dilemma.

"So," concluded Billy Ray, "I know I want to be the absolute best, and I know about a lot of the little things I need to do to get there, but I don't have a master plan for getting there."

"What you need," said the guy in the red hat, "is a strategy for becoming a star. Or if we can cut out the Hollywood, a formula for becoming the best: Maybe the best in the world, and maybe even the best of all time, but certainly the very best you can be. And believe it or not, I can make this pretty simple for you. All you need to do is pay attention to four things, and you'll be all set.

Let's start off with one of the most misunderstood of these four critical building blocks: ability. Call it 'aptitude,' 'genetics,' 'talent' or whatever else you want, but never forget that each of us is unique, and the downside of this is that some of us have more or less of certain attributes than we might like.

The key here is to pick your battleground with care, Billy, always trying to be honest with yourself about which arenas allow you compete at your strongest. And don't forget this idea of competition, because if you are out to become the best in the world, or the best of all time, you have to try to pick a competitive arena that gives you the biggest advantages over everyone else.

It's easy to get sidetracked on this one, and think that you didn't spring from the gene pool of your first choice, or even that you ended up with nothing at all that can really put you on top, but that usually just means you aren't looking around with an open eye. For example, the people who are too blocky to be at their best in bodybuilding contests, might be great candidates for lifting, and for the lifting types, those with long arms who suffer on curls and benches, can excel on deadlifts and cleans. *Everyone* has some special talents—they just need to discover them.

The second key is focus. How many people do you know who are training for bodybuilding one day, powerlifting the next, and just loafing on the third? How many people do you know who are always wildly enthusiastic about what they are doing but, funny thing, what they are doing seems to change almost every thirty seconds? And of the champions in any field, how many haven't been doing whatever they do for years, many years?

Someone once told me that the reason the Olympics were originally only scheduled every four years is because it was felt that four years was the minimum time it took to produce a champion of that caliber. Talk to top athletes today you are more likely to hear about preparation periods of more like two Olympiads.

Don't forget that medical doctors, lawyers, and scientists with Ph.D.s all spent about that much time in school after they *started* college. So when we are talking focus, we mean a longstanding commitment to one field of endeavor. Remember the old line: 'Jack of all trades, master of none.' You simply must stay focused to be the best.

The third key is effort, and it is very closely related to the need to stay focused on what you want to achieve. When we talk about staying focused for at least a few years, and probably something more like a decade before you hit top form, we're not talking about just going through the motions. We're talking about working hard the whole time.

In fact, we're talking about working progressively harder the whole time—handling more intense training if you're a bodybuilder, and more weight if you are a lifter; absorbing ever-more information if you are a student, and so forth. You need to keep the pressure on yourself or you not only won't go forward, you will slide backward. And if that's not a bitter enough pill to swallow, remember that at least for things physical, it's usually much easier to go backward than forward. In other words, in a couple of misspent months, you can literally undo years of training. So keep the pressure on—first to not slide backwards, and second to keep progressing toward your goals.

The fourth key to becoming the best is probably the least understood of all: luck. The truth is that not everything will ever be under your control. You can have the right abilities, stay focused on your goals, work like nobody's business, and still come up short. That's the risk—the uncertainty of your final result—that often turns the knees of the would-be bests into jelly. You have to understand that things might go south even when by every rational indicator, they should be heading due north.

One of the big problems with this luck factor is that it's tempting to attribute all of one's ills to "bad luck" and just throw in the towel, when you really made an error in one of the three areas mentioned earlier. In fact, hard work often masquerades for good luck, just as bad judgment, poor focus, and laziness can be misrepresented as bad luck.

It's hard to prove, but chances are good that if you go through each of the first three steps according to the plan, good luck will usually find its way to your doorstep. And if it doesn't, remember that the mark of a true champion is how he handles himself after a crash: It's easy to be gracious and appear in control when you're on top, but how do you fare when you're not? The mark of all true champions is their ability to rebound from adversity—even if it means reversing directions and changing their original plans when genuinely stonewalled in their efforts to succeed.

"Ability, focus, effort and luck—those are the four keys to becoming the best," summed up the guy in the red hat, "so go home Billy and assess your performance—honestly—with an eye to each of these areas. And let me know how you do."

Billy Ray thanked the man and headed for the door, already determined that he was surely going to hit his goal, no matter if it took several tries and even more years to get there. Yes sir, Billy Ray was on his way to becoming the best.

34 Don't Blame The Sauce Bernaise

Let's talk basic French sauces for a minute. As in Hollandaise and Bernaise.

Even if you might not find handmade Hollandaise at every truck stop along I-25, it's in enough demand that you can even buy its namesake in a can or an envelope. Bernaise, on the other hand, springs from the same basic roots (your low-fat/pre-contest favorites: butter and egg yolks), but the addition of vermouth, shallots and tarragon take the basic product in a different direction, one that is far less travelled.

So much so, in fact, that sauce Bernaise just might the most memorable item after your first trip to a multi-star restaurant. And because of its relative rarity, sauce Bernaise has lent its good name to a psychological phenomenon that might be singing a nasty little song in your ear.

You probably still need to be convinced that French cooking has anything to do with your training, so let's follow you on your first visit to a French restaurant—easily recognized because it's called "Chez something-or-other," the waiters refuse to make eye contact with the customers, and the prices on the wine list would make you consider calling Citibank for an emergency increase on your credit card limit.

Luckily for you, however, you are being treated by your wealthy and urbane uncle, who just happens to be passing through town and wants to treat his favorite nephew to his "first real meal." Naturally, therefore, your uncle did the ordering, and among other things, you ate steak smothered in sauce Bernaise. There were countless new things both before and after—including liberal splashes of champagne—but in your mind, *the* exotic introduction of the evening was to the sauce Bernaise.

The next morning, feeling lousy for whatever reason, you considered what might be causing your discomfort and, *voila!*, in your mind's eye you spot the villain: *It must have been the sauce Bernaise!*

"The "Sauce Bernaise Effect"

One of the areas that has long intrigued psychologists is how people explain the events around them. We're not talking about simple things like why people fall over when George Foreman punches them. We're talking about more subtle things like how you explain the complex successes and failures in your life—how you come to grips with life's ups and downs.

Psychological research has demonstrated that we have a strong inclination to label whatever stands out as *the* most memorable event as being the cause of things, regardless of whether the two events are closely related. So even if the latest flu bug has been mowing down everyone around you, and even if you put away somewhere over a dozen glasses of champagne at the dinner with your uncle, if it's the sauce Bernaise you remember most, it's the sauce Bernaise that most likely will be named as the culprit when the next morning finds you feeling ill.

Let's see how "the sauce Bernaise effect" can affect your future performances. We'll call our example "first time at the Nationals" for emphasis, but think of this pattern as applying in the gym, at school or on the job just as easily. Follow the main points of the example, and then consider a personal application or two.

First Time at the Nationals

It's been a longer road than you ever might have guessed, but here you are, sitting pretty at your first national-level contest. If you are a bodybuilder, you did your homework: The early years were spent developing size, while always striving for improved symmetry and shape. Gradually, you mastered what you saw as putting the finishing touches on your physique and learned how to shed excess fat and water almost at will.

After cutting your teeth on local contests, you scored big in a regional event and laid out a one-year pre-contest plan for your debut at the nationals. You planned your training and diet cycles meticulously, developed and mastered a posing routine and had your tan down to a T. On paper everything was perfect, and the way you saw things you were a shoe-in for the top five and with a little luck, you could hit the top three and maybe even... .

The problem was that when they started calling out names, you didn't even make the first cut! Nearly squashed by your disappointment, the first thing you could think of was that the contest was on the East Coast, and since you were from California, the judges were biased against you.

Same sort of thing goes in lifting. You might have bombed out in a contest where you expected to hit the total that would put you on an international team representing the United States. And in explaining your disappointing performance, you might point out things like the fact that they had used an Olympic-lifting bar at the powerlifting contest or that "there seemed to be something strange about the platform, because so many guys were missing lifts."

These sauce Bernaise-type explanations might provide some momentary consolation because they create the illusion of understanding the situation, but in the long run they will prove counterproductive—simply because they miss the point and therefore set you up for future disappointments of the same kind.

For example, if you really looked lousy compared to the competition it might not have mattered if the contest were in Tampa, Chicago or your hometown, so what you really need to do is come to your next show even better prepared to do battle. Or if you continue to open with weights you would like to lift, versus what you are capable of lifting, you will continue to bomb out far too frequently.

And if you really just let yourself get done in by a handful of small irritants that you should have taken in stride, the next time a lifting contest doesn't use your favorite brand of plates, you are once again poised for disaster.

The moral of our tale is simple, but always worth remembering:

> When you're hit with disappointment,
> Or suffering from malaise,
> Do yourself a favor:
> Don't blame the sauce Bernaise!

35 People Power

"I believe that this study of psychology has been a great help to me. For instance, I seldom could lift my challenge dumb-bell when alone, or even with just one or two friends there. Give me a big audience and an important occasion and I always was able to rise to the occasion and never even thought of failure." —Thomas Inch, turn-of-the-century English strongman and sole conqueror of his "unliftable" challenge dumbbell

They come in all sorts of sizes and shapes—from little and skinny to big and fat—but most of them have two legs, two arms and one head. Despite their wide variety of forms, most have an uncanny ability—one that's rarely discussed but is undeniably powerful: They can boost your gains just by being there!

What we're talking about is how having people around you when you train can actually make you bigger and stronger, and the best part is that you'll get this gain without turning to another miracle split routine or another chemical enhancer. Here's how it works.

Being around people has a generally arousing effect. Physiologically, this translates into a quicker pulse, raised blood pressure, faster respiration, and psychologically, a feeling of tension, or what the Bulgarians have called "mobilization readiness." This is the familiar "fight or flight" reaction which has been protecting the species since its earliest days, and it's what also prepares you for another battle with big iron.

The truth is, training without this edge would be about as smart as expecting big gains from a low protein diet. Being an intelligent person, you try to train smart, so you decide to look into getting some added boost from your fellow man.

To start off, not all people are equally aroused by others. For example, the highly trained guards at Buckingham Palace would probably be immune to the presence of anyone, even the Queen herself. Also, the arousal value of people differs in magnitude and direction: Picture your grandmother first, then switch to your favorite swimsuit model or matinee idol. What's generally true across all people, however, is that having others around gives them a little added shot of physiological and psychological fuel.

Everyone has probably had a training partner who was perfect for always helping you squeeze out that one more rep which makes us all grow bigger and stronger. Thanks, Alice. And some of you have also had the experience of training in a gym where there was someone who irritated you and if he happened to be in the gym when you were training, well, you always had all the motivation you needed for a little extra effort. Much as you'd like to run over this guy with a cement truck, the truth is, just having him around your gym put 50 pounds on your best front squat and over an inch on your arms. Thanks, George.

These are clear-cut examples of how having people around can make you bigger and stronger, but we want to focus on an even more basic process—the way other people can make you stronger just by being there, in a process research psychologists call "social facilitation." And just in case you're afraid that social facilitation has all the instability of this month's wonder supplement, you'll be happy to learn that the idea has been kicking around longer than the plate-loading barbell.

In 1897 a fellow named Norman Triplett noticed that bicycle racers rode a lot faster in the presence of others than they did alone. Triplett was credited with beginning the field of experimental social psychology with his research based on this observation, and he was able to demonstrate the social facilitation effect under tightly controlled laboratory conditions: Children were able to wind up fishing reels a lot faster when in the presence of others than alone.

Since then researchers have tested the idea in a variety of settings and even though there have been exceptions, the general finding is that just having other people around can boost your performance.

"O.K., so 'social facilitation' might work, how do I put it to work in my training program?"

Simple—expect to train harder when others are around, because you probably will. That's why we call this phenomenon "people power."

"You know, I've noticed that I get an extra hit when I'm in contests a couple times a year and that's nice, but to really make impressive progress I need something that works on a regular basis. Is there any way to use this people power stuff to boost my training all the time?"

"Absolutely."

Train with other people at least some of the time is the first moral of this story. Even if you primarily work out alone, make it a point to get out and do some training in public from time to time. We're not just talking your big trip to the famous hardcore gym down the road either, but recommend that you make some pretty regular trips to any gym where a couple of people might be watching you, even if only out of the corners of their eyes.

If you want to put a little added twist in this program, make it a point to go to a new gym every once in a while—don't be surprised if this turns out to be one of the best ways around for breaking some of your PRs. In fact, if you're having problems with a sticking point and just can't seem to budge it, start gym-hopping and see if you don't break into new territory very quickly.

There's a catch to social facilitation, one that goes beyond the fact that it won't produce 30 pounds of muscle overnight: The price of gaining the arousal boost is that your so-called "dominant response" will prevail when you're surrounded by others. Here's what that means.

Let's say that you have a longstanding tendency to lift your hips off the bench when the weights get heavy, and only recently have you learned to keep your glutes glued down no matter what. And let's say that you've been stuck at a certain weight for who knows how long and would do just about anything to make some progress, even going so far as to try this people power stuff.

So off you trot to that hardcore gym across town, where you not only don't know anyone, but also get that sinking feeling as if you just walked into the wrong bar.

What will happen in this situation is that if you actually stick around and start training, you might well pop right through your old bench press limit, but the price you'll pay for this "advance" is that you will probably revert back to your hips-up style. That's what the dominant-response syndrome means: You'll revert to your most familiar response pattern.

Being the smart trainer you are, however, you manage this situation by easing into your bench press training on your gym-hopping days and by sticking to your well-oiled squat, where you could maintain your groove in a dark basement with rats chewing on your toes. Since we all know what miracles can be wrought by intensive squat programs, it's no surprise that you made dramatic gains in overall size and strength from this approach—not to mention how your old bench PR now reads like ancient history.

Finally, if you're desperate about getting back at an old training partner who once stole your date and is now threatening to take away your state title too, start whispering in his ear about the advantages of home training. Talk up the idea to the point of getting him to train exclusively at home—tell him you can be training partners once a week or so. Then, every time you're supposed to show up to train, cancel at the last minute and head off to a new gym. Chances are good that he'll get punier and punier, as you get bigger and stronger: Just another case of people power!

36 The Feedback Factor

When people make extraordinary progress in their training, it's a sure bet that they have solid information systems supporting themselves. Information is power, and gains in the gym are not immune to this equation, so let's see how to develop the sort of information system that will accelerate your gains. We'll start with the basics and then concentrate on the main event: the feedback factor.

Information and Performance

Whether you are training as a bodybuilder, powerlifter or Olympic lifter, your progress will be greatest if you have a clear-cut goal in mind. Indeed, the importance of goals is so well accepted that it's the most commonly discussed information system element in weight training circles. Beyond your long term goals, you must set subgoals and define accomplishments to mark your path along the way.

Most intelligent trainees get this far, but the next step—understanding why each accomplishment is important—sometimes gets short shrift. Saying "that's what Lee Haney does..." might inspire effort for a while, but it's good to know *why* Lee Haney does it and even better to know *why* you should too.

Even this much of an information support system will already put you ahead of someone who is just in the gym "to make progress" and numbly marches through the routine his buddy scratched out for him. But if you really want a high octane information system, you need to add a feedback loop: something that tells you whether you are on the right track, and how close you are to your goals.

The Hawthorne Effect

Over half a century ago the Western Electric Company conducted a worker productivity study at its Hawthorne plant. Not only has this project stood as the most famous and influential investigation of its kind, but it also—after correct interpretation—provides dramatic evidence supporting the power of feedback to boost performance. Here's what happened at Hawthorne, and how it applies to getting bigger and stronger.

The researchers in this study were interested in learning what influenced the plant workers' productivity, so they moved a group of them to a special room where variables such as illumination and rest periods could be manipulated and the results on productivity could be measured. What happened was that no matter what the researchers did, productivity improved—even if the lighting and rest conditions were poor!

For years this curious set of results was interpreted to mean that if you just paid attention to people they would produce more. And in some circles the study was cited as evidence demonstrating how Mickey Mouse most productivity enhancement schemes really were—since anything and everything seemed to help in the Hawthorne study.

After resting comfortably on its laurels for fifty-odd years, this interpretation got a strong jolt when an enterprising researcher named Parsons re-examined the original study and demonstrated that, lo and behold, along with whatever else was being done in that experimental room in Hawthorne, the workers 1) were getting feedback on their performance, and 2) their pay was tied to their performance. Suddenly "the Hawthorne Effect" was cast in a whole new light and what had seemed to be a spongy set of results now stood on the bedrock of behavioral theory: When you tell people how they are doing, and make it worth their while to perform well, their performance is boosted. Usually dramatically.

"Cute story," you say, "but I'm interested in biceps, squats and power cleans—not assembling electrical relays. What's the Hawthorne Effect got to do with me?" Plenty, because the moral of the story is that proper feedback loops are probably the most powerful element in an effective information system. Here's how it works in the gym.

Let's say that you look in the mirror and based on what you see, you decide that more muscle mass is the order of the day. Since you know about the importance of setting clear-cut goals, you want to define a quantitative goal—not just something wishy-washy like "getting bigger." You know that some of the most fabled bulk-building programs in history can pile on around five pounds a week, so that becomes your starting point for exemplary performance.

Working the numbers around a little, you decide to try to pack on around 15 pounds of muscle in the next month. You carefully select a routine designed to take you to your goal, and settle on one that you've heard has worked wonders for a lot of people. To frost the cake, the routine you selected also makes it clear why you need to do each of the things recommended in the program. Now for the feedback portion.

When you are striving for large gains in muscle mass, your principal bench marks come in the form of changes in your appearance, measurements and bodyweight. Naturally, then, primary tools for evaluating your progress include the mirror, the tape and the scale. Because you need to keep track of not just where you stand at the moment, but even more importantly, what sort of progress you are making, you need to use these feedback tools at different points in time and track your progress. You need to be systematic about it, and that includes not just writing down the results of your observations and measurements, but also analyzing the raw data to determine if you are on the right track.

The next step is to either maintain your course of action, if things are going well, or to make adjustments, if your progress toward your long term goals is falling short of the standards you originally set. Apply the same approach whether you are cutting up, specializing on a body part, or whatever.

If your primary interest is bodybuilding, then you will definitely want to take photographs at regular points in time, and especially at key junctures in your training: Before and after major bulking up/trimming down programs, and each time you compete, for example. As obvious as the photo records sound, you would be amazed at how many not-quite-up-there bodybuilders are completely haphazard about taking photos, relying instead on their memories when it comes to how much sweep they have added to their thighs, or how their biceps have a whole new peak this year, and so forth.

And don't use the excuse that you don't have Mike Neveux at your disposal either: We're not talking major artistic expression here; merely adequate documentation would be a major boost to most bodybuilders' feedback systems. You also shouldn't feel that you don't want to be photographed because you don't quite look like a Mr. O contender yet. Consider these photographs as personal or confidential as, say, your checkbook, your private phone directory or your diary.

If you are a lifter, the bottom line in any feedback system is whether your PRs are increasing. Toward that end, analyzing your training log and contest results will tell you whether or not you are progressing toward your goals. In addition to tracking this bottom line, lifters also need to keep an eye on the technical aspect of their performance—an area that increases in relative importance as the technical aspect of the lift increases, relative to the strength component. For example, since technique is a major factor in the snatch, but a minor one in the deadlift, getting technical feedback is much more important in the snatch than in the deadlift.

The expert's eye is very useful for providing technical feedback, so naturally, having a knowledgeable coach at hand is invaluable. And one of the ultimate feedback tools is having videotape coupled with expert analysis—pointing out both the strengths and weaknesses of your performance. But even if you don't have access to a world class coach, don't underestimate the value of videotaping your performance: Study it, and for added insight, compare it to tape of an exemplary performer.

Let's say you live hundreds of miles from the nearest qualified Olympic lifting coach, and you're trying to learn how to do squat snatches. And let's say that it turns out that your major weakness is your speed. When you watch yourself on videotape and then look at a world champion, the message will hit you between the eyes. Then, armed with vivid images of yourself compared to the experts, you will be able to tackle the problem head-on.

Finally, when it comes to getting feedback on your performance, remember that a little knowledge isn't a dangerous thing: Instead, it just might the most potent training tool you'll ever find.

37 Massive Motivation

While it's true that there certainly are some training routines that are nearly guaranteed to work and others that are nearly guaranteed to fail, the vast majority fall somewhere in between the two extremes. And it's also true that whether you are training on a super-routine, or something a little more ordinary, just how much progress you will make often boils down to one not-so-simple factor: your motivation.

Motivation is what makes one athlete get up at 4:30 A.M. to be in the gym by 5:30, for a full training session before school or work. Lack of motivation is what keeps another in bed. Motivation is also what keeps people of the first type focused on a specific mission, while those of the second type are changing their targets almost daily. And it's motivation that creates a magnetic tension between the person and his goal, while a lack of motivation ensures that others just bob around randomly.

"O.K.," you say, "no need to sell me on the need for plenty of motivation—just tell me what it is and how to get some more."

Motivation De-mystified

Purely and simply, motivation is the presence of anything that initiates behavior. The most fundamental kind of motivation springs from what psychologists call "unlearned drives," which are tied to basic physiological requirements and, in short, physical survival. Because most of us spend most of our lives far from the edge of death, we tend to discount the importance of basic physiological needs for such things as oxygen, water, food, warmth, etc. Spend a night as an exhausted, dehydrated, freezing climber enduring a forced bivouac, and the primacy of drives will become amply clear.

In modern society, with basic survival assured for most people, the majority of our motivation comes from "learned drives," or what some psychologists prefer to call "needs." Learned drives have no intrinsic relationship to survival, but instead have acquired meaning through your social context. Achievement, recognition, and the pursuit of such symbols as wealth are examples of learned drives.

Once again, if you doubt the mere social value of these things, try to stay warm with your college diploma, or to stave off your hunger and thirst by munching on a handful of $20 bills when you're stuck on the proverbial mountainside.

So it also goes with muscular development and strength: In days of yore, the biggest and strongest, very simply, ruled the earth. Pundits might note that now it's the smallest and weakest who have inherited this mantle, but even if things haven't completely reversed themselves, it's only a very small minority of iron tossers who train to literally ensure their survival, or even to enhance their prosperity.

As for the rest, the motivation to spend their leisure time in the gym—straining, grimacing and panting—is hard for non-trainers to understand. That's something you shrug off, at least most of the time. What is of concern, however, is those times when *you* start to wonder just why you are pounding iron, those times when you start to lose your edge in the gym. What's the bedraggled trainer to do?

Without getting embroiled in psychological theories, let's reveal the mysteries of motivation enough so you can establish your own internal "motivation meter" and keep yourself high on the power curve.

A Portrait of Motivation

Let's walk through the chief characteristics of motivated behavior, so you can get a handle on both where you stand in terms of motivation, and can also get some insight into how you might focus your efforts for a boost in motivation and performance.

1) *Arousal*: Motivation is arousing; it energizes your behavior. You can frequently spot this type of arousal in two related forms. First, when you are engaging in the target behavior (i.e., what you are motivated to do), you attack it with a vengeance. Second, when you are not engaged in the target behavior, you are restless and are often distracted by thoughts related to whatever is motivating you.

How do you measure up on this count? Are you limp as a dishrag when you hit the weights, or do you march through your reps with the backbone and determination that leaves no question about your intentions? Do you find yourself looking forward to your workout or avoiding it? Is your training something that brings out the be(a)st in yourself, or is it just a cue for excuses about how tired/sick/burned out you are?

In a nutshell, highly motivated trainers can drag themselves into the gym when they really are hurting and still knock out a stellar workout, and the unmotivated can come into the gym with every possible reason for being fresh, but then wimp out on all their tough reps.

Self-Evaluation: If your energy level is flagging, be sure that you are giving yourself a fair shake. Is your schedule overloaded? Can you re-schedule your training for a time of day when you have a little more go-power? Are you flat out overtrained? Are you eating well and getting sufficient sleep and relaxation?

Stack the odds in your favor energy-wise by changing as required: your training time, training routine, diet, outside activities and rest schedule. And remember, don't just throw in the towel and say, "I'm too busy to be able to change things for the better." Sometimes the best way to improve your situation is to do less of some things—which should be music to the ears of the overcommitted.

2) *Direction*: Motivation gives meaning and direction to your life. When you are motivated, things start to fall into place, because it not only gives you an overall goal, but it also gives shape to a game plan which makes it easier to evaluate what you should be doing at every step along the way.

If you frequently find yourself either at a loss for what to do next ("I'm bored"), or torn between very different choices ("Is it pizza and beer, or water-packed tuna and nonfat cottage cheese for supper?"), that's a hot tip that you might not have your sense of direction running at full tilt. In fact, people who are under-motivated are often finding themselves with "nothing to do," while highly-motivated people "never have enough time."

Self-Evaluation: What are you trying to accomplish this workout? How about this month? At the end of the year, what would you like to be able to say you have done?

Setting goals and sticking with the plan for reaching them is one of the toughest battles you face in training, but make a start by committing to something for the next month or so. And once you set your goal, wild horses shouldn't be able to drag you away from it.

3) *Tension*: Motivation creates a feeling of tension that is always drawing you toward your goal. In that sense, motivation is like magnetism, because you are continuously being pulled—mentally and

physically—toward the object of your attraction. And in fact, the only way to relieve the tension is to reach your goal.

This tension-creating aspect of motivation is closely related to its arousal ability, because once a highly-motivated person reaches his/her goal, not only does the tension disappear, but the energy level drops. In fact, this tension, in itself, can be reinforcing to many people, and when they reach a goal, they experience a big letdown because they enjoyed having the added zip of being highly motivated to reach some pinnacle.

Self-Evaluation: Are you steadily pulled toward everything related to meeting your goals? Are you more frequently pulled toward something other than your supposed goals? Just what are you attracted to? Did reaching a big goal leave you feeling disoriented?

No need to waste your time fooling yourself into trying to do what you don't really want to do. Sit down and figure out what you really want to do and then do it. Remember that not all goal-related activity has to be extremely intense, so make use of this fact to reinforce your progress rather painlessly. And as you draw near one goal, be sure to set another.

When you are highly motivated, there's almost nothing you can't accomplish, and when you're not, all the talent in the world will do you little good. And to make things even nicer, motivation is free—readily available to anyone who wants some. So what are you waiting for? It's time for you to develop massive motivation.

38 Fear of Success

Fred really wanted the muscular mass and mighty lifts he dreamed of. Or did he?

On the one hand, Fred was one of the most faithful trainers you could possibly hope to find. It wasn't just that you could practically set your watch by Fred's arrival in the gym, although that was certainly true. Nor was it just that he logged more hours in the place than just about any three members put together. There were plenty of other indications of Fred's pursuit of excellence.

For starters, Fred did his homework on anything and everything related to training: You could quiz him on any contest result, competitor statistic or training principle and it was like money in the bank that Fred knew the answer. Fred had scoured the ends of the earth for any and all information related to his chosen sport.

And if that was too abstract, take a look at his training diary: not just the usual pounds-and-sets-and-reps notes, but a complete list of everything he ate or drank, pulse rates, mood indicators, injury descriptions, and just about every-thing else short of weather reports. Fred's training diary contained more facts and observations than a lot of local newspapers, and his analyses looked like something for an Honors science project.

Fred really seemed to have everything wired for fast track progress, and if you asked him, he would be quick to tell you that his training was going great.

What was funny, though, was that to an observer, Fred had really been stuck at his current levels of size and strength for a long—very long—time. How could that be? After all, nobody but nobody could rival Fred's commit-ment level. Or could they?

Commitment to success really boils down to commitment to progress, so Fred's long term stagnation was the first big hint that something was rotten in Denmark. And without dragging out the ink blots and the black leather couch, the contrast between Fred's perception of his progress and everyone else's perception of his progress was interesting from a psychological perspective. Very interesting.

Besides the lack of new PRs, there were other signs that cracked the image of Fred as the absolute master of his training progress.

While he might fool a casual observer, a sharp eye would note that Fred basically bailed out on his heavy sets. All of them. It didn't matter that he might give the outward appearance of a maximum effort—he psyched up beforehand with great dramatics, he huffed and puffed mightily in the middle of the set, and he fairly limped away at its conclusion, often muttering something about "not feeling quite right," or some nagging injury. But a trained observer would note that Fred's will cracked on his heavy sets, and he surrendered before the battle even got intense. Fred had beaten himself before his hands ever grabbed the weight.

And if you missed the subtleties of Fred's mental collapse on his top sets—the ones that create the progress—all you had to do was step back and watch Fred on his final warm-ups before the big ones, and compare that to what followed. After all, when you saw him blast up 220 with plenty of gusto one minute and then completely collapse with 230, you had to wonder whether Fred's mind had somehow exaggerated the importance of those ten little pounds.

It had, and that was the real problem: Fred suffered from what psychologists call "fear of success." Let's take a quick look at three ways it can rear its ugly little head and ruin your progress.

The Basic Pattern

Social psychology researchers in the 1970s had noticed something unusual: Despite all the talk about how everyone wanted all the success in the world, it was clear that some people, some of the time, actually did their best to *avoid* success. With a little more investigation, the picture emerged that some people *fear success* because of the consequences associated with it.

For example, women sometimes actually feared too much success in school because they thought it might lead to social rejection. And minority group members sometimes faced similar conflicts: Success in the larger world could be feared because it was sometimes seen as a barrier between the individual and his ethnic group.

This type of fear also hampers iron athletes. For example, women might fear rejection because they have gotten too big and too strong for some people's ideas of femininity. We even heard of an attorney who was afraid that juries might think he was stupid on the basis of assuming his imposing physique implied "all brawn and no brains."

If you are caught in this type of bind, your best bet is to develop a social support system consistent with your goals. In other words, try to avoid the specific people and social groups that pressure you to avoid success in your chosen field; simultaneously, actively seek out people and social groups that endorse your goals. As your confidence increases, you will be able to withstand more and more criticism without being seriously shaken, so you will be able to branch out from your initial support group. But why push things? Take them one step at a time, beginning by using the safe haven approach to boost your confidence.

The Hero-Worship Trap

There's plenty of the basic fear of success pattern around, but there's another pattern that's even more common and holds back even more people. We call it the hero-worship trap and here's how it works.

Unlike the basic social version, the roots of this fear lie in the person's view of himself: Whether or not nearly everyone likes to think of himself as a leader, most of us aren't because the burden is too great. So most people actually prefer to follow. And one of the easiest ways to follow is to pick a leader.

This is what creates the hero cult—not mere admiration for someone, but flat out adulation and hero worship. This might seem like a harmless pursuit that at worst makes a lot of money for the heroes and their agents, but a direct result is that it puts a lid on the progress of the hero's followers. Here's how.

Let's say you worship so-and-so. We're talking serious idolizing here, as in seeing a large part of the world in the context of so-and-so and frequently relating what you do and what you see to your hero. We're not really concerned with you learning constructive things from demonstrably capable and successful people—that's beneficial. We are concerned, however, with your getting so carried away that you think of nearly everything in relationship to your hero. When that happens, you will always limit yourself to what your hero has accomplished.

"Not a terrible fate," you say, "since he has homes on three continents, is driven around in a Rolls.... I could learn to live within those limits."

You probably could, but the problem for you is that you might not do best trying to follow precisely in your hero's footsteps. Where he went right, you might do better going left, and, heaven forbid, what if you could actually exceed your hero in some pursuit? Hero worship limits your progress by locking you into a tight little box. It's not just that there is only one way for you to succeed, but also that you are afraid of ever outdoing your hero, at anything. After all, if you beat your hero, then he would lose some of his lustre and you would have to stand on your own two feet.

The best way to free yourself from the hero-worship trap is to first admit that, perhaps, your hero isn't completely perfect. Admit to a few chinks in his armor, and then start to acknowledge that some other people have something to teach you. Try to be selective in your attention to several people who can serve as worthy role models, and use them as springboards to let yourself unfold. Finally, begin to accept some responsibility for guiding your own development.

Low Self-Esteem

The third primary way fear of success retards your progress is a cousin of the hero-worship trap because it also involves avoiding success as a way to avoid having to reshape fundamental perceptions. Instead of requiring that you reshape your perceptions of another person, however, this third form is a technique for avoiding the challenge of reshaping how you think about yourself.

Let's deal with a painful, yet real stereotype. Suppose that early in life you received inadequate reinforcement of your basic worth, or even worse, had more than an occasional source telling your that you were basically worthless. The result would be a psychological scar, analogous to the scar you would carry from being burned or cut physically. Even if you wanted to, it would probably take a while before you could develop a truly positive self-image under these conditions.

One of the problems with lugging around a negative self-image is that you can become afraid to succeed because all you know is that you are a worthless failure. Without getting too melodramatic, the ultimate form of this situation would require that if you were to succeed, you would destroy yourself, figuratively speaking. And even if you aren't completely crazy about yourself, it's pretty tough to just toss out what you think of as yourself.

If you are caught in this bind, you need to start building a more positive self image, one step at a time. Be sure to note each little success you have and begin to remind yourself of them throughout the day. Pretty soon you might be able to admit to a radical new thought: Maybe you're not so bad after all. When you get that far, you will be able to make some good progress, because once you have a positive self-image, you can more than handle the idea of making progress. In fact, once you have a positive self-image, you will expect and even demand that you make progress.

39 Supercharging Your Self-Esteem

Two guys start training at the same time, on opposite sides of the same town. One expects to make great progress, and before too long, he has made solid gains and starts aiming toward entering his first contest—which he plans to win. The other fellow begins without expecting much for his efforts, and some time later, he is ready to quit—he hasn't made much progress and doesn't see that changing down the road. What's the difference between these two?

"Genetics," you say, knowingly. Actually, the difference is just about as far from genetics as you can get: It all has to do with what's between their ears, and that, fortunately, is subject to change.

What's going on here is part of the potent psychological phenomenon called "self-esteem." Differences in this little bugger produce some extraordinary results, like putting two people at the same point on the figurative mountainside, where one works his way to the top, while the other crashes to the bottom.

Self-esteem refers to a person's evaluation of his own worth. And it's such an important aspect of your overall self-concept that "self-esteem" and "self-concept" are often used interchangeably.

People with low self-esteem are characterized by feeling discouraged, depressed, isolated from others, unlovable, fearful of angering others, and so forth. People with high self-esteem are characterized by feeling successful, self-confident, optimistic, free of anxiety, expressive, active, and so forth.

In more specific terms, people with high self-esteem expect greater success for themselves and they march forward to make it happen. Conversely, people with low self-esteem expect less from themselves and run their lives within these confines. Given these opposite expectations, you can see how low-esteem people get caught in an unending downward spiral:

1) Low self-esteem leads to expectations of little success,

2) which lowers one's aspirations, efforts and accomplishments,

3) which reinforces low self-esteem.

Then the loop repeats itself.

Similarly, you can see how people with high self-esteem ride an escalator to ever loftier achievements:

1) High self-esteem leads to expectations of great success,

2) which increases one's aspirations, efforts and accomplishments,

3) which reinforces high self-esteem.

Then the loop repeats itself.

In case you think this is a lot of hooey, you should know that research has found that, among other things, people with high self-esteem select tougher goals, are less conforming, are less vulnerable to persuasive messages, and generally conduct themselves with greater competence.

Self-esteem packs a lot of leverage, with the effects of your self-esteem level getting multiplied in a chain reaction process. Thus, in research that led people to feel good about themselves, it was found that they selectively paid attention to other positive information about themselves, and people who were led to feel bad about themselves paid more attention to other negative information about themselves.

Think of this process as being like emotional inertia: When you start rolling in one direction, such as feeling either good or bad about yourself, you will tend to keep rolling in the same direction.

It's also important to understand that once your level of self-esteem is firmly established, you tend to bias incoming information: For example, a hardcore high self-esteem person will explain away a failure, and a hardcore low self-esteem person will explain away a success. The moral here is that if you have high self-esteem you can weather more than one emotional storm, but if you have low self-esteem, you need to wage a relentless battle against your limiting, negative view of yourself.

Pumping Up Your Self-Esteem

With self-esteem playing such a powerful role in your life, what can you do to boost yours? Our recommended program for pumping up your self-esteem has two components:

1) *cognitive*, which is based on what you think, and

2) *behavioral*, which is based on what you do.

Let's see how the pieces fit together.

To begin the cognitive component of your training, you need to develop an awareness of what you say to yourself *about yourself*. If your internal dialogue runs something like, "Come on Champ...way to go..." you are already on the right track and probably don't need to change a thing. If, however, your internal dialogue runs something like, "It probably won't do any good, but...Nothing ever works for me...I sure blew it when..." then you need to make a big change. Here's what we would like you to do.

Start to think about things that make you feel good about yourself. And don't say "nothing," because *everyone* has something that makes him feel at least a little proud—it might be a past accomplishment, a personal feature, a skill, or even a dream you have about something you would like to do. Absolutely anything will do, as long as it makes *you* feel good about yourself. The emphasis is on you because other people may discredit or ignore things that would otherwise make you proud of yourself. Don't fall into this trap of trying to please others at this point—just stick with what makes you feel good about yourself.

Try to come up with several strong positives, but even one will do. Think of these positives as being something like your psychological supplements—swallow them in the morning and at night, with other feedings in between as needed. Minimally, run through your positives when you first wake up and as you are getting dressed for the day, with another round as you are getting ready for bed. If something pops up during the day that makes your self-esteem shake, pull out your positives and start gulping them down.

The second prong of your attack plan centers on what you do, and this is where your iron exploits are perfectly suited: Not only will you make your best training progress ever, but you will also gain far-reaching psychological benefits as a result. Do this right and not only will your biceps and bench press soar, but your self-esteem will gain mass so fast that you can start to feel like a completely new person in less than two months.

We want you to pick a specific training goal: Maybe it's to add half an inch to your arms, or to gain 20 pounds of solid bodyweight, or to boost your power clean by 30 pounds. Your exact goal doesn't matter; it just needs to be measurable and realistically achievable in two months. This is not the time to shoot for ultimate results—it's the time to pick a worthy goal that you will absolutely, positively make.

The matter of being measurable is critical, so don't stop your goal-definition with something like "I want to look better" or "I want to get stronger." Define better looking or stronger in terms you can measure: inches, pounds, and so forth.

Write your goal at the top of a piece of paper, and underneath list your basic training program for reaching it. Take a look at your goal and ask yourself if it's realistic. If not, modify it until it is. Once you have a realistic goal, examine your proposed training program and assess whether it's really the best way to achieve your goal. If you have any doubts about your goal or your training program, stop and do some research—read, consult experts, watch other people, and so forth. For this program to work, you must be 100% committed to both your goal and your training program.

After making any adjustments necessary to your goal and program, go to the bottom of your piece of paper and write the number 8 by the left edge. Write your goal on this line. Go up a line and write the number 6; go up another line and write the number 4; go up another line and write the number 2. Above the number 2, write down where you are at the moment, in terms of your goal.

What you now have at the bottom your piece of paper is your starting point and your desired goal, with three blank lines in between. Split the difference between these two points and right the result next to the line marked 4—this is your midpoint goal. Split the difference between your midpoint goal and your starting point, and write it by the line marked 2. Split the difference between your midpoint goal and your final goal and write it by line number 6. You have now defined two-week subgoals that will lead to your overall goal in two months.

C arry this piece of paper around with you and keep reminding yourself of your overall goal, your program for reaching it, and what you need to do to reach your next subgoal. At each two-week marker, record your level of accomplishment. Each time you reach one of your two-week subgoals, you automatically gain another positive to add to the cognitive portion of your training.

If you have done everything right, you will be right on track, and eight weeks later, you will have reached a very worthy goal: Not only will you have bigger arms, a mightier bench, or whatever you targeted, but even more important, you will have proven that *you* can control your destiny, that you are competent and that you are a force to be taken seriously.

You will not only have gotten bigger and stronger: You will have supercharged your self-esteem.

40 n Ach: Not Just for Naturals

Harvey Lippinscott is one of those people who only knows one way to do things: the best way possible. For example, when Harvey was a kid and had to make an insect collection for his grade school science class, he wasn't content to simply snag a couple of yellow jackets and Monarchs in the back yard and then mount them on an old piece of styrofoam, like the other kids in his class.

Instead, Harvey spent every free moment day after day stalking the most exotic bugs in his general area, and his nights went into making a fancy wooden case to display his six-legged trophies. And that's how Harvey has always attacked everything in his life.

The Johnson twins lived across the street from Harvey, and where Harvey went north, they went south. Not that anyone could say the Johnsons weren't a likeable pair, for they were, but it was just that they preferred hanging out with their pals to doing serious work, and rather than striving for greatness, they set their sights right where most of their buddies were aiming—about in the dead center of the scale.

For whatever reason, Harvey and the Johnson boys both got interested in muscles the summer before their senior year in high school. Even though the guys on both sides of Maple Street shared a common goal—getting a lot bigger and stronger—you would never have guessed it from watching their methods.

The Johnson boys trained at the high school weight room, which consisted of a dilapidated Universal gym, a rickety bench, a couple of semi-straight exercise bars and a small pile of plates, many of which were the infamous vinyl-coated variety. A standard workout involved talking baseball with the other guys for two and half hours, with about 12 sets of bench presses and 18 sets of curls sneaked in between. Their approach to nutrition was just as simple: cold cereal for breakfast, burgers and Cokes for lunch, and if things went right, pizza for supper. Even though the Johnsons liked hitting the gym, if someone suggested a movie or a trip to the beach instead, they were game.

Harvey, meantime, had made a deal with his dad: In exchange for cleaning out a section of the basement and relocating a lot of boxes to the attic, Harvey had claimed a zone for setting up a home gym. After two weeks of combing the want ads and searching garage sales, Harvey had landed a solid bench, a pair of squat racks, two decent bars and 300 pounds in iron plates. As far as workouts went, Harvey stuck with the proven winners, so three times a week he spent about an hour on the basic exercises.

His diet was equally straightforward: plenty of nutritious food and enough milk to float a canoe. With twelve weeks of vacation and three workouts per week scheduled, it was no surprise to see Harvey's summer training log had complete records for 36 workouts.

Three months later, the Johnson boys could bounce their pecs, barely, and there was a new walnut on their upper arms, so they were pretty happy with their training progress.

Harvey emerged at the end of the summer wearing all new clothes—about the only things that still fit him from June were his socks and shoes. Where Harvey had once been an average flat-chested, thin-shouldered, spindle-armed and -legged teenager, now he looked like a minor boulder—thick, round and solid everywhere.

And while the Johnsons were already talking about skiing, Harvey was setting his training goals for the end of the year—with some pretty big numbers figuring into his plan.

What is it about Harvey? Why is he driven to excel? Why does he do everything so intensely and well when most people do everything so lackadaisically? Ask a psychologist and you're likely to hear about need for achievement, or *n* Ach.

The Need for Achievement (n Ach)

People who are high on the *n* Ach scale are just like Harvey: they are driven to excel. This is a behavioral pattern can emerge very early in life and it tends to be applied to a wide variety of the individual's activities. So, *n* Ach is already observable in nursery school-aged children, and the pattern shows up across a range of situations.

And while it's easy to focus on the idea that high *n* Ach individuals are competitive, it's important to realize that they aren't just motivated to outperform other people—they can simply be striving for the high standards they have set for themselves.

We might say something like *n* Ach is a "broad cognitive structure developed through the process of socialization" or we could just say that *n* Ach is, in effect, an attitude you develop based largely on how people react to you. For instance, firstborn children tend to score higher on *n* Ach than later born children, due to the fact that mothers tend to interact more with firstborns and are more likely to challenge them toward achievement.

This process continues in school, where children not only learn very quickly that a premium is attached to high achievement, but they also develop a marked tendency to evaluate their own performances compared to others. Of course, in an achievement-oriented society such as ours, tremendous pressure is put on people to compete and excel.

What IronMind® wants to emphasize about *n* Ach, though, is that it *can* be divided much more democratically than, say, perfect muscle insertions.

First, we acknowledge that *n* Ach is correlated with ability, which makes good sense since capable people tend to do well, which brings them praise, which increases their chances of doing well, which.... It's pretty simple to see how that one works. But what isn't often brought out is that *everyone* can raise his or her level of *n* Ach—and the result should be better results in whatever he or she does. Here's how that works.

If you want to boost your own level of *n* Ach, begin by picking one or two little things that you do well. A lot of people get stuck at this stage because they dismiss their abilities simply because they haven't done something on the level of having won a Nobel prize or an Olympic gold medal. What you need to do is to think in terms of *anything* you do well, and then build on that area of success. You will extend this success in two directions:

1) You will keep raising your performance standards in this first area, and
2) You will apply ever-higher standards to other areas of your life.

For example, let's say that one thing you are really great at is detailing your car. "Not such a great talent," you say.

"More than enough to work with," IronMind® replies.

Following the two-stage plan of attack, you first bring your detailing up another and yet another notch—getting to the point where other detailers are asking, for example, just how you got those seats to look so sweet. Second, you ride this wave into new territory: For example, you take the same sort of focus and effort you put into detailing and apply it to the chemistry class you are nearly flunking. If you follow this plan you will turn yourself into a high-achiever even if you were a 9th-born who was never encouraged to do anything as a child.

Many people have used this approach to transfer a bodybuilding/lifting success to create success(s) in other areas of their lives. For example, after dramatically improving themselves physically—and proving that they can succeed—they took the next step and applied the same set of expectations and discipline to school, their profession, or whichever area of their lives they chose.

And the reverse also works. People who come into bodybuilding or lifting with a string of successes in other areas tend to set higher standards for themselves in the gym, and they work to ensure that they meet these standards.

So just because you might not have inherited a genetically-perfect body, and just because you might not have been molded from the cradle to become king of the world, it doesn't mean that you have to slog along in the mire of mediocrity. Start small, stretch a little, and keep reaching a little higher and little wider as you pick up steam. What you will end up with is a self-created level of achievement orientation that will knock down just about any barrier ever to pop up in your way.

41 Farewell To Fear

B ig things were waiting for Ray Bigelow if he could just add 25 pounds to his bench press. It wasn't simply that he would win the semi-major bet he'd made with one of his gym buddies. Nor was it that he would then be able to break the state record. No, this lift was bigger than just those two things, because in another 25 pounds, Ray would hit what had seemed like the weight of the world to him when he first entered a gym. If he made that lift, *Ray* would be impressed with himself.

Ray was no fool about something as important as hitting this lift, so he meticulously planned how he would reach his goal: His training, diet and rest were mapped out in impeccable detail. And just as the storybooks would have it, good things came to Ray by virtue of his efforts: five pounds here, ten over there, another five here and—presto!—he was within spitting distance of his goal. The problem for Ray was that he'd reached that point a couple of months ago and hadn't budged since. And there was a good reason, too. Ray was scared blind of the target weight.

Unbeknownst to Ray, a fellow gym-mate, one Terry Deming, was going through a similar battle. Terry had gotten into weights as an extension of a fitness program, and before too long, the barbell bug had bitten and Terry had become a steadfast bodybuilder. Now Terry might not be the focal point of IFBB contract negotiations, but that's not to say there wasn't some potential there for Terry walking away from some pretty impressive shows with an armload of hardware, not to mention the title. Terry was built and dearly wanted to compete, and shows were just waiting to be won. There was one small problem, however: Terry never entered a show, due to an extreme case of stage fright.

Perhaps fear is limiting your life in a similar way, whether the feared situation is in the gym, at home, on the job, or wherever. What's to be done?

A Few Words About Fear

Fear is an emotional response to a specific perceived danger or threat. For example, Ray is afraid of a certain weight in the bench press, and Terry is afraid of appearing before large crowds. If you aren't sure you understand what fear is all about, consider their extreme form, called "phobias." Most people can get jelly-kneed and produce a racing heart, sweaty palms and a knot in their stomach just by thinking about being placed in a phobic situation. Common phobic stimuli include heights (acrophobia), closed areas (claustrophobia), and open spaces (agoraphobia). So even if you just dream about yourself dangling from a cliff, chances are good you will produce all the classic symptoms of fear.

Fears can be established after just one encounter with a frightening experience (e.g., getting bitten by a pit bull), and they can also exist without direct contact with the feared situation (e.g., a 400-pound bench press). Some fears are essentially universal (like fear of the dark), and others are more limited (like fear of crossing bridges), but for all their outward variety, they all operate about the same way.

The important things to remember are:

1) Once established and if allowed to run its own course, fear is very durable;

2) Fear leads to avoidance of the feared situation, which both limits your life and helps maintain the fear; and

3) Specific fears can be wiped out, often amazingly quickly, using the right techniques.

Let's see how.

Facing Off With Fear

Fear gets its powerful hold on your life because it limits your options, primarily because when you fear something, you will do *anything* to avoid it. And when you avoid something, it's not just that you have boxed yourself in; you have also virtually guaranteed that your fear will be maintained. After all, when you avoid something, how can you ever learn that, maybe, it's not worth fearing after all? It's no accident, then, that the best way to reduce or eliminate a fear is to go face-to-face with it.

"Easy for you to say," you growl, "because you're not the one who has to stand nearly-naked in front of all those people or try to lift a weight that could flatten me like a pancake." Actually, facing off with your fear(s) can be a lot easier than you think. Let's map out a program for reducing your fear in three easy steps, using a technique called "systematic desensitization." We'll show you how you can use this tool to empower yourself and crush your fears.

Systematic Desensitization

Developed by the psychiatrist Joseph Wolpe, systematic desensitization is a powerful, portable, flexible technique that has proven to be extremely effective at eradicating specific fears. In a nutshell, systematic desensitization works by teaching you to stay calm in the face of feared events, and it does this through a process called "counterconditioning." In a very simplified form, Wolpe's logic runs like this: You can block a fear response if you can teach the person to relax when facing a feared situation. And that's exactly what systematic desensitization attempts to do. Here's how you put it to work for yourself.

First, you need to create a hierarchy of feared events. For Terry, for example, a hierarchy of fear for appearing in public might go like this: attending a show would be at the low-fear end; being backstage would be at the intermediate-fear level; walking out on stage would be at the absolute-terror end of the scale. Whatever your fear, develop a hierarchy like this, coming up with half a dozen to a dozen graduated levels of feared situations.

Second, teach yourself deep relaxation—the exact relaxation technique you use isn't critical, as long as it works. Our preferred form of relaxation is based on a technique called "progressive relaxation," which teaches you to first tense and then relax each part of your body. Start with your toes and work your way, step by step, up to your scalp. You should be able to learn effective relaxation in just a few practice sessions.

Third, pair the fear-producing stimuli with the relaxation response. As you would guess, you begin with the least-feared situation on your hierarchy (e.g., attending a show), all the while maintaining your state of deep relaxation. If you stay calm while imagining a given situation, you move up to the next one; if you become anxious, you try again, or go down a level on your fear hierarchy. Step by step, you continue in this manner until you have stayed relaxed through the most-feared situation on your list.

When Ray Bigelow heard about systematic desensitization, he immediately got to work outlining his fear hierarchy and learning deep relaxation. Two weeks later he popped up a bench 10 pounds over his goal, and he was so impressed that he told everyone in the gym about the latest weapon in his training arsenal. One of the crowd, Terry Deming, was paying particularly close attention. Maybe that's why a month later, Terry ordered a couple of posing suits.

42 Tom And The Towel

Someplace between your ears is a little switch that largely determines not just how big and strong you will ever get, but also how successful and satisfied you will be with your life as a whole. Forget fancy neurophysiological or cognitive process labels—just think of this mechanism as your "quit switch."

Let's drop in at a local gym, where we are fortunate enough to have two aspiring Olympians training, and see how the quit switch affects what each puts into his training and what each gets out of it. Then we can draw some conclusions to help you with your own training. Our example involves a couple of weightlifters, but remember: The process and conclusions apply across the board—whether you are a bodybuilder, a powerlifter, a surgeon, a student or a shoe salesman.

Looking at our two Olympic hopefuls, we see that both are about the same age and although neither one has yet represented the United States in international competition, they both dream of making the '96 Olympic weightlifting team. Let's watch them train, and check the gym's PR board to evaluate their progress.

Our first lifter, Pete, isn't exactly beginning with a perfect body structure for weightlifting—in fact, on a couple of key points, he is put together the opposite of the ideal. Maybe that's why he looks a little awkward, but no matter, because he has a lot of desire and that's why he not only makes all his workouts, but also keeps trying hard even when he doesn't make any progress for a couple of months. His efforts have recently been paid back with interest, because he has hit so many PRs in the last couple of weeks that his numbers on the board are changing faster than stock quotes. And all this progress has earned him a new nickname: "PR Pete."

Our other lifter, Tom, has a better body structure than Pete and is just as zealous about making his workouts—he spends so much time in the gym, you would suspect he was getting paid just to show up. And he doesn't shy away from trying for new records, either, so you would think that his progress would put Pete's to shame. But the truth is that his numbers might as well be carved in stone as written on a blackboard—they seem to be about that permanent.

To get a clue as to why Pete and Tom have such wildly different performance records, let's taker a closer look at them in the gym under two very specific conditions:

1) Let's watch what they do when they miss a heavy lift, and
2) Let's watch them squat.

The first condition is of interest to us because how people handle frustration is an essential indicator of where their quit switch is set. The second condition is of interest because progress on the squat is central to meeting their overall goals, and is largely related to how hard they work. Thus, how you squat also provides insight into your quit-switch setting.

Handling Frustration

When Pete misses a lift, he usually scowls, maybe kicks the bar and after muttering a few choice words, he paces back and forth, exhorting himself to make a good lift, while also reminding himself of a key technical point (e.g., "keep pulling" or "shrug and reach"). Whether he tries the same weight again or whether he drops down, the important point is that he keeps going at that point and he ends his workout on a strong note of success—even if not with a new PR.

When Tom misses a lift, some real drama ensues: He yells curses that would make a drunken sailor blush; he jumps up and down; sometimes he rips off his lifting shoes and hurls them across the gym and storms out; sulking in a corner is SOP for Tom after a miss. And when Tom misses a lift, he rarely drops down. Instead, he usually tries—and misses—the same weight again. And again. And again...with the same histrionics following each miss, and each miss looking a little more automatic than the one before.

Raw Effort

Watching Pete squat isn't a pretty sight. It's not just that his relatively long legs and short upper body make for a somewhat ugly squatting style. And it's not just that his wide stance makes the whole thing even less picture-perfect to watch.

Those things are bad enough, but the real horror is in how he attacks his sets, grinding out reps that look like certain goners, and then doing another two or three on top of it. It doesn't matter to Pete if it takes him forever to come up with the weight, or if he turns purple and gets pretty gnarly in the process—if his program calls for five reps with 190 kilos, that's exactly what he makes.

Tom, on the other hand, looks cool when he squats: He has the classic upright stance, which he maintains flawlessly throughout his reps, and he has his groove so wired that he might as well be a well-lubricated piston gliding up and down in a cylinder. It's downright inspiring to watch him, as he descends slowly—in perfect control—and then explodes upward at his bottom point. And so it goes through his first few sets.

In fact, Tom keeps everything together so perfectly up to his heaviest set that you can just about feel him smashing his PR squat. What happens on the next set is that after another trademark descent, Tom makes it to the sticking point and—wham!—he hits a mental wall, gives up, and dumps the weight. It's like money in the bank: Tom throws in the towel just when he should be hitting his stride.

Think of Pete as being like a football player who makes a lot of his gains on "second effort," what he accomplishes after most people would have simply quit. Pete is just like the halfback who is initially bounced back by the defense, only to cut his way to a touchdown, or the quarterback who nails a big completion even when his primary and secondary receivers are covered. Tom is like a receiver who goes down in anticipation of the defense closing in on him—no wonder he never gains any ground!

Obstacles are bound to be a part of your life, both in the gym and out, so you need to develop effective strategies for dealing with them. Think of yourself as being a great running back, and think of obstacles as being like the line you are trying to penetrate. For some people, simply bulling ahead works: They can put down their heads and keep pounding straight ahead until they open up a hole. Other people do better to head outside, maybe with a cut or two thrown in. Still others reverse the field or simply go airborne.

The critical thing is that you need to concentrate on persevering until you conquer your obstacles, and if one thing doesn't work, you must try another. If you keep running the same doomed play over and over again, you are destined to quit in the face of obstacles. Instead, if one thing doesn't work, try another, so if you get stopped straight on, try going over, under, around or through the obstacle, and keep going until you break through.

H ard work is the usually the handmaiden of success, and there's an apocryphal story about the father of a self-made mega-millionaire that bears repeating. "Your son sure is lucky," a man says to the father.

"Yes," the father replies, "and I've noticed that the harder he works the luckier he gets." Enough said.

43 Killing The Clock

A funny thing has been happening in sports lately: There have been a lot of successful comebacks, and a lot of guys who were supposed to be has-beens are making big splashes. Nolan Ryan. George Foreman. Jimmy Connors. Renaldo Nehemiah. Albert Beckles. Leonid Taranenko. What's going on? Are these guys onto the fabled Fountain of Youth? And at the other end of the spectrum, how about all those six- and seven-figure tennis pros who aren't even old enough to drive themselves to their tournaments? Is the Diaper Brigade taking over the world?

Time was when you could make good sense of something as straightforward as age: Your twenties were pretty much it, because before that you were too young, and after that, you were too old. Somewhere along the line, that rule seems to have been discarded, because now people of all ages are doing it. And they keep doing it better and better. Just what is this thing called age, and how much impact should it have on what *you* can do?

Age seems to be something like education when you're applying for a job: You never have the right amount. Just as job interviewers delight in telling people that they are overqualified or underqualified, most people most of the time seem to be the wrong age for what they want to do.

The critics might open with such condemning classics as "he's still wet behind the ears," or the eternal "he's over the hill." Somewhere in between are the hopeful "wait until he matures" or the apologetic "he used to be one of the great ones." So what happens is that when you're young, you sit around wishing you were older, and when you're older, you sit around wishing you were younger. *Quel dommage!*

So while it's certainly true that there is an undeniable biological component to one's age, people rarely talk about the psychological and the social sides. The pity of this omission is that even if the biological component marches forward without missing a beat, why would you ever give up control of the mental aspect of the process? Let's examine that idea for a minute.

IronMind® has explained how social beliefs and social pressures create an incredibly powerful reality: In psychological research laboratories, most people will actually kill another person if so directed by an authority figure. And, also in the lab, most people will go along with what the group says, even if it's the opposite of what's staring them in the face. Scary stuff, to be sure, but this type of research should alert everyone to the need to guard against being pressured, socially, into thinking black is white and up is down.

Not as dramatic as murder but tragic nonetheless is the idea that someone would not do what he or she would like, and would not achieve what he or she is capable of, simply because other people say they are too young or too old to chase their dreams. Why limit yourself by conforming to somebody else's idea of what you can or cannot do at a certain age?

"Nice pep talk," you say, "but come on. Teeny-boppers don't make it big in the Iron World, and neither does the geriatric set. There's a reason why they have bubble gum and rocking chairs, and neither one makes it in the gym or on the platform."

Think so. Well let's see.

Mention Steve Reeves today, and you will get a lot of responses. Calves. Shoulders. Handsome. Movies. All these things are true, but when he won the Mr. America title in 1947, one of the most remarkable aspects of his victory was his age. Reeves was just 20 years old, and not only did he turn the physique world on its ear with his win, but he was regarded as having defined a new, modern look. How's that for someone who wasn't even old enough to vote? And let's not forget that Arnold Schwarzenegger was a mere high school lad when photos of his bulging biceps started hitting the American physique magazines.

And at the other end of the spectrum, ever heard of a fellow named Albert Beckles—even if people debate his exact age, everyone places him in at least his fifties. Can you imagine a man in his fifties or sixties competing in—and winning—professional bodybuilding contests? It's true. Not that Al is an isolated case of a bodybuilder competing at an age when most men are planted in their recliners, remote control units glued to their hands. In terms of the classic physique stars, John Grimek, Reg Park and Bill Pearl all won the Mr. Universe contest when they were about 40. And even if he's no longer competing, take a look at 50+ Larry Scott—if you wouldn't want to trade for the premier Mr. O's arms, you are doing extremely well.

"O.K., so you can *look* pretty good whether you are young or old," you say, "but what can you *do*? Good lifters don't come in all ages."

They don't?

First, let's talk raw strength. Three-time World Champion powerlifter Rickey Dale Crain first made the muscle mags as a ten year old—he had just deadlifted 200 pounds at 66 pounds bodyweight. I know a lot of grown men who can't deadlift 200 pounds, even though that's about what they weigh.

And as for the should-be-retired set, just remember Karl Norberg, who, among other great feats, bench pressed 460 when he was 80 years old. Just think, if they'd had bench shirts then, Karl could have done a quarter of a ton as an octogenarian! Karl's fame had spread so wide in the Iron World that Arnold Schwarzenegger once came to the Sports Palace in San Francisco just in the hope of meeting him. And if you still think you must be weak later in life, consider Doug Hepburn, who is training to do a standing press with 300 pounds when he is 70 years old!

Olympic-style weightlifting would seem to be the branch of the Iron Game most dependent on the age trap. After all, you not only have to be very strong, but you have to have tremendous explosive ability and downright speed. And while speed might be the gift of youth, successful Olympic lifters are very polished technically, which takes many years of work. So Olympic lifting should really be the province of the mid-20s—or should it?

One of the most productive lifters produced by the U.S. and one of history's greatest all-around strongmen, John Davis, won his first World Championship at the tender age of 17. Another American, Pete George, won his first World Championship as an 18-year old high school student. These youthful conquests supposedly fueled the Bulgarian lifting machine and when 10-year old Naim Suleymanoglu displayed an aptitude for the sport, his Bulgarian coaches encouraged him to lift, and lift some more. Thus, the "Pocket Hercules" broke his first World record when he was barely 15 and won his first World Championships when he was 16!

At the other end of the spectrum, Norbert Schemansky, brought a bronze medal in weightlifting back to Detroit from the 1964 Olympics—impressive enough in itself, but "Ski" was 40 years old. And now, 35-year-old Leonid Taranenko appears to be a good prospect to win a gold medal in weightlifting at the '92 Olympics—12 years after he won his first Olympic gold.

Einstein proved that time is relative. That's the theory. The practice is apparent in all the above examples. So whether you are eight or eighty-something, or anywhere in between, what are you waiting for? Isn't it about time you forgot your age and focused on what you want to do? Isn't it about time that you killed the clock?

44 Leaky Logic

There's a funny thing that goes on in our heads: We don't treat all pieces of information equally—sometimes we give things far more weight than they really deserve, and sometimes we give them far less. "No problem," you say, "it probably all comes out in the wash." But it doesn't, and because this process can have an adverse impact on everything from how you train to how you eat, it's worth learning a little about an example of what psychologists refer to as "information processing errors."

Suppose you are in the market for a new 4 x 4, and you are leaning toward a Toyota—they have a reputation for holding up well, you like their styling, the price is right, etc. Being somewhat prudent, though, before you plunk down your hard earned money, you wander over to the library and dig up one of those consumer guides that rates products based on large-scale owner surveys. You don't have to be a Harvard economist to understand the charts: The Toyota you've been eyeing gets unusually high ratings, especially compared to one of its competitors—Jeep. At this point, with your brain working rationally, you and Toyota seem like a done deal. But wait.

The next day you run into one of your buddies and when you tell him about your plans to buy a Toyota, he minces no words:

"A Toyota!" he says, "my cousin's neighbor bought one of those. What a piece of junk. The thing blew some kind of seal the second day he had it and then one of the wheels fell off.... He sure wishes he had gotten a Jeep instead."

At this point, if you were perfectly rational, you would take this one case, add the results to the million and a half reported in the consumer survey and recompute new average scores—which would turn out to be virtually identical to the original ones, with Toyota scoring high and Jeep scoring low. What happens instead is that you forget all about the million and half positive cases, and treat the one negative case as if it were typical, and vice versa. So the next day you buy a Jeep. You think you made the right decision, until you blow a seal the second week and then lose a wheel shortly thereafter.

We'll give you another example a little closer to home. Some critics of Olympic-style weightlifting like to say that the sport is unnecessarily dangerous, using flawed logic and allusions to non-existent numbers to claim that one's wrists, shoulders, back, and just about everything else is at grave risk whenever you do a power clean, let alone a squat snatch. To round out the picture, the same critics are usually big on football.

For the moment, never mind that the facts roundly contradict their claims about weightlifting, but consider only the following: At the 1991 World Championships a freak accident occurred, resulting in a B-session lifter being paralyzed after he was struck squarely on his neck by the bar after he missed a jerk.

Does it matter that such an accident, to anyone's memory, has never occurred before? Or does it matter that, on the other hand, that it's virtually certain that every year football will produce multiple cases of paralysis, not to mention at least one death? The likely answer is that this one case—the wild exception—will now be used to bolster the claim, "Weightlifting is an extremely dangerous sport," and the demonstrably dangerous activity, football, will continue to be condoned by the people who criticize weightlifting.

The exact reasons why our brains work like imperfect computers aren't clearly understood, but here are some conditions that create bias in how you treat information—chances are good that if you understand how you might be misled by phony reasoning, you can better defend yourself against making related errors.

1) Authority figures can get away with murder, and in fact, the right authority figure will be able to convince you that up is down and down is up. For example, suppose that you think Dr. So-and-So is the be-all, end-all authority on training. Even if the rest of the world tells you that you need to, for example, eat sufficient protein for muscular growth, the right authority might convince you that 50 grams of protein a day builds all the might and muscle you ever might want.

To guard against being duped by authorities, watch out for arguments that try to persuade on the basis of the authority's reputed credentials, rather than specific reasons. And, as the bumper sticker says, "Question authority," because unless you are dealing with prima donnas, reputable experts will be happy to explain their positions. And don't be fooled by the "it's too complicated for me to explain to you ruse"—smart people can simplify complicated matters, just as stupid people can complicate simple matters.

2) People whom you know or examples that are close to home have more influence on you than does a pile of abstract data. This is how you get caught in the "But my uncle said this stuff worked for him," even if every nutritionist in the world panned the supplement.

When you are trying to evaluate something, try to step back from the issue and look at the issue in general, not just in terms of how it relates to one specific person you might know or might have heard of. Remember the car-selection example, and don't fall into the trap of ignoring a mountain of evidence in favor of one oddball occurrence. It's no accident that research scientists have formal procedures for dealing with aberrant data—they use sophisticated statistical techniques like simply tossing out the unusual result.

3) As a special case related to both of the above points, always beware of the person who bases his entire argument on the grounds that "this is what worked for me." Sure, what worked for one person might well work for another, but chances are good that you want to play the odds: Suppose that 90-some percent of the world gets big and strong by doing squats and drinking milk, but someone comes along and says, "I always made my best gains on Dynamic Tension and corn flakes."

Yes, you might be like this fellow, but chances are good that you are not. Always be open to doing things differently, but remember that when you have overwhelming odds in favor of one thing versus another, the smart money plays the odds.

4) You will tend to work around the available data to find support for what you already believe. Funny thing about the car-selection process is that once you buy a Jeep, you will notice every good thing ever written about them, just about every one of them on the road will catch your eye, etc. Whereas before you bought one you might have been neutral, once you joined the Jeep owners' club, your perception became biased in favor of reinforcing your decision.

We all like to be right, and one of the most convincing ways to reinforce our beliefs is to keep looking for evidence that supports the wisdom of our choices. Nobody likes to make mistakes, but it's better to admit an error and correct it than to keep repeating it in an effort to save face.

So keep your wits about you as you evaluate everything from how to train, to how to eat, to how to choose a new truck: Chances are good that if you avoid leaky logic, it won't rain on your parade.

45 Gains From Brains

Chris Wilson hadn't really planned it, but things had just turned out that way: One day, while rummaging through a pile of *Playboy* magazines at a garage sale, he stumbled on an older issue of *Iron Man* and there, bigger than life, was Reg Park.... Chris was hooked immediately, and figured that if he ever got 17-inch arms and hit a 315-pound bench press, he would be as happy as anyone could be. So the bug had bitten.

For the first six months or so, it was all Chris could do to stay out of the gym in between his Monday-Wednesday-Friday workouts, and while he wasn't turning the bodybuilding world on its ear, he was making steady progress, getting bigger and stronger by the week. In fact, about one year into it, basic bodybuilding routines had pushed Chris through two sets of clothes, and he was benching close to double what he had been squatting in his first days of training. Chris knew he was onto something good, so he kept at it.

Without going overboard, Chris kept increasing his training volume and after two or three years of steady bodybuilding, he was putting in two-hour sessions six days a week. By now, it was obvious to anyone that Chris worked out: His legs might not have been that much larger than Lee Haney's arms, and his squat was about half of Ken Lain's bench press, but by any other standards, Chris was thick and strong—fully looking the part of someone who worked out with excellent results.

A funny thing had happened along the way, however, because even though Chris had never really lost his initial desire to get as herculean as possible, there were times when his resolve dropped as soon as he hit the gym: In the morning he was fired up to train, but by the middle of the afternoon, he was starting to feel some aches and thinking about some things he really needed to take care of.

As it got closer and closer to the time he was supposed to hit the gym, these reasons for not training that day loomed ever larger in Chris's mind, and believe it or not, he was even starting to skip workouts. And in some ways even worse, his training quality was slipping on the days when he made into the gym: His mind wandered, and his training weights, reps and sets were all starting to slip. Even more extreme, entire movements were dropping from his program.

In themselves, these things might not have been tragic, but the problem for Chris was that he still wanted to meet his original bodybuilding goals, so when he broke training, he got depressed. And it wasn't as if the respite was recharging his enthusiasm when it actually came time to train next: Even if he skipped a workout or two, it was just as hard for him to muster the enthusiasm to make his next one.

And when he tried taking two weeks off, he found that it was 20 times harder to get himself back on track. Chris was bummed, so he decided to talk things over with a fellow who was said to successfully blend psychology and strength sports.

"...so you see," Chris concluded, "I still want to make progress, but I just need a little help getting motivated enough to do the work required to take the next step up. Any ideas?"

"Ideas are my specialty," thought the good doctor, but he didn't want to appear arrogant so he just said, "sure." Then he went on. "You have a marvelous tool at your disposal that you aren't fully exploiting. That tool is your brain, and the way we're going to use it to get you through this little slump is going to be fun. In fact, it's going to be a lot like a children's game of sheer imagination."

Chris had nothing personal against Mister Rogers, but if that's the kind of thing this guy was thinking about, it was time to move along.

"Don't worry," said the good doctor, almost as if he had been reading Chris's mind, "we're not going to be doing anything you might think is silly. We're just going to use a process called 'eidetic imagery' and put it to work for you. Specifically, we're going tap your ability to form images that will help you progress in the gym. Let's walk through it step by step."

"True eidetic imagery is a mental picture that is so clear that it's like actually looking at something. For example, people said to have photographic memories, can glance at something and then form such a clear mental image that any detail can be recalled—just as if they were still looking at the original object. Not everyone has this ability, but everyone can, with help, form clear mental images. In your case, we're going to help you form the type of mental images that will spur you on when you don't really feel like training. The bottom line is that this process will give you the type of results you are looking for.

"Sounds good," said Chris, trying to be polite, but he didn't think this business had anything to do with bigger biceps. In fact, he was trying to figure out an excuse he could use to just get up and leave.

"You probably think this sounds like the usual visualize-success B.S.," said the good doctor, once again appearing to read Chris's mind, "but for starters, think about how it was you got started on this Hercules thing. A picture of someone, right?"

Chris nodded.

"And then you started to picture how you might be, right?" asked the doctor.

Chris nodded again.

"So this imagery thing might have some basis in fact, right?" the doctor asked.

"I guess," Chris said, "but if it worked for me then, why isn't it working for me now?"

"Because it's time to take your application of imagery up another notch," said the good doctor. "And here's how you do it."

"We are going to create a little video, starring you, that you will play in your mind. In the first scene, you are considering what got you interested in training in the first place. Next, you will review some of your goals, and the progress you have made along the way. Don't try to wave off your accomplishments at this point, either. The more you have had to struggle for each step forward, the more meaningful that accomplishment should be—regardless of the actual amount of forward progress you have made. Close your eyes, relax and start in on this scene now, please."

Chris did what he was told and as soon as he started to smile a little, the good doctor knew that Chris was on track.

"The second scene in your video involves developing ways to trick yourself into training hard, even when you don't want to. This is what we call 'developing a coping strategy,' and it just might be the most important aspect of your entire video, so put some effort into both developing the strategy and then visualizing it.

For example, you might tell yourself that you are only going to do your warm-up sets and nothing else. Then, after your first warm-up set, you tell yourself that you will do just one more. Set by set, this is how you sneak through some of the best workouts in your life. Another example is the 'big bribe'—rewarding yourself with something for a getting through a good, honest workout. Play with this scene until you have a clear image of a coping strategy that works for you.

Now, your internal video cuts to the final scene: how you have handled your best workouts. These are the workouts where everything was flowing right and you pounded out one more rep after one more rep. Focus on one of these workouts that you *know* made you grow by leaps and bounds. Really get into how you rocketed through one of workouts, and if you are doing a good job directing this video, don't be surprised if you start to breathe a little faster and get sweaty-palmed to boot.

And just in case you are going to tell me that you've never had this kind of workout, go ahead and make up one. And if you want to boost the octane a little on this one, think of how hard Reg Park used to train, and then jump into his shoes."

By now Chris was grinning like a drunken monkey because he had just gotten a major jolt of inspiration from the most powerful source of all: his brain. He barely stopped to thank the good doctor as he bolted for the door.

"Got to hit the gym," were his last words.

46 Slow To Grow

Danny Simpson was one of those people who made an impact just by being there: Danny exuded so much nervous tension that you could feel it anytime you came within five feet of him. Danny usually was on his feet, pacing and gesticulating wildly, and when he did sit, he would perch on the edge of his chair with his body compressed and leaning forward—as if he were a human cannonball or missile poised for the launch signal.

But you didn't even have to see Danny to know he was one wired hombre: His voice packed so much tension that you got the impression he could knock people over just by yelling a few choice words at them. Not that his words were likely to be just a few, though, because Danny talked a mile a minute and he was at least as likely to finish your sentence as his own.

Danny had the sort of behavioral profile that suggested that, among other things, he was more prone than average to heart disease and a host of related, unpleasant outcomes. And while he wasn't out to have a coronary, Danny had other—bigger, if you will—concerns that worried him more: like how to fill out his shirts, and maybe even how to move up a size or two.

Danny wasn't in a race to get his pro card, but he sure didn't want to spend another year dreading going to the pool because of what he looked like. And he also wanted the personal satisfaction of knowing that he was strong, even if he never competed in a sport, or even entered a lifting contest.

The problem for Danny was that he was training pretty sensibly and eating pretty well, but he just wasn't gaining the way he would like to. In fact, he seemed caught in a spiral of being sore and that's about all from his training. And in general, Danny frequently felt run down by the end of the day, had trouble sleeping soundly, and rarely got through a day without throbbing temples or a burning stomach.

Danny was no dummy, so he realized two things: 1) his excessive nervous tension was keeping him from gaining because he was wasting a lot of energy, and 2) maybe there was a psychological tool or two that he could use to reduce his overall tension and thereby increase his gains.

"It's worth a try," he said, after he scheduled an appointment with his local sports psych type, "because I should know pretty quickly whether or not he has anything to help me." Armed with hope, Danny went back to thinking about how his arms would soon be stretching out his shirt sleeves.

The sports psychologist was having his own fantasies, reading "Road & Track" and mentally picking between a Viper and an NSX as his daily driver, when Danny showed up and brought the good doctor back down to earth.

When Danny came into the doctor's office, he noticed the guy's diplomas hanging on the wall, was dutifully impressed, and thought he better be prepared to bare his soul. After all, if that's what it would take to get bigger biceps, that really wasn't such a high price to pay.

While Danny awaited the doctor's signal to start describing his childhood, he assumed his characteristic position on the guy's couch: Seated on the edge, Danny was leaning forward with his elbows on his knees. His whole body was coiled and even his teeth were noticeably clenched. If you looked closely, you could see that Danny was literally in a constant state of vibration. "I'm a little tense," he told the doctor, who wanted to reply, "you don't say," but had the good sense to just say, "yes."

"Yea," Danny continued, "I guess I'm always on edge, and I think maybe that's why I haven't been able to make very good gains in the gym. I mean, I train right and eat right, but maybe because I'm so nervous, it takes away whatever I need to grow. Can you help me put a lid on my overall tension level?"

"No problem," said the doctor, trying to sound brave, but secretly he was just hoping he could get Danny out of his office before he either self-destructed from his internal tension, or maybe vibrated the sofa into little pieces. "For starters," the doctor said, "make yourself comfortable on the couch."

"Here it comes," thought Danny, "all the stuff about the girl next door.... ." The doctor interrupted Danny's thought with the instructions to just lie there with his arms at his sides and to uncross his legs.

"I'm going to teach you a technique called 'progressive relaxation.' It was invented over half a century ago by a fellow named Jacobson, but all you need to remember is that it really works if you give it half a chance. This technique will quiet your whole being, from head to toe, from your mind to your body. You don't really need a technical understanding right now; just think of this technique as helping you achieve extreme relaxation."

"Sure," thought Danny sarcastically, but he tried to sound convinced when he said the same thing to the doctor. Danny was grinding his teeth wondering when his fifty-minute hour would be up, so he could leave.

"What we're going to do," said the doctor, "is teach you to become aware of your own tension levels, so you can negate them. You are going to see that deep relaxation doesn't involve any real effort on your part—it's simply a matter of not being tense. To learn how to become deeply relaxed, we're going to start by teaching you a little more about tension. The idea here is that if you can better recognize and understand tension, you will be able to reverse the pattern and achieve extreme relaxation. Ready to start?"

Danny nodded.

"Since you're a bodybuilder, let's begin with the *numero uno* bodybuilding muscle, the biceps. And since you're right handed, let's start with your right biceps. What I'd like you to do is flex your right biceps and hold it for a few seconds, paying close attention to what that feels like. Do that, please, and then don't do whatever you were doing to make the muscle tense. Try it now, and practice this cycle a few times."

The doctor could see from Danny's face that he was somewhat skeptical of such a simple procedure, but as he kept watching, the doctor could see that Danny was having the "ah ha" experience of getting his first taste of deep relaxation.

They repeated the procedure with Danny's other arm, and then worked through his thighs and calves, one at a time, and then in order, his stomach, his lower back, his upper back and neck, and finally, his facial muscles. For each target area, Danny first tensed the muscles, noted what that felt like, and then let the tension slide away. Danny wouldn't have passed for a mythical Eastern master, but by now, his face had assumed a new-found calmness and he wasn't generating sparks of electricity the way he had been only a short while before.

Randall J. Strossen, Ph.D./*IronMind*   **131**

After Danny had finished the series of tension-relaxation cycles, the doctor let him remain in his state of deep relaxation for about fifteen minutes before gradually rousing him.

"So what do you think?" asked the doctor.

"Amazing," said Danny. "I've never experienced anything like that before."

The doctor smiled, told Danny to run through this drill at least once a day for the next few weeks. After he got proficient at it, he could just apply it as needed, but for now daily practice was required.

Danny left the doctor's office feeling as if he had just awakened from a terrific night's sleep and was raring to build biceps the size of baseballs. And the good doctor, meantime, was wondering if he got a Bugatti, where he'd get it serviced.

47 Know When To Go

Tim Kramer was one of those people whom you'd guess would succeed at anything he tried: He was goal-oriented, could be serious to a fault, had an uncanny ability to focus on something, wasn't easily mislead by irrelevant details, and so forth. Given all this, you would think that when he took up bodybuilding, that he would have made great progress. In fact, his progress was so miserable that he was tempted to write off his failure to date as being due to horrible genetics and go back to working on the software he hoped would make him the next Bill Gates.

Ralph Hudson, on the other hand, was an easy going kind of guy: Even if he didn't give you the impression that he was sleeping on his feet, he usually walked slowly, talked softly and generally seemed pretty laid back. So when Ralph took to the gym, you might have guessed his lack of overall intensity would have kept him from making progress. In fact, Ralph might not have been dealt world championship caliber genetics, but nonetheless, he began placing in regional lifting contests in less time than it took a lot of people to pick a major in college.

Tim wasn't making progress for the same reason that Ralph was, and that reason is what psychologists refer to as "arousal regulation." Let's take a quick look at this phenomenon and see how you can put it to use in your quest for reaching your bodybuilding and lifting goals.

Arousal Regulation and Performance

Arousal involves both a physiological component (such as increased blood pressure and heart rate) and a psychological component (such as a feeling of alertness) that combine to prepare you for action. And while it would generally seem to make sense that running at full tilt leads to optimal performance, there truly are times when "Less is More" (see Chapter 5 for more on this). This basic idea has become fairly popular among iron athletes, but what isn't so widely known is the exact arousal pattern that can separate success from failure—inside the gym and out.

Over 25 years ago, an ingenious psychological researcher named Fenz decided that a great way to study arousal was to monitor parachutists as they approached the big jump. Early in this research program it was learned that— surprise, surprise—parachutists displayed signs of increasing arousal as they got closer and closer to that fateful step. "Any moron could have guessed that," you say, "so tell me something I didn't know—something that will help me get huge arms and the strength to squat with a pile of big plates." Hang on another minute.

As this research program unfolded, something emerged that proved to be the key to regulating arousal for peak performance: It was discovered that this pattern—arousal increasing as the launch time drew near—was limited to novice parachutists; the veteran jumpers started off with a similar pattern, but after the early increases in their arousal levels, they had arousal *decreases* up to jump time. In fact, even though the experienced parachutists had initial increases in arousal, the subsequent decreases were so marked that they were almost at their normal arousal levels at the time of their jumps. Hmmm—so maybe like a lot of other things, when it comes to arousal, timing is everything.

Closer to home, a Bulgarian researcher named Genov, working with top weightlifters, compared arousal levels for successful versus unsuccessful attempts, both under normal circumstances and when the lifter was primed for action. Consistent with the ideas above, it was learned that the unsuccessful lifters were *more* aroused under normal circumstances, but *less* aroused when it came time to perform. The case for timing being critical to effective use of arousal is looking pretty potent.

"O.K," you say, "but what do I do to control my arousal level—it's not like I can just flip a switch to go up or down."

At least initially, it won't be as easy for you to regulate your arousal level as it is to, say, regulate how hard you hit the gas pedal in your car. Nonetheless, think of the process as being analogous: You want to be able to control your arousal level the same way you control how hard you step on the accelerator in your car, or where you set the thermostat in your home. And while we don't have time this month to go into each of these techniques in detail, here are some basic tools that you can use to step up or scale down your arousal level.

The key to scaling down your arousal level is to learn how to relax at will, using any of the standard techniques. For example, last month IronMind outlined a technique called "progressive relaxation." Progressive relaxation systematically teaches you to recognize and eliminate tension in your body, and it's a skill that, properly employed, could put you on the road to big gains. If you are new to progressive relaxation, or any of the other structured relaxation techniques, keep practicing until you can hit a relaxed state quickly and completely.

Aside from overall tension, another principal cause of inappropriate arousal is anxiety and fear, and a very powerful tool for countering either is "systematic desensitization," which is outlined in Chapter 41. In a nutshell, systematic desensitization teaches you to stay calm in the face of progressively more threatening stimuli. Stick with systematic desensitization for a while and you should be able to laugh at your worst nightmare.

On the other hand, suppose that you have no trouble hanging loose, but when it comes time to put the pedal to the metal, you come up short. What can you do?

The first thing you need to do when it's appropriate to get jacked up is to maintain your attentional focus—you have a job to do and this is the time to do it. Suppose that you are very familiar with a certain turn on a race course, and under good conditions, you can take it at around 70 miles per hour. When you take this turn at 30, you can whistle "Dixie," discuss supply-side economics or do just about anything else you might choose while driving.

Trying to take the turn at 80 or 90, however, means that you had better take care of business, or you'll be in for a crash. It's like that when you are training or performing for top performance: When the money is on the line, don't let your mind wander.

A second key arousal-generator is "self-talk" or "self-instruction" in the form of both inspiration ("I can do this...") and instruction ("Keep your chest up..."). Remember that your brain can lead your body and that language is a window to your brain. Talk yourself into becoming the substance of your dreams.

And whether you need to psyche up or down, remember to make good use of our old standby, imagery. If you need to calm down, picture yourself being calm, visualize tranquil settings, imagine a role model staying cool in the circumstances that are upsetting you, and so forth. If you need to psyche up, imagine yourself on the brink of a do-or-die situation, visualize a successful athlete attacking a comparable situation with a vengeance, and so on.

When Ralph Hudson heard about this arousal regulation business, he just shrugged his shoulders and said, "Sounds like what I do anyway," so he just kept doing what to him came naturally. And he kept getting bigger and stronger.

When Tim Kramer heard about this arousal regulation business, it was a very different story. First, he sat down, and as he was prone to do, laid out a program to make better use of his ability to get charged up. He started off by making a list of the situations where he usually came in overwired and noted how he would use a structured relaxation technique to remove a bit of the edge.

For example, now Tim realized that he spent too much energy obsessing about his training, and when he actually came in the gym, he was already down to half a tank of gas. Second, Tim even made a secret note of some things that he worried about, recognizing that worrying was just a waste of energy that could be better utilized for some positive outcome.

Tim planned to attack these fears with a self-administered systematic desensitization program. For example, Tim secretly admitted that he hated to squat, in part because he was afraid of getting crushed by the barbell. Finally, Tim jotted down the times he really did need to be on, and he planned to take all the energy he had squandered inappropriately and apply it during these critical times.

For example, Tim decided that because he needed muscle mass quickly, he would really go for broke on his benches, rows and squats, shooting for added reps or more weight each workout.

Three months later, it was as if Tim had discovered a secret routine: He had gained something like thirty pounds and was benching his old squat weight. Asked the secret of his success, he winked and said, "Timing—you just have to know when to go."

48 Willy Worry

Willy hadn't exactly gotten sand kicked in his face, but that didn't diminish his desire to build himself a better body—bigger, more shapely, and stronger. So Willy set out to do just that, and his first step was to buy a muscle magazine and read it from cover to cover.

For whatever Willy might have lacked on the physical front, he was no mental midget, packing around an I.Q. that allowed him to inhale and digest myriad bits of information faster than most folks could tie their shoes. So when Willy emerged from his studies more than a little dazed and confused, there must have been some good reason for it.

What Willy had run into was advice from some quarters that said certain machines (theirs, of course) were the be-all, end-all in terms of building muscle mass; other camps openly sneered at machines, said they were on earth to keep the geeks away from the free weights, and argued for barbells, pure and simple. And some experts cheered for pyramiding, while others called for drop sets, and still others extolled the virtues of one-set-to-total-failure. Do this all twice a day, six times a week, or once every four days—depending on whom you talked to. And as long as you either moved the weight very slowly or very quickly, again depending on who was speaking, you would gain.

As if this weren't already confusing enough, Willy had read about the need for high-protein diets, the hazards of same, and everything in between—from the merely anabolic to the anti-catabolic!

In the face of this conflicting advice there were two paths Willy could go on, and he unwittingly chose the one more-travelled—Willy took the way to Worry, and with all he had spinning around in his head, it really was worry with a capital W.

A Few Words About Worry(ing)

Willy might not have known it, but psychologists have been considering worry for some time. In a nutshell, worry involves lingering over whatever is bothering you. For example, Willy kept going over and over whether he should really be doing five exercises per bodypart, or five exercises for his entire routine, and considering the two choices made him ever more anxious. So Willy was walking around with a knot in his stomach, a lump in his throat, sweaty palms and a dizzying stream of chatter in his brain.

If we sat down and made a list of Willy's training worries, it would be fairly staggering: It would range from the type of equipment to use and how to use it, to the content and frequency of his routine, to what went into his mouth, and if he was really getting nutty, it even included the color of his T-shirt. Remember, worrying is the psychological equivalent of spinning your wheels and so no matter what the tach says, you're going nowhere.

If worrying is the psychological equivalent to being stuck in the same place, problem-solving is the psychological equivalent to getting some traction and walking away from the mess. Let's see how Willy might get a little traction—something to grab on to—so he can make some progress.

The first rule is to prioritize your concerns. If you have a lot of things batting around in your head, make a list of them, and if your list is too long to easily prioritize, quickly sort it into two piles: the critical and the not-so-critical items. For example, Willy might decide that it's critical that he know what his routine was going to be, but he can temporarily shelve any concerns he might have about his T-shirt.

Once things are prioritized, chances are good that you will discover that when you make one decision, others will automatically fall into place. For example, Willy might decide that an abbreviated routine of the basic exercises is the proven road to success for him, so that's the way he should go. It then follows that he doesn't have to worry anymore about machines vs. free weights, five exercises per bodypart vs. five per routine, etc., etc. because his first decision simultaneously answered a host of follow-up questions that had been bugging him.

"But how to even begin making decisions?" you wonder, with more than a little worry. "What if you make the wrong decision?" No need to worry about this one any longer, because Willy cleared this hurdle, and you can too.

For starters, remember that you are engaged in a constructive activity—problem solving—and that your goal is to find solutions, not to increase your concerns or otherwise add to your indecision. You might begin by trying to step back from the situation and imagine that someone has come to you with the exact set of questions, problems if you will, that are puzzling you. This person has come to you because while you might not be a famous authority in the field, you have done some research, and if necessary, can do some more. Well, what do you think? Based on the evidence, just what should this person do?

For example, Willy had faced the primary question of how to pack on some muscle mass, and while he had read about a lot of different ways to skin this cat, the method that kept popping up as the tried and true technique involved tooth-grinding effort on the basic exercises. So even if he might have been tempted by some other approaches, at least when he stepped back a little from the problem, the solution was obvious. In fact, the solution was so obvious that Willy could make the decision with some confidence, at least when he considered how he would advise another person with the same problem.

Setting your course and moving off the dime, like this, is the first step toward overcoming the incapacitating effect of worry. But to stay on track, to maintain your momentum, you need to have a couple more tricks up your sleeve.

First, you need to learn when to put on psychological blinders—just as a horse might do better under some conditions to have its peripheral vision limited, so might you. Thus, once you have made a basic decision, make it easier for yourself to live with it by not going out of your way to confront alternatives.

Suppose you are in the market for a new bike, and after months of agonizing whether this one was going to be a Yamaha or a Honda, after you finally buy the Honda, do you keep going back to the Yamaha dealer? Not unless you cross the street to look for trouble. It's the same thing with less concrete decisions: Once you have made your decision, don't look back.

Second, remember that what appears to be an overwhelmingly massive commitment today can probably be reversed at some later point in your life. And if the monumental decisions that have been keeping you awake at night involve your training, this is most certainly true. The beauty of this realization is, of course, that what had once seemed ponderously significant, now shrinks in stature to the level of whether you choose a Big Mac or a Whopper today—the other option is readily available any time you want it.

So Willy once had been mired down in worry—spinning his wheels and going nowhere. Now, armed with a few simple tricks, he dug out and was blasting down the road. And about his only concern now was why he spent so much time and energy worrying in the first place. But will he worry about it? Naah.

49 Sex-Role Stereotypes

Doug Jones had been bitten by the bodybuilding bug, and in mere months of benching, squatting and rowing his heart out, his progress was something to behold. Sure, he was no Mr. Olympia threat—now or in the foreseeable future—but for a guy who used to wear small T-shirts and was nicknamed "The Weed," he was becoming somewhat formidable in size and shape.

In fact, Doug's gains were so solid, that he was even thinking about entering his first show the following year: He was eyeing a local all-natural contest and thinking how he'd feel standing in front of all those people, holding the winner's trophy, of course.

The proverbial fly in the ointment, however, was some ribbing Doug had always gotten, even if in small doses. "Bodybuilders are a bunch of sissies, always parading around in their underwear," his pal Joey used to tell him, "and if you keep hanging around with them, you'll become one too." Doug might not have needed to have any concerns in this area, but Joey's warning kept rattling around in the back of his brain, distracting him.

Across town, Jill Robinson had gotten introduced to Olympic-style weightlifting by her volleyball coach—he told her that working on the Olympic lifts would greatly improve her explosive power, with tremendous positive transfer to her VB game. In fact, not only did Olympic lifting put some serious height on her vertical jump, but it also was helping Jill develop a killer spike. Besides those benefits, Jill found that she liked training on the lifts. The problem was that even though she definitely wasn't getting any fewer looks on the beach, she didn't want to "become like a man," as one of her friends kept warning her.

Once again, sex-role stereotypes threatened to upset the apple cart. But isn't this the natural order of things? Aren't men and women as different in mind as in body? And never the twain shall meet, right?

Masculinity, Femininity and Androgyny

"Masculinity" and "femininity" refer to personality characteristics; they are the psychological counterparts to the labels "male" and "female," which refer to physical characteristics. As you would guess, men are generally expected to be masculine, exhibiting such characteristics as aggression, ambition, and independence. And women, accordingly, are generally expected to be feminine, exhibiting such characteristics as empathy, warmth and nurturance.

During the 1970s, these traditional notions of gender-based personality characteristics took some heavy flak, in research laboratories as well as on the streets and in the courts. One of the most significant developments on the research front was the idea that masculinity and femininity were not represented by a single dimension, where being more of one meant you were automatically less of the other.

Instead, masculinity and femininity were now seen as two separate dimensions, which meant that a person could simultaneously have significant measures of both characteristics, without either one being diminished by the other. In other words, someone could be both independent and ambitious, while also being warm and empathetic.

Referring to this blend of masculine and feminine characteristics as "psychological androgyny," Dr. Sandra Bem developed a scale to measure it. Lo and behold, not only did she find that men and women *could and did* simultaneously possess both masculine and feminine characteristics, but she also hypothesized that ideally-developed people contain the best of both worlds when it comes to sex-type characteristics.

In a nutshell, Bem's argument was that the androgynous person would be most adaptive to the situation—reacting with appropriate masculine traits at some times and appropriate feminine traits at other times, rather than being locked into one stereotypical pattern or the other. Remember, we're talking generally-accepted, appropriate behavior, so psychological androgyny isn't just another name for swishy men or butch women.

A Case Study

I have a buddy named Steve who can give all of us a good lesson in sex role stereotypes. Let's meet him.

Fresh out of high school, Steve joined the Marines and headed to Vietnam—that's exactly the sort of guy he is. Twenty-some years later, he's still proud of having been a Marine and when things started heating up in the Persian Gulf, he walked around wearing a T-shirt showing cross hairs on a military camel caravan, with the caption, "I'd fly 10,000 miles to smoke a camel."

Steve spends his days as a San Francisco cop, where he battles crime—sometimes hand to hand. At night, he coaches weightlifting, and if the kids don't produce, he might refer to them using what the dictionary calls "vulgar slang." Or, he might just walk over and—on the spot—hoist hundreds of pounds just to make his point.

If you need a few more details, Steve is missing a couple of teeth, from fights of course; he gets his hair cut "high and tight," smokes big cigars, and bottom line, is definitely not the sort of person to get into a brawl with—no matter which martial art you have mastered.

At this point, it doesn't take an Einstein to write off Steve as some ultra-macho meathead, but wait.

Steve is also the kind of guy who sometimes has his lifters over for lunch, and while you probably wouldn't be surprised to hear that the menu might well be hot dogs and baked beans, you might not predict that he'll worry aloud about whether he has enough milk for everyone. And you would probably never guess that he might fold the napkins two or three times—just to get them perfect. And if there's a baby or little kid around the gym, Steve's usually the first one over to find out the little tyke's name and make it crack a smile.

And even if it's just a matter of his lifters making reservations to go to the Nationals, Steve worries about them like a mother hen. He'd probably do their laundry for them if he thought it was necessary. He's also the kind of guy who can call me and end the conversation with, "Love and kisses, darlin'," without making me nervous.

This, sports fans, is a case of psychological androgyny in action.

Meanwhile, back in Doug's gym, in between his sets of gut-busting squats, Doug was beginning to choreograph his posing routine in his mind—somehow the idea of artistic expression no longer seemed to get in the way of the focused aggression and driving ambition that were pushing him through his workout. And across town, Jill—after listening attentively to a friend's problems over lunch—was in the gym power snatching more than a lot of the freshman football team could handle.

Fueling their efforts, both Doug and Jill had transcended their sex-role stereotypes, and instead, had learned to pick the best of the masculine traits and the best of the feminine traits, applying each as appropriate. More than doubling their options, this approach was allowing Doug and Jill to pursue their dreams. In fact, Doug is looking like a shoe-in for his first show, and Jill, well, watch for her in Atlanta in '96.

50 Flexing Your Rights

It's just another Monday night in the gym, and as usual, things are backed up around the bench pressing stations. Artie Nelson just wants to bang out a few sets, so he can hit the shower and get home in time to catch a little pro wrestling before calling it a day. Instead of already being halfway through his benches, Artie is still in line, feeling more like he's in the deli on Saturday morning than maintaining his warm-up and pump in the gym.

Finally, it's Artie's turn and just as he finishes stripping down the bar for his first set, some bazooka ambles up and says, "Man, I'm running a little late tonight, would you mind if I crank out three fast ones with four and a quarter?"

Of course Artie minds, but he numbly says, "O.K." and watches as "three fast ones" turns into another tooth-grinding, ten-minute delay as the guy does a set, rests, does a set, rests, and does another set—the whole time sitting on the bench as if it's his throne and nobody dare even think about cutting in for a set.

As things turn out, the next day, in another city, Sue Burkett finds herself in a psychologically-similar situation at work: It's performance review time, and Sue feels that she has more than earned a raise, a pretty big one at that. After all, Sue reasons, she was the one who brought in the XYZ account that was peanuts at the time, but is now her company's third largest customer. And wasn't Sue the one who never missed a day of work and always had suggestions for cheaper, faster, better ways to do things?

Unfortunately, Sue's boss didn't seem to see things the same way: It wasn't that he dismissed Sue's contributions, but it was just that, he said, times were tough and everyone had to live with a little tighter belt. "...the truth is," he concluded, "we're even going to have to delay putting in the lights for our new tennis court at home." Sue was ticked, and she could feel her temples pounding, but all she said was "thank you" when she was told her salary would be frozen for another year.

Artie and Sue, like many people, are having difficulty standing up for their rights—they are letting other people push them around.

Getting Pushed Around

The sad truth is that most people, most of the time, let other people push them around. There was a time when it was fashionable in pop psychology circles to focus discussion of assertiveness training on women, but the fact is that men also need all the help they can get in this area. And lest you think that this whole idea of people letting themselves get pushed around is either a paranoid delusion or a rare event, consider the following piece of research:

Based in New York's Grand Central Station, a researcher waited outside a phone booth and when a businessman finished his call, the researcher said he had lost a ring and asked the businessman to empty his pockets. Would you be surprised to learn that 80% complied with this outrageous request? Even though this was one of the most audacious tests of passivity/assertiveness, the pattern of results, 80% compliance, fits squarely with other pieces of related research!

Asserting Your Rights

Everyone has had the feeling of being swindled—whether in terms of time, money, emotions, or whatever—and it's not a pleasant feeling. In fact, when you let yourself get steamrolled, bad things are happening to both your mind and your body, things that spell S-T-R-E-S-S. For example, stress-related anger stimulates the release of norepinephrine, a hormone that boosts your heart rate and constricts your blood vessels, which means that your blood pressure increases.

And even if you don't end up with heart disease or an ulcer, the added stress could leave you with anything from a headache to diarrhea, and a lot of things in between. One of the things in between is no gains in muscular size and strength. In fact, weight training is so stressful, that anything you can do reduce stress in the rest of your life will only help you get bigger and stronger. Faster.

Think of your ability to weather stress and to recuperate as involving energy. And think of energy as being like any other resource—your supplies will be limited, so use what you have wisely for best results, or squander it and have little to show afterwards. Thus, you probably learned long ago that if you are trying to make big gains in mass and power, you not only need to be selective in terms of what you do in the gym, but you also need to be selective in terms of what you do outside the gym as well. It's the same thing with your emotions: If you subject yourself to unnecessary stress, your bodybuilding and lifting progress will suffer as a result.

One of the prime reasons for people lacking appropriate levels of assertiveness is that many of us are walking around with the mistaken idea that it's not polite to stand up for our rights, and there is a general notion that being assertive is the same as being aggressive or rude. Let's talk about these ideas.

When you are confronted with a situation that produces conflict and stress for you, there are three basic ways you can react:

1) non-assertively ("Sure, boss...whatever you say..."),

2) aggressively ("How would you like some free orthodontal work?"), and

3) assertively ("I can understand why you say that, but I think that...").

Let's see how these options stack up.

The problem with responses in the first category is that you avoid an immediate confrontation, but your stress level will rise and you will later suffer for playing the role of the submissive wimp. In fact, that night you will probably stew over what you wished you had said to assert your rights.

The problem with responses in the second category is that escalation might create a little short-term relief, but chances are good that later on, aggressive responses will also create added stress. What often happens when you blow up is that you later feel guilty or foolish.

R esponses in the third category are appropriate because they will leave you with the feeling that you stood your ground and expressed yourself directly, honestly and politely. In essence, these last responses do not produce stress because they leave you feeling good about yourself and how you handled a potentially troublesome situation—even if you don't always get your way.

So when the guy tried to cut in on Artie's benching time, Artie could have said, "I understand; I'm running late, too, and have to finish my benches and be out of here in fifteen minutes or I'll miss the Hulkster. How about if you work in with me?"

And Sue could have empathized with her boss about his tennis court, but still expressed here disappointment and frustration—speaking frankly, firmly and politely. If she felt bold, she might conclude by pointing out that if they bought him a Honda instead of a Mercedes as the company car, they could more than afford to give her the raise appropriate to her contributions.

The next time you feel exploited, remind yourself that it's perfectly all right to put yourself first sometimes. And you have the right to your opinions and to be treated fairly, and most of all, you have the right to say, "no" and "I disagree." Exercise those rights and you will not only feel better about yourself, but you'll also live a longer and healthier life by avoiding unnecessary, destructive stress.

If that's not enough motivation, remember that the stress you avoid creates the opportunity to gain more size and strength, so look at managing these difficult situations as an adjunct to your training: Each time you assert yourself appropriately, you'll be on your way to bigger biceps and a mightier bench press.

51 Harry And The Have-To's

Harry Ketchum was a normal child: He rode his bike, fought with his brother, ignored his sister and every time his parents said "No!" Harry planned to run away from home. The operative word here is "planned" because Harry's intentions were never translated into action, largely because he always lacked what he saw as the key ingredient required for a successful escape.

For example, when Harry was five and was miffed because his parents wouldn't buy him a dog, he plotted his liberation, but quickly realized that until he got a big flashlight and a little tent, the great outdoors might be a bit too spooky for his taste. So Harry concluded that he had to have a flashlight and a tent before he could put his plans into action and make his life perfect. For weeks, all Harry thought about was how to get that flashlight and the tent, and just how wonderful everything would be if he had them.

Harry's life continued in this way, and at various stages he decided that if he only had X, life would be perfect. It didn't really matter that this pattern had progressed from flashlights to skateboards to motorcycles to muscles—the pattern was always the same: "If only I had [blank], everything would be perfect...I absolutely have to have [blank]," had become Harry's refrain.

And when Harry decided he had to have something, he was the picture of persistence: Day and night he was preoccupied with the object(s) of his desire, to the point where it became somewhat dysfunctional. Thus, when Harry got the idea that he had to have something, he developed a level of focus that might have psychologists mumbling words like "obsessive" and "compulsive." "Obsessive" means that you are locked into a certain idea, or set of ideas, and "compulsive" means that you are locked into a related set of behaviors.

When Harry got the have-to's, about all he did was think about and try to move toward the object of his desire. So, when Harry was about fifteen, he seized the idea that he "had to have muscles" and that was what he thought about day and night. Besides thinking about muscles, he had adopted a couple of new behavioral patterns, such as measuring his right arm something like 15 times a day, everyday.

Before too long, Harry had a stack of muscle magazines that might worry the local fire department, and he had spent so many hours pouring over their contents that he could identify the owners of countless body parts—whether they were attached to heads or not. And as a direct result of what he had been reading, Harry was regularly reminded that the world has wonder supplements, nearly the equal of banned substances, and if he just used them, it would mean more beef on his biceps, a smaller waist and various other wondrous things. So Harry had to have this one, and next month he had to have that one.

Not that Harry's have-to's were limited, now, to food supplements. There were have-to-have workout clothes, have-to-have pieces of equipment, and certainly, have-to-have training routines. And to cap things off, Harry wrote letters to experts far and wide, pleading his case for the secrets he had to have to make the progress he wanted. Harry was hooked on the have-to's and while a lot of people were prospering from Harry's orientation, one them certainly wasn't Harry.

For starters, Harry had painted himself into a corner as far as his daily happiness went: Since he was always looking to the future and whatever magic wand he thought it held, Harry was virtually barred from enjoying his present situation. For example, after he had packed on 15 pounds of high-grade muscle, instead of saying, "Gee, my arms are up an inch, my chest is up two—that's terrific," all Harry could mumble was, "if only I had some of that new supplement, I would have gained even more. I have to have some of that stuff."

But that was just the beginning, because not only was Harry unable to take pleasure in his progress, but he also started to slump because he didn't have what he saw as crucial tools for his progress. "What's the use in even trying," he muttered, "my gains won't be half of what they could be if only I had... ." So now Harry fell into a vicious circle:

1) First he discounted his progress because he didn't have access to something he felt would help him even more, and

2) then he started to soft-peddle his efforts because, after all, he was competing with one hand tied behind his back, and

3) his reduced efforts cut back his gains, which

4) reinforced the wisdom of his original conclusion: He had to have X.

Harry was in trouble, because even when he got whatever he felt he had to have, something new always popped up and you know who had to have that, too.

One day Harry decided that enough was enough and it was time to talk to somebody about himself and the have-to's, so he made an appointment with his friendly neighborhood sports psychologist—who, fortunately, just happened to have more than a passing interest in lifting weights.

Harry described how he always felt his training was handicapped by not having some critical tool or other, and how he was discouraged—and was even starting to think that his whole life, not just his training, was affected the same way. The psychologist listened, asked Harry some questions about how he handled a few typical situations, and then nodded in a way that left no doubt that he was sure he understood matters. The psychologist had seen some pretty bad cases of the have-to's before, and he decided that this was not the time for highly technical language or fancy theoretical constructs.

"Harry, you're not really nutsy, it's just that your attention has gotten a little out of focus," began the psychologist. "You have fallen into the trap of believing that you, or your existence, is somehow flawed and that some *thing* can make your life perfect," he continued, "which is always the easy way out. Of course, this is precisely what the folks on Madison Avenue want you to think."

"The easy way out?" asked Harry, "you've got to be kidding. Do you know what I go through, always being blocked the way I am?"

"The reason that the have-to's are the easy way out has nothing to do with the frustration or anguish you might be suffering. They're the easy way out because they allow you to avoid the sometimes painful conclusion that things like your vision, boldness and effort will control your destiny far more than anything you can grab, put on your body or swallow. It's actually pretty hard to just seize responsibility for what you want to do and not just look for answers in magic wands," concluded the psychologist.

"Media hype?" asked Harry, amazed that someone could think he was being sucker-punched as much as anyone believing some ridiculous detergent commercial. "You mean to tell me that the world isn't filled with things that work better than others? Do you really believe that some supplements aren't better than others, that some routines aren't better than others and that some pieces of equipment aren't better than others?" Harry's eyes were getting a little brighter, because this conversation had gotten his blood pumping.

"Of course there are," said the psychologist, "but the point is that all these things really depend on your effort and that's the key: The world's best training routine doesn't work for you—what it does do is reward you for your hard work. In fact, one of the funny things about the 'great routines,' is that they are usually based on incredible effort, and the harder you work on them, the better you gain. The same thing is true about the top pieces of equipment and the top supplements: They work if you work. You, not they, are the critical success factor."

Harry was starting to feel a little like Dorothy, about to leave Oz with a new understanding of where to look for answers. "Thanks much," he said standing up. "I'd better get going: Today's a heavy training day and I don't want to be late."

The psychologist nodded and thought to himself, "Bet he hits a couple of PRs."

52 It's The Mind That Matters

Dear Dr. Strossen:

I enjoy reading your column in IRONMAN magazine every month and have greatly benefited from your advice, but was wondering if you sometimes exaggerate how people can rise to the occasion and solve their problems... .

This question is fair enough, especially because sometimes it's pretty hard to separate the wheat from the chaff when it comes to bodybuilding and lifting advice. This is an ironic situation not only because bodybuilding and lifting are such concrete activities, but also because what is presented as apparent scientific fact might prove to be nothing but sham, and what appears to be the most outlandish of claims might turn out to be utterly accurate.

Without getting into the rigors of formal research for evaluating different claims, case studies are one of the most powerful ways to get a sense of what works and what doesn't. Let's take a look at a case study that addresses the question raised in this letter by looking at a teenager who might be fairly typical if he weren't hooked on weights.

From a bodybuilding or lifting point of view, Scott Muriel has genetics that fit squarely in the middle of the curve, but that doesn't keep him from making exceptional gains, because he makes good use of his most important body part: his mind.

After fooling around with a basic bodybuilding routine, Scott started talking to the Olympic-style weightlifters who trained in the back room of his gym. Unfortunately, on his very first workout, he kept getting talked into trying to snatch heavier and heavier weights—never having done snatches before, and certainly never having been taught how to bail out, he eventually got stuck in a bad position and had to be taken to the hospital because there was some concern that he had dislocated his elbow. As things turned out, it was just a strain and Scott was back training, a little tender, but much wiser for the experience.

After this rude introduction, his lifting progressed smoothly and no small part of his progress was due to Scott's insatiable appetite for information—he even bought translated copies of highly-technical Russian training manuals and inhaled their contents. Before too long, Scott was lifting in the National High School Championships.

One day Scott decided that some more muscular size and strength would be a definite boon to his lifting career, so he incorporated portions of the *SUPER SQUATS* routine into his training—most notably, the ferocious 20-rep squats. As Scott's fortune would have it, the first day his squat weight really took him to the pain zone, he had a particularly enthusiastic audience urging him on.

By about the twelfth rep, Scott looked like dead meat and felt even worse, but the guys at the gym were screaming like banshees and kept dragging Scott through rep after rep until he got the full twenty. This proved to be a fateful set because even though he was semi-delirious with fatigue, Scott decided to walk a couple of blocks to a convenience store to get something to eat. What happened on the way back is history.

Literally hobbling, Scott made it to the store, but on his way back, his legs could take no more and he simply lay down on the middle of the sidewalk. If this had been in a big city, it might have gone unnoticed, but in a suburban neighborhood of expensive homes, people just don't take naps on the sidewalk so a concerned citizen called an ambulance.

When the medical team arrived, one thing led to another and before long, Scott was in the hospital, and the doctors were trying to perform a spinal tap—which would have been bad enough, but given Scott's unusually well-developed spinal erectors, it took the medical team over half a dozen tries before they got the needle where they wanted it. The next morning they released Scott and told him that—surprise, surprise—he had only been very tired. Scott spent the next week and a half in bed recovering from the medical tests, and to add insult to injury he got a hospital bill that looked like a ransom note.

Undaunted by all this, Scott was back training as quickly as he could, and shortly afterward he added a strenuous part-time job to his full-time schedule at school and substantial responsibilities at home. Once again, his pals at the gym did him no favors by, one day, coaxing him to try the training routine being used by the handpicked Olympic hopefuls who train in Colorado Springs. Scott's back couldn't take the program and before long, he just plain couldn't even squat.

By this point, just about anyone else would have thrown in the towel, but not Scott, he just switched back to the *SUPER SQUATS* routine, but substituted hip belt squats. In the first two or three weeks, his presses behind the neck went up 20 pounds, his benches went up 30 pounds, and both his bent over rows and hip belt squats went up 40 pounds. Not too shabby. Oh yes, his bodyweight increased 10 pounds.

Scott's work schedule remained heavy, and his back wasn't rehabbing as quickly as he had hoped, so he made a couple of adjustments in his program: Most notably, he cut back his already basic program to just the core exercises and added frog kicks to his routine. In another three weeks, he added another 30 pounds to his benches and rows, and another 40 to his hip belt squats. And his bodyweight increased another 10 pounds, bringing his total bodyweight gains to 20 pounds in about five weeks.

As far as his diet went, Scott didn't use a single food supplement the entire time. What he did do was follow a nutritious high-protein, high-calorie diet and was fanatical about drinking at least two quarts, and generally a gallon, of milk a day.

Adding twenty pounds of muscle literally transforms a typical person and Scott was no exception—he's starting to look as if he's wearing shoulder pads under his shirt, and his thighs make his pants bulge right down to the knee, shouting "strength" every inch of the way. And for anyone who thinks that all he did was pile on a lot of lard, it should be noted that Scott's chest-waist differential more than doubled in this five-week period—a little over a month ago, he was fairly straight up and down, but now he's got the telltale taper of a successful bodybuilder.

As we said at the top, Scott was blessed with average genetics from the shoulders down, but because he had the good sense to use his mind—to seek out good information, ignore bad advice even from well-meaning people, to analyze and adjust his program along the way—and to never, ever quit, he's made more progress in the last few weeks than many people make in a lifetime of training.

Exaggerate the good things you're capable of doing? Not hardly!

53 When Ignorance Is Bliss

E ven if you might not have heard of him lately, Henry "Milo" Steinborn remains one of the great figures in Iron Game history. Let's introduce him and use an example from his career to illustrate how a little ignorance can produce a lot of bliss.

While a prisoner of war (WWI), Milo trained with barbells fashioned from tree trunks and following his release, he came to America, where he astounded everyone with his physique, his lifting ability and his reliance on a hitherto little-used movement: the flat-footed squat.

Best known for upending a 550-pound barbell, getting it on his shoulders unassisted, performing a rock-bottom squat with it, and then returning it, Milo was a real iron man: He combined the top standards of both the bodybuilding and the lifting worlds in one body. In fact, he displayed the required attributes of strength, speed, endurance and agility to such a degree that the dean of Iron Game historians, David P. Willoughby, placed Milo in the elite "Super Athlete" category.

As far as his lifting went, Milo wasn't just good in the squat. In fact, it was really because he was so good in the snatch and clean and jerk that other people paid close attention to how he trained, and thus noticed his penchant for very heavy deep knee bends. The simple truth is that Milo was so utterly magnificent in the quick lifts that he would playfully walk into a gym and one-hand snatch 200 pounds and one-hand clean and jerk 250 pounds without even removing his coat! And the story was just as impressive when it came to using both hands. In fact, Milo could perform a two-hands clean and jerk with 350 pounds when that was truly a world-class lift.

One day when Milo was going after a 350-pound clean and jerk, a funny thing happened: He missed the lift. Whether or not he then uttered a few choice words I don't know, but on his next attempt, he won the battle with gravity and rammed the bar overhead. The only unusual thing was that the bar had been misloaded and actually weighed 375 pounds.

The story goes that Milo was so ticked at missing a weight he knew he could lift, that he attacked it with added vengeance on his second attempt—and what he didn't know, the true weight of the barbell, certainly helped him. Therein, iron athletes, lies a big story about a little trick that can help pack inches on your biceps and give you a pile of new PRs.

Our Old Friend: Mental Rehearsal

Medical doctors sometimes get ribbed about their overreliance on a simple prescription: Take two aspirins and go to bed. If this advice weren't accompanied by a large bill, it might not be such an easy target because it really works amazingly well in a wide variety of situations.

But the M.D.'s aren't the only ones to have latched onto a simple formula with far-reaching applications: Talk to just about anyone even only vaguely related to the field of performance enhancement and you are certain to get an earful about mental rehearsal. "Just picture yourself succeeding," they advise, "and success will soon be yours." Lest you think this advice is hogwash, remember that the technique has gained such widespread popularity for one very simple reason: Like taking aspirins and going to bed, it works amazingly well.

Aside from the fact that you will likely need more than just one strategy if you are going to master your mind, the problem with visualizing success is that sometimes you just can't stop the little voice that is whispering, "I'm not really sure I can do this." This is no small point, for our research at IronMind® has demonstrated the need at times to simply stifle negative cognitive input, rather than enhance the positive. In other words, sometimes it's more important to not say bad things to yourself than it is to load up on saying good things.

Visualization, of course, gives you the chance to perform mental dress rehearsals designed to be as identical as possible to the real thing and creates the opportunity to load up on positive self-instruction. What we are going to show you now, however, is a very simple strategy for doing something very different: stopping the negatives by, essentially, attacking your target on blind faith. Let's set the stage with some research.

Psychological Ambiguity

Michael Mahoney, a distinguished research psychologist, provided a valuable demonstration of this mechanism with some work he performed with some of the nation's top Olympic-style weightlifters.

In a nutshell, Dr. Mahoney had lifters go for maximum lifts on the snatch under two conditions: the lifters either knew how much weight was on the bar, or they didn't. There is no need to get bogged down in the niceties of Mahoney's research design, so please just accept the fact that he adhered to a level of scientific rigor that might even make a Ph.D.'s head spin, and you can have every confidence that this was a high-grade research project. The results indicated that on average, the athletes lifted more when they did *not* know how much weight was on the bar. So much for the advantages of staring your nemesis straight in the eye.

How to Use This Technique

In coming up with possible explanations for why the results turned out as they did, Dr. Mahoney suggested three possibilities:

1) some athletes might have been "liberated" from a mental barrier,

2) not knowing the exact weight on the bar might have allowed the athletes to concentrate more on their technique, and

3) the sheer ambiguity of the situation might have increased the athletes' arousal level.

Let's briefly consider each of these possibilities and see how a little ignorance can help your training.

Mental barriers are a significant factor in all areas of athletic performance. For example, it is well documented that when watershed records are finally broken, it results in a flood of performances exceeding the old record. To get around such mental blocks, some lifting coaches consciously work to have their athletes miss as few lifts as possible in training, to keep their confidence high. "Why risk having an athlete keep missing a certain weight and develop a mental block toward it?" they ask.

Consider your warm-up sets: What are you concentrating on, the weight or the movement? Exactly. So doesn't it make sense that you should do the same thing when you get to your big-time weights? At the opposite end of the spectrum, you might have a powerlifter smashing his forehead into the bar to get himself psyched for the big numbers facing him on the squat bar, or you might have a bodybuilder thinking nothing but, "This will be a PR if I get 12 reps with this weight."

The unknown certainly can give you a few extra RPM and to confirm this with your own experience you need look no further than the feelings associated with anything from first dates to solo walks in the dark: Uncertainty can turbocharge just about any situation. And a few extra revs can often help boost athletic performance.

So how to put this idea to work for yourself? First, when facing a PR weight, forget about the usual advice to mentally picture the weight in intimate detail and to keep telling yourself how you are going to "blow the 450 right through the ceiling." Instead, think of the weight—if you must—as being only moderately heavy and concentrate on using your best form and highest level of confidence to attack it.

For example, let's say you are trying to squat 405, and 375 is a weight that is heavy for you, but is one that you can lift with authority. When you get to 405, if you must think about what's on the bar, tell yourself that it's about 375. The idea is that with 375, you will approach the lift brimming with confidence and will focus on your form, rather than being preoccupied with the actual weight. What we want to avoid is any possible fears and self-doubt associated with your ability to lift what's really on the bar. To help you believe that the weight is only around 375, don't load the bar with four 45's on each side, but use three 45's and some small plates.

You can extend this approach by asking your training partner or coach to occasionally overload the bar for you. Another great way to break through possible mental barriers is switch back and forth between pounds and kilos. For example, aside from the fact that he was emerging as the world's strongest man, there was another very good reason why the great Vasily Alexeev was the first to break the monumental 500-pound clean and jerk barrier: Vasily wasn't lifting 500 pounds—he was lifting 227-1/2 kilos, and who ever developed a mental block at the number 227-1/2?

Operating with full knowledge is generally a good idea, but don't forget that there are times when a little ignorance can produce a lot of bliss.

54 High Machs In Muscledom

Once upon a time, long before the first plate-loading barbell, there lived a certain Prince of Florence who counted among his advisors one Niccolo Machiavelli. Nick, as we'll call him for short, might have spent his childhood quietly pulling the wings off insects and rolling the smaller kids in his neighborhood for their lunch money, but for whatever reason, he grew into a world-renown philosopher whose advice largely boiled down to, "Do whatever it takes to get ahead." Lying, cheating and deceit were just tools of the trade, according to Nick.

Of course, studying Machiavellians, as Nick's followers are called, is usually confined to things outside the bodybuilding and lifting worlds, but what about all the ways you are manipulated in your quest for a bigger, stronger, better you? Don't you buy food supplements and pieces of equipment, not to mention books and magazines—and in each case, how might you be manipulated by one of Nick's understudies?

Let's begin by taking a brief look at these people called Machiavellians and see how they work. We'll wrap up by giving you a few tips for protecting yourself from their evil ways—hopefully leading to added inches on your arms and more pounds on your bench.

Meeting the High Machs

No, so-called high machs are not the Native American counterpart to Chuck Taylors—high Mach is the label psychologists give to people who exhibit a lot of what our old buddy Nick talked about. For starters, high Machs are the ones who get the big scores on psychologist Richard Christie's test of Machiavellianism. High Machs, for example, believe that the best way to handle people is to tell them what they want, and that trusting people is asking for trouble. Ask a high Mach, and you'll hear that people have a vicious streak that will appear, given a chance. Are these guys paranoid, or what?

Low Machs cling tightly to such basic moral precepts as, "There is no excuse for lying to someone." Knowing that, you can predict how they view just about any situation.

High Machs are masterful at manipulating people for personal gain. For example, research psychologists devised a standard experiment where one high Mach person, one medium Mach person and one low Mach person are given the task of dividing $10 among themselves. The only catch is that the money can be divided as soon as any *two* of the people agree on how to split up the money.

You might guess that most of the time, each of three people walks away with three dollars and some change. Instead, what usually happens is that the high Mach person walks away with about $6, the medium Mach pockets about $3 and the low Mach gets about $1. High Machs, you see, gain at the expense of the people around them.

And don't think the junior set is immune to Machiavellian tendencies, either. In one test of the "Kiddie Mach" scale, 10-year olds were paid for each bitter-tasting cracker they induced another child to eat. The high Mach kids coaxed and coerced other kids to eat more than twice as many of the experimental crackers as did the low Mach kids. If these high Mach kids are selling Kool Aid in your neighborhood, watch out.

Muscle Mach-ery

The history of competitive bodybuilding is filled with examples of even ace bodybuilders being psyched out by their more Machiavellian competitors—who might do anything from hiding someone's favorite posing trunks to giving misleading advice, or worse. Pre-contest, high Mach bodybuilders might convince already too-smooth competitors to add even more size and will keep a straight face while dishing out the misinformation: One of the things that distinguishes high Mach people is their uncanny ability to size up other people's weaknesses and then exploit them. High Machs will latch onto these soft spots and look their victim squarely in the eye while selling him or her the Brooklyn Bridge, for a good price.

Despite all the bodybuilding stories of underhanded psychological manipulation, the all-time most potent performance goes to a weightlifter, whose con job gave him a gold medal few think he would otherwise have won. Here's how the scam went down.

Turn back the clock to 1964, and draw a bead on the Tokyo Olympics—weightlifting, in particular. In the sport's glamour class—the superheavies—things boiled down to a gold medal battle between the highly-touted Russian Yuri Vlasov and his upstart countryman Leonid Zhabotinsky, with American superstar Norbert Schemansky in for the bronze.

Entering the clean and jerks, Vlasov had a five-pound lead on his countryman. Zhabotinsky opened with a 441 clean and jerk, which he made; Vlasov answered with a good opener of 452. Zhabotinsky waited as Vlasov made a strong second attempt with 463. Zhabotinsky called for a world record 479 and barely did a deadlift, before limping off the platform, clutching his back and looking for all the world as if he were on the way to the emergency ward.

Vlasov naturally assumed the gold was now his, and probably eased up on his third attempt, with the same weight—which he missed. He still should have won, right? But wait, what's this, the other big Russian was back from the dead and made what was described as a "flawless clean" and "a very strong jerk." Was Zhabotinsky's Olympic gold medal a miracle? Not hardly—it was one of the great examples of Machiavellian manipulation in the history of sports: Vlasov was just plain suckered out of being a gold medalist in two consecutive Olympics!

Stop Being Suckered

In the muscle business, most people assume that the high Machs are just the highest-profiled, most crassly-commercial moguls in the industry. And that's the danger to the average bodybuilder and lifter, because things go much deeper than that.

What would you think if the same outfit that rates a food supplement is the one that sells it? Or what if you knew that the big claims for this or that were only the result of fees paid for the testimonials? And what if someone claimed nearly miraculous results for a certain program but forget to mention that the athletes who made the program famous were notoriously heavy drug users?

More subtle and maybe more insidious, what of the folks who might like to convince you of the wisdom of their programs by enticing you with images of physiques you could not possibly obtain no matter what you did? And what of all the support gear manufacturers who lobby for more and more lifting aids on the basis of purported safety?

Caveat emptor, let the buyer beware, should be your motto whenever you are a consumer, and certainly so when you are in the muscle market—whether you seek advice, equipment or supplements. This approach, of the buyer accepting a lot of responsibility, is certainly more difficult than blindly accepting whatever is laid before your eyes, but the reward will be more progress, for less money, and much greater overall personal satisfaction.

Oddly, you might be your own greatest enemy when it comes to being swindled by the high Machs of the world. Remember how we mentioned that high Machs could sense an easy mark? Consider the view of Yellow Kid Weil—sometimes regarded as the top con man of this century, a con man who was considered to be "an equal-opportunity swindler" because he dealt in all manner of fraud. The Yellow Kid told Nobel-laureate novelist Saul Bellow, "I have never cheated any honest man, only rascals. They may have been respectable, but they were never any good. They wanted something for nothing. I gave them nothing for something."

55 The Man In The Mirror

There's a lifting coach I know who is quick to point out that his charges have two primary enemies: gravity and the man in the mirror. Because gravity seems more obvious and because it's of little concern to bodybuilders, let's concentrate on the second point and see how you can be your own biggest enemy when it comes to building bigger biceps and making heavier lifts.

Pop psychologists forever remind us to be our own best friends, that we really are okay, etc., etc., so how can it be that we commonly prove to be our own worst enemies, especially when it comes to gaining muscular size and strength? Unless you are openly self-destructive, the ways you trip yourself up aren't always so apparent and more often than not, they spring from good intentions. Let's consider three ways you can get in your own way, and what you can do about each.

Discipline

Think of discipline as being the great leveller among people: Extra discipline makes up for lack of talent, and the lack of discipline quickly siphons away extra talent. This is why it's commonly found that the most disciplined, rather than the most gifted, people rise to the top, and this is just as true in bodybuilding and lifting as it is in other pursuits.

It's important to remember that most people are pretty good about the discipline aspects of their training: For example, most of the time they at least largely follow their diets, stick to their training routines, and so forth. As you would guess, mostly doing the right things has its rewards: Most people make pretty decent progress. What we're interested in here isn't pretty decent results, however; we want to put you on the path to exceptional results and that requires exceptional discipline. Consider Maurice Jones.

In his prime, Maurice Jones was considered to be the most massively muscular man in the world and was dubbed "The Canadian Hercules." When I describe him, I say something like, "think of a cross between John Grimek and Doug Hepburn and you will start to get the picture." Maurice Jones was once considered to be among the world's strongest men, and was known for his tremendous endurance as well: It wasn't just that his regular training included pretty serious running in Stanley Park—he was renowned for loading a pack with rocks and then running up mountainsides.

Talk to anyone who knows him well and a recurrent theme immediately stands out: Maurice Jones had tremendous self-discipline, which was reflected by his training—along with his results. It wasn't just that he never broke training, but get this: He never missed a single workout in his first five and half years of training.

Discipline takes many forms in the Iron Game, and usually the most obvious forms—such as following your diet, grinding out those tough reps, hitting all your workouts, and so forth—present the fewest problems. It's the more subtle areas that can trip you up. Consider, for example, your enthusiasm.

Pretty often, when people call or write us for training advice, they present a training routine that has mixed elements from several different sources. This is a fine idea in principle, but what sometimes results is a mishmash of training approaches that to some extent are self-canceling. So far, at least, we haven't yet run into anybody who was simultaneously training to gain and lose weight, but we've seen some routines that came pretty close.

The usual cause of this problem is that the person's enthusiasm was pulling him or her toward a handful of very different training routines and goals at once. Our usual advice in this type of situation is to recognize that one of the major challenges facing everyone who trains is to stick with a good program long enough to allow it to work, and to accomplish this, you need to, first, truly believe in the way you are training, and second, shut out thoughts of other training programs until your next cycle.

Performance Anxiety

Performance anxiety refers to those nasty feelings of uncertainty and self-doubt that might crop up exactly when the heat is on. Generally, performance anxiety is only discussed in the context of public performances, but you need to recognize is that choking under pressure isn't limited to moments like stepping out on stage in your first pro show or making an appearance in a major lifting contest.

Performance anxiety also crops up when a cellar dweller sees that his workout today calls for knocking out a set with five more pounds than he has ever done before in his life. In a nutshell, performance anxiety can attack you anytime you have to act in a specified, challenging manner.

Generally, discussions of how to manage performance anxiety concentrate on reviewing relaxation techniques, with the sound logic that if too much anxiety is hurting your performance, a little relaxation will reduce your anxiety levels and improve your performance. This is good advice on the whole, but we'd like to have you add a couple more skills to your repertoire.

First, focus your attention on the immediate task, without the excess baggage of what this task "means" in a larger sense. For example, let's say your best bench for five reps is 280 and today's workout calls for 285 x 5. On the one hand, you could simply focus on the immediate task of benching 285 for five reps, or you could make it into something bigger.

Thus, you might tell yourself that if you miss the 285 x 5, you will be off track, and in a nutshell, a veritable failure. In fact, you might remind yourself that if you miss this lift, you aren't just a failure as far as your training goes, but in the rest of your life as well. Now that you are a little off balance, remind yourself that the last time you tried to bench 285, you squeezed out two reps and you felt as if that almost killed you.

Of course, these latter things are what you don't do. Just concentrate on benching 285 for five, without any extra psychological baggage. And if per chance you fall short of this goal, don't belittle yourself; just resolve to try your best to make it next time.

The second twist we would like you to use for managing performance anxiety involves putting extra arousal to work for yourself. Remind yourself, and it's true, that the anxiety you feel is like extra energy that you can harness for the task at hand. Ever try for a PR when you were emotionally flat? The weight went nowhere, right?

On the other hand, if you ever happened to try a big lift when you were really ticked about something, chances are good that the weight felt pretty light. This is the type of energizing effect you should try to capture from performance anxiety: Try to put the uneasiness and agitation you feel to work for yourself. Try to make your extra arousal an ally, not an enemy.

Self-Efficacy

Eminent Stanford University research psychologist Albert Bandura has done much to demonstrate that our beliefs about our ability to produce certain results are strongly linked to the results we obtain—so if you don't believe you can do something, you are beaten from the start.

In the glory days of American weightlifting, one of the true superstars was "the boy wonder," Pete George—who won his first World Championship when he was a mere 18-year-old. Pete George went on to win five World Weightlifting Championships (plus getting the silver medal in two others), along with an Olympic gold medal (and silver medals in two other Olympics). Not content to rest on his laurels at this point, he went on to become a successful orthodontist.

Our purpose in raising the example of Pete George isn't to review his many accomplishments in detail, but rather to point out that he made full use of his mind and his belief in his own ability when he lifted. His coach, Larry Barnholth, once noted that Pete George was "the finest pupil a coach could ever want...his imagination was UNLIMITED." And Pete George was fully aware of how what went on in between his ears affected his performance on the lifting platform: He once wrote that the question of whether a certain weight will be lifted is already decided before the lifter grabs the bar!

Discipline, performance anxiety and self-efficacy—three areas where you can become your best friend or your worst foe. Manage these areas correctly and put the man in the mirror on your side!

56 Psychological Tests: One Red Light

No matter what he did, Bob Spivey was one of those people who always liked to have an edge. And so it was that when Bob started bodybuilding, he not only made sure that he knew everything there was to know about genetics, training, diet and equipment, but he also went the extra step to have his personality assessed—to see if he had the right stuff, psychologically speaking, to succeed.

Up until the point of getting his bill, Bob found the testing process pretty painless: It just seemed like taking a test in school, except that instead of asking him about the Magna Charta, second derivatives or basal ganglia, this test quizzed him on his personal preferences, his thoughts about certain situations, and so forth. And like most of the tests he had taken in school, Bob thought some of the questions made sense, some didn't and most were some place in between.

As a result of taking his test, Bob was told, for example, that he was fairly high in leadership and need for social approval, fairly low in risk-taking, and overall, a pretty well-adjusted individual. Bob, evidently, had nothing between his ears that definitely stamped him as terribly unsuited for bodybuilding, and had a couple of things that seemed to be in his favor, so off he went, in full pursuit of his dreams of size, symmetry, cuts and all the rest.

Perhaps you, too, have thought about having your personality analyzed, or are just a little curious about how personality tests came into being and what they might or might not do for you.

Psychological testing might be fairly new to athletics in general and bodybuilding and lifting specifically, but it's a game that has been played for over a century. Sir Francis Galton began testing people for such things as reaction time, sensory acuity and strength of movement in 1882, using a questionnaire that was an important forerunner to those that would follow. And in the 1890s, Alfred Binet began to measure intelligence, work which went on to form the basis for one of the most popular I.Q. tests used today.

Because the common practice was to name the test after yourself and because anyone with 500 milligrams of brains could think up some kind of test and because, for a long time, no one really worried too much about whether the tests performed as advertised, the number of personality tests absolutely exploded over the next fifty years, becoming something like a full-employment law for psychologists.

Think about how easy it was to become famous or to at least stay busy: All you had to do was decide that you were going to measure, say, "bench pressing aptitude," write up a few questions (e.g., "Do you like to do it on your back?"), name the thing after yourself and go into business. And if you didn't have the desire or ability to invent your own test, it was even easier to make a career for yourself administering someone else's test.

Before all the Ed.D.'s, Ph.D.'s and other test-wise types take the other side by discussing the advanced psychometrics of sophisticated test design, let's look at the process of test development without hiding behind any fancy language.

The goal of testing is to support science in its quest to observe, describe, understand, predict and control—in our case, bodybuilding success. We hope that by administering our test, we will know *who* will do well and *why*. This will help us sort potential winners from losers and also help us make more people winners.

To meet these goals, tests have to demonstrate two properties: reliability and validity. Never mind that each of these takes several different specific forms and that each is defined in terms of a formal statistical equation, because both concepts can be explained so that a twelve year old will understand them.

Reliability refers to how consistently you get the same measurement. Let's say that you measured your arm 39 times in the past three days, always using the same procedure. Even though you might have been standing in front of different mirrors, at many different times, etc., your arm always measured about the same amount. That's consistency—that's reliability. Reliability means the test is stable. You wouldn't measure your arm with a rubber tape would you, so why not demand some stability from a psychological test?

Validity is the other test for tests and it deals with whether or not you are really measuring what you claim to be. To evaluate validity, you look at whether your test can predict what it's supposed to. For example, predicting bench pressing ability based on color preferences will probably flunk the validity test: Some top benchers will like blue, others green and all the people with lousy taste will like brown, no matter what they bench. The same thing for weak benchers. This test doesn't have any validity because knowing someone's color preference doesn't tell you squat about what they can bench. On the other hand, testing people with dips will probably be valid since the big dippers will tend to be the big benchers. Validity just means the test really predicts what it's supposed to.

Most personality tests are reliable. That is, they produce the same score for the same person in the same situation, day after day, no matter who scores them, etc. Validity is where the rubber hits the road for tests and that's exactly where most tests blow up.

The opposite of validity is things like bias or discrimination, and it's no accident that the psychological testing business ran into some very serious legal and ethical problems with the Equal Employment Opportunity Commission: Tests that consistently picked white males over, say, black females for certain jobs sometimes turned out to not really measure things related to job performance. They just weren't valid; i.e., they didn't measure what they claimed to measure. This pattern hardly surprised contemporary research psychologists because the personality theories underlying many of these tests had been under fire for some time.

In sports, this issue hit the fan in a very big way in 1971, when the Players' Association of the NFL instituted a ban against the use of psychological tests as a hiring tool. This was the result of some overzealous psychologists giving a bunch of personality tests to players and then telling management whom to keep. It was a nice job for the psychologists, while it lasted, but it killed some football careers. Based on just about any psychological research you'd care to review, the smart money would bet against this approach when you put it next to actual samples of performance: The personality tests just won't hold up.

In the Iron Game, powerlifters have been tested psychologically, using what is called the "mental health model" of athletic performance. This overall approach states that athletic success and positive mental health are "directly proportional" and successful competitors will be less "neurotic, anxious, depressed, schizoid, introverted, confused, fatigued, [or] low on psychic vigor" than unsuccessful competitors. The powerlifting research generally followed this pattern, by reporting low tension, depression, anger, fatigue and confusion, but high vigor among some successful lifters and low vigor among others. The results of the vigor measure seemed tied to exactly when the test was administered, so reliability draws at least one red light. How about validity?

Don't you think that sometimes you lift more the angrier you get? Don't you sometimes flex your muscles, think "stay tight" and do other things to increase your tension as you psyche up for a big lift? Of course you do, and yet these are the very things that are supposed to predict your failure as a lifter. The bottom line is that because the relationship between anger/tension, for example, and lifting ability depends on a lot of factors, it going to be extremely hard to predict your lifting ability based on your anger/tension test score. Thus validity also gets at least one red light.

All this is not to say that every psychological test is hopeless or that all attempts to apply them to bodybuilding and lifting are misguided—but the buyer should beware. We give them two white lights because some tests work pretty well—even if generally they are *not* the ones for measuring broad personality traits. And there's always a possibility that a super test will be developed: Maybe the next hundred years of research will be more productive than the first century was.

Until such a test emerges, however, don't worry if someone tells you that your psychological profile doesn't match their famous iceberg—that's probably less important to your bodybuilding and lifting success than the color of your shirt. And after all this, if you still insist on having an excellent predictor of the psychological characteristics required for bodybuilding or lifting success, just ask: "How bad do you want to be good?"

57 Labels As Limits

Labels are a funny thing: On the one hand, there are real benefits to their shorthand descriptions and efficient definitions, but on the other hand, they act as filters, with some distortion becoming inevitable. Consider first how labels can affect the merely insane, and then we'll turn our attention to how labels can affect some real crazies—bodybuilders and lifters.

On Being Sane in Insane Places

You might not be able to tell a Maserati from a Lamborghini, or—blindfolded—a Bud from a Coors, but even on your worst days you'd know who should be in a mental hospital and who shouldn't. Or would you?

Psychology professor David Rosenhan had himself and seven other ostensibly normal people call different mental hospitals and deliver a standard complaint that began, "I hear voices, unclean voices..." and thereby get themselves admitted. Other than this introduction and altering their name and job-related information, everything else they said was truthful, and the "pseudopatients" acted in their normal manner once in the hospital. What happened to these people is pretty scary.

First, they were labelled as "schizophrenic," which is considered a very severe form of mental illness (one was labelled "manic depressive," considered to be a somewhat less serious condition). Second, once this badge was hung on them, it influenced how their every action was interpreted by the staff and even the most outwardly normal behavior was tainted by the label. For example, walking around would be seen as "engaging in schizophrenic motoric behavior" and so forth. These pseudopatients were never discovered by the hospital staff and when their release was won by spouses and colleagues intervening on their behalf, they was discharged with the diagnosis of "schizophrenia in remission."

On a personal note, yours truly once had the unique experience of spending a day visiting the locked ward of the VA hospital that provided Ken Kesey the material for "One Flew Over the Cuckoo's Nest." One of my strongest memories from the day was that after watching a group therapy session, I commented to one of the staff that one of the patients seemed pretty well-adjusted to me. "He's a sociopath," I was told, "and he's only pretending to be normal." Okay.

So much for garden-variety insanity. Let's see what can happen to true crazies, like bodybuilders and lifters.

The Case of the Hard Gainer

One of the most prevalent labels in bodybuilding today is "hard gainer," intended to describe all of us who are not genetic freaks, or mere naturals, in the Iron Game. Surely this is a reasonable and potentially-useful label, one that can productively guide decisions on everything from how to train to what to eat to what to expect for one's efforts. But what is the cost of this label? For all its merits, what are the downsides of applying this label to yourself?

For starters, "hard gainer" is negative, but let's not even dwell on how that can take the wind out of your sails. Let's just proceed by reviewing how the label itself—and its connotations—might affect someone who might be a good candidate to wear it.

Imagine a 5' 9" male with 6-3/4" wrists and 8-3/4" ankles. It's not just that he pushes the scale to a mere 155 pounds, but he also has apple-on-a-stick calves, short biceps, high lats and just about every other bodybuilding malady you can name. Since he's obviously not packing around much muscle mass, despite several years of persistent training, he's a good candidate to be called a "hard gainer."

Once he adopts the label, he can easily become reconciled to never making very good progress at bodybuilding or lifting. He might come to believe that he will be lucky to build a 16-inch arm, for example, or that he will never display anything beyond moderate levels of strength. He might turn this into self-fulfilling prophesy by arbitrarily restricting his goals, his training intensity, his training volume and even his poundage progression. In a word, he might guarantee the end result of mediocrity.

On the other hand, he might consider things a bit more before throwing in the towel. As he continues his analysis, he might even continue to make occasional use of labels, carefully choosing only those that are non-judgmental, specific and constructive.

As a first step, he takes a long hard look in the mirror and says, "I'm ectomorphic, no doubt about it." Along with having a light bone structure, the idealized ectomorph tends to be quite cerebral, so it's not surprising that the analysis didn't stop at this point.

"Being an ectomorph," he says to himself, "I'll never threaten Paul Anderson in terms of sheer muscle mass, but other guys with a bone structure like mine have gotten pretty husky. Besides, even if being an ectomorph puts some ultimate limits on the size factor, that's just part of the story. From a bodybuilding perspective, even if I have to give up gargantuan size, it says nothing of symmetry or cuts—in fact, I can still be pretty lean looking even after putting on a lot of size, unlike a lot of mesomorphs who might begin to look like stuffed sausages along the way."

From this point forward he has adopted a more positive outlook and can begin to realize his actual physical potential, appreciating it for what it is, and not set arbitrary mental limits for himself based on a label. Not only has he left the door open for some respectable results in terms of achieving a symmetrical, well-defined physique, but he has also not closed his mind to the possibility of making some striking progress in the size department.

If he needed some added inspiration, he reminded himself of some the light-boned people who achieved stellar physiques even though they weren't the sheer mass monsters. If that wasn't enough, he made a mental note that history has proven that you don't even have to have a 7-inch wrist to build a Mr. Olympia-winning physique—witness Frank Zane.

Turning his attention to strength, our man could simply stop at this point and write himself off as having the lousy leverage common to a hard gainer, and settle for mediocre strength levels, but he doesn't. Instead, he does a bit more thinking—for himself.

"Lifting leverage is a funny thing—what's good for one lift might be terrible for another, so it doesn't take Einstein to figure out that there must be at least one lift on which I can excel," he says to himself. Taking to heart this idea that lifting, in some ways, is much more democratic than bodybuilding, he realizes that, "Besides, lifting is part mental, so maybe I'm not a complete washout as far as strength goes" and takes an inventory on how his lifts go.

For starters, as part of the ectomorph's territory, he is fairly high-strung so with a little training, he finds that he can use this nervous energy to his advantage on lifts that require explosiveness or a high arousal level. In addition, the very anatomical features that give him lousy leverage on presses and curls, work to his advantage on deadlifts. With a little research he finds that Bob Peoples—a legendary deadlifter who could pull more than most 300-pound monsters—was a relatively slender man who only weighed around 185 when he was deadlifting well over 700 pounds several decades ago.

And so on.

What we end up with is a fellow who, instead of wringing his hands about being "a hard gainer," squares off and assesses his strengths and weaknesses and always using his head, forges forward with his training.

R ecognizing that muscle mass is, naturally, in short demand on his frame, he attacks the super bulk and power routines with a vengeance—and quickly outgrows two sets of clothes for his efforts. Along the way, he pushes his deadlift to respectable limits, power cleans more than a lot of real beef hounds, builds an arm that is large by any mortal standard, and in general, accomplishes quite a lot. What he didn't do was limit himself from the outset, think negatively, or spend an excessive amount of time feeling sorry for himself because he bore the burden of being a pitiful hard gainer.

Instead, he went beyond the limits of the label: He thought, he trained and he gained.

58 Bouncing Back

To look at him, George had made all the right moves—he was on his way to becoming a partner at his law firm and it showed: He drove a fancy German car, lived in a condo that smacked of *Architectural Digest*, was known in many of the most expensive restaurants and clothing stores in town, and had a night life that seemed like one unending party. Then one day his bubble burst.

First, George got canned at work. And if that weren't enough to take the wind out of his sails, he found that with no cash, the rest of the life he had been leading came crashing down in a hurry. It wasn't just that the Bavarian Beauty sped away with the repo man, and that he was holding onto the condo by a mere thread, but somewhere along the line, his self-esteem and self-confidence had taken it on the teeth in a very big way—and that was the biggest loss of all.

The exact form and texture of your fall might not be the same as George's but you can pretty much bank on the fact that at least once in your life, you will take a big hit on the teeth—one that will put you on the ropes, if not actually drop you to the canvas. What you do at that point is critical and is far more under your control than you might imagine. What we would like to do is give you some pointers for picking yourself up, brushing off the dust and coming back better for the experience. Let's talk a little about getting dropped and bouncing back.

For starters, don't make the mistake of assuming that your position at the top of your own Mount Olympus is secure, as this in itself could put you on a quick trip downward. The ancient Greeks called excessive pride or self-confidence "hubris" and they knew that the gods were prone to slap down uppity mortals. Learn to foster a little humility along the way and your fortune, even if not perfect, will be better for it.

Remember, too, that misfortune, at the life-altering stage, is incredibly democratic: Young and old, rich and poor, male and female all are susceptible to the big bang. Finally, remember that even if you escape a cataclysmic shake-down, your mettle is still likely to be seriously tested at least once in your life. So, what to do when that happens?

Your survival strategy has to begin with the fundamental belief that you will pick yourself up. This might sound self-evident, but you would be surprised at how many people go down for the count the first time they are tagged and that's all she wrote. Champions, of course, have the ability to get up, beat the bell and often rally for a victory. And don't make the mistake of thinking this is just a cliched Hollywood script or that it is just limited to boxing.

About fifteen years ago a kid from Nevada started showing up for bicycle races in the San Francisco area. Even early on, it was apparent that there was something special about him: It wasn't just that he could pedal away from most of his competition at will, but he also had tremendous heart, because whenever he crashed, he was back on his bike in a second, chasing down the pack, instead of heading for the sidelines like a loser. Years later, Greg Lemond made his mark on the world, and don't think for a minute that his intestinal fortitude wasn't a key to his success. Always keep this image in mind: To win, you must pick yourself up when you fall.

When you take a big hit such as losing your job or getting dumped by your significant other, your major emotional hurdle is likely to be depression. In extreme clinical cases of depression, it is as if your will is paralyzed, and severely-depressed patients lose their desire to get out of bed, get dressed or even, literally, to move. You might not hit these extreme depths, but the tendency will be the same: You will want to pull within yourself and just not do anything.

Because depressed people find a sense of comfort in their immobility, it takes a little dynamite to get them going, but move they must or they will perish. The situation is something like that faced by climbers stranded on a mountain in extreme conditions—if they succumb to the urge to fall asleep, they will freeze to death, and if they wish to live, they will have to make an effort to stay awake and do whatever they can to generate and conserve body heat.

When your life takes a big slap in the face, you might be tempted to forget your workouts, but that would be a huge mistake. As odd as it might sound, training is actually one of the best ways to help depressed people get on their feet—literally and figuratively. In fact, more people have walked, run and lifted their way back to good mental health than the pharmaceutical industry might care to acknowledge.

Proper exercise is progressive, so you can do as little or as much as fits your requirements and abilities. Extremely depressed people might begin with the smallest of efforts, but can work up to Olympic-level routines. And you don't have to have a big budget to train—for example, when George had to give up his racquet club membership, his personal trainer, and even his state of the art mountain bike, he still had a pair of running shoes and he began to jog. After a few weeks, he was also hitting selected stations at the fitness course in a local park. Within months, he had a small pile of weights at his place and was pumping iron three times a week, along with morning runs several days a week.

George's workouts literally transformed him, replacing his borderline depression with energy and gave him the strength of carriage and bounce in his stride that brought him back from the near-dead.

Complementing his training, George also began to rebuild himself from the inside out as he came to learn that while he had once seen himself as the center of the universe, something larger lurked out there. This new belief helped George put things in perspective and gave him the inner strength to keep on trucking even when things looked hopeless. Whatever its precise form, spirituality enriches lives and helps people tough out tough times.

Finally, tapping his training-generated energy and his broader spiritual perspective allowed George to see that while some doors had closed for him, others had opened. In fact, George began to focus on the opportunities presented by the sudden change in his circumstances, rather than dwelling on the unfortunate aspects it presented. He might end up at another law firm, or running a surf shop in Baja, but whatever, he was determined to make use of the fact that he hadn't just lost his job—he had gained the opportunity to find one better suited to him.

At this point, it no longer really mattered what happened to George next because he had already won his battle with Fate—George had fallen, but more important, he had bounced back.

59 The ABCs of Progress

Fred Keller had gotten started lifting weights when his big brother let him come along to a garage gym workout one day—while his brother and his pals benched their hearts out, Fred was put in the corner and shown how to do presses and curls. So Fred curled and pressed, pressed and curled, and did the whole thing some more. For the next three days, Fred's arms were too sore to even comb his hair, but he was hooked—from that fateful moment forward, Fred became an iron warrior.

One of the things that Fred liked about training was that he was making progress, adding a quarter of an inch to his arms here, five pounds to his squats there, and before he knew it, a couple of years had passed. The 25-pound plates that had once looked so big and felt so heavy to Fred had now given way to a pair of 50s on a lot of his exercises, and his arms, by now, weren't much smaller than his legs had been in his early days.

But all was not rosy in Mudville, for one day Fred realized that he had a problem: He was stuck, seriously stuck. In fact, it had been so long since Fred had hit a PR on any of his lifts or moved a critical measurement that he was starting to identify with glaciers, even if only small ones.

So Fred did what any normal American kid did—he hit the marketplace, looking for a solution. And while he tried a variety of the latest supplements, as well as experimented with a series of purportedly advanced training programs, nothing really seemed to bump Fred along the road to progress.

Fred was ready to throw in the towel, when he came across an article on sports psychology and decided that he had nothing to lose by seeing if a sports psychologist could do him any good. To be honest, Fred wasn't very optimistic, but he figured, "What the heck—it can't be any more of a boondoggle than some of those supplements and courses I've bought." After making some inquiries, Fred located a fellow who was supposed to have proven himself useful when it came to solving training problems with the careful application of some grey matter. So Fred gave him a call.

Never having talked to a psychologist before, Fred wasn't sure to expect: Would he find an introspective, German-accented, black leather couch type or a shy turtleneck and corduroy sports coat college professor type or a crystal-wielding new-ager? Fred was surprised, but relieved, to find what seemed to be a normal guy who was cursing the person who told him to reset the clock on his computer in a way that might have just reformatted his hard disk.

When Fred described all that he had been through in his efforts to get back on the road to progress, the psychologist nodded supportively and said, "Don't worry, we can give you a simple tool to help you on your way.

You have been trying a little too hard, in some ways, to get back on the path to results, and also have been looking in the wrong places. We're going to simplify things and focus on the control center for your world: your brain."

Fred could go along with the first part, and as long as the second part didn't mean brain surgery, that one would be okay too.

"Let's bring things down to the most basic terms," the psychologist continued, "and consider the primary elements that shape your training behavior. Let's see what you might be doing to keep yourself locked into your present levels of strength and development. And let's see what you might do to pull yourself out of this rut.

I could tell you about heuristics, cognitive transformation models, and contingency plans, but let's keep things simple by reducing the issues to the ABCs."

Fred had no aversion to theory, but at the moment he was big on action and results, so the good doctor was starting to make sense. Fred nodded his agreement, encouraging the psychologist to go on.

"No matter how complex your training behaviors are, we might reduce our explanations of them to three stages:

1) antecedents,

2) behaviors and

3) consequences.

I'll tell you what each of these means and how you can use your understanding of them to stimulate some progress in your training.

Antecedents are what happen before your behaviors to stimulate you to act. We're going to focus on what psychologists might call cognitive antecedents, which in your case is nothing more complicated than what you are thinking about before you start training.

Behaviors are what you do—in your case, the act of training is the set of behaviors that are of interest to us. So think of your behaviors as everything from banging out curls, to fighting for one more rep, and so forth.

Consequences are what happen after the specific behavior and this can be everything from what you think to yourself to physical actions."

Fred didn't think this business sounded too exciting, but with the carrot of renewed gains staring him in the face, he was willing to let the psychologist continue.

"What you are probably doing right now is running through an unproductive ABC sequence, with things going something like this:

A: You say to yourself, 'Well, I guess it's time to train, even though I haven't made any progress for a long time.'

B: So you go through a lackluster workout, mechanically grinding out just what you have been doing steadily for the last umpteen workouts, or even less.

C: Afterward, you tell yourself, 'See, I'm just stuck.'"

Fred nodded in agreement because the psychologist's analysis was right on.

"What you need to do is change the pattern along the following lines:

A: 'It's time to do curls. Last workout I curled 100 for 8 reps—I bet that if I really try, I can squeeze out an extra rep.'

B: You do your curls and hit the ninth and maybe even the tenth rep.

C: You say to yourself, 'Nice work—I knew I could do it. Next workout I'll go to 105 or 110 pounds and see if I can hit 6 reps.'"

Fred's mama hadn't raised a fool, so he couldn't help but break in at this point.

"Sounds good when things go according to the schedule, but what do I do when I crash and burn on the set?"

"No problem," said the psychologist, "just use the same system.

A: 'It's time to do curls. Last workout I curled 100 for 8 reps—I bet that if I really try, I can squeeze out an extra rep.'

B: You do your curls and the bottom falls out after the 8th rep.

C: You say to yourself, 'Well, I didn't hit a PR, but let's see if I can do another set of 8 reps...' or maybe you say to yourself, 'O.K., I didn't get the 9th rep this workout, but next workout it's like money in the bank.'"

The psychologist could tell that Fred was chewing this one over and was looking as if he believed in the system enough to give it a try. He knew his case was won when Fred said, "So I really have the ability to program my progress a lot more than I have been, if I just use the system you outlined."

Fred stood up, ready to have the best workout in a long, long time.

After Fred had gone, the psychologist muttered to himself, "The next time someone tells me to re-run the setup program on my computer, and I almost wipe out my hard disk, I'll give them some free orthodontal work. It's as simple as ABC."

60 Derailed By The Detraining Phenomenon

Phil Hinshaw thought he had finally gotten a handle on how to train properly: After years of earnestly blasting away on this split and that, he read about the virtues of training less frequently than some people wash their cars. Some of the advocates of these less frequent training schedules were downright rabid about their recommendations so Phil was soon among the followers.

In no time flat, Phil went from training six times a week to four times a week to three times a week to twice a week to, near-Nirvana it would seem, training just once every five to seven days. To be sure, at least at first, Phil started to make fresh progress, so the system must be right, right?

A little doubt about the perfection of this system first crept into Phil's brain because he had noticed something funny: At first, when he cut back on his training, he certainly felt fresher and clearly was able to make better progress.

As time passed, however, the gains slowed down and besides only making infinitesimal progress on the physical front, Phil noticed that something funny was also going on between his ears: It was actually getting harder to train on schedule and easier to skip a workout on the basis of being not quite 100%, whether due to incomplete recovery, injury, or what-have-you. One of Phil's buddies thought Phil was turning into a head case so he gave Phil the phone number of a certain sports psychologist who had something more than a passing interest in lifting weights.

The psychologist was immersed in his own problems, wondering why it was that he didn't seem capable of teaching his dog anything—old tricks or new—but with the selflessness of the consummate professional, he pushed aside his own concerns to fully concentrate on Phil's. "Dumb dog," he thought to himself one last time before inviting Phil to describe why he was there.

"...and so," concluded Phil, "this less frequent training business might have some holes in it. What do you think?"

"Have you ever heard of the 'detraining phenomenon'?" asked the psychologist?

Phil shook his head, thinking it sounded like an accident about to happen.

"Detraining," explained the psychologist, "is like training in reverse: Instead of your body adapting to the increased load of training and becoming bigger and stronger for it, detraining causes your body to become smaller and weaker because you aren't taxing it as much as you had been or as much as you could.

Even if you hadn't heard of this phenomenon by its formal name, you already noticed that when you quit training your arms, for example, they got smaller, and when you came back from vacation, just about all of your lifts were down. That's detraining: Your body adapted to the decreased demands you were placing on it and the result was to lose size and strength."

Phil nodded, not liking what he was hearing, but the good doctor had his attention.

"So while it is true that overtraining stymies your progress, so does undertraining. Here's how. After you train, you need a certain amount of time to recover, but beyond that amount of time, your body will start to lose what it has just gained. Think of Sisyphus, in Greek mythology, who was condemned to forever push a boulder up a hillside: For each two steps he took uphill, he slid back one. The detraining phenomenon is like that because it causes you to lose some of the forward progress you had otherwise made.

And don't think this is mere academic theory, either. If you ever have a chance to watch the Bulgarian weightlifting team train in the last week before a major contest like the Olympics or the World Championships, you will see some heavy, heavy lifting just a couple of days before they hope to do the lifts of their lives. The reason why they keep going heavy right up to the big moment is that they don't want to lose any of the strength they worked so hard to develop."

"So having too much time in between workouts is just as bad as having too little, right?" asked Phil.

The psychologist nodded and couldn't help but wish it was this easy to communicate with his dog.

"But what does this have to do with the mental slump I seem to be caught in? Why has it been getting easier and easier for me to skip my workouts, even though they are less and less frequent? Shouldn't it be the opposite?" asked Phil.

"It's because there is a psychological parallel to the detraining phenomenon," said the good doctor.

Just as your training routine conditions your body, and it rebuilds itself bigger and stronger for your efforts, your mind also adapts to the stimulus of training. If you doubt this, just consider what happens when you miss a lift you wanted to make or don't hit your full complement of reps on a key set. You're bummed, right?"

Phil nodded, because he could remember how whenever he missed a key lift or fell short on a key set, it was very hard to stay focused and positive for the rest of the workout—the big temptation was to just blow off the whole day.

"Conversely," continued the psychologist, "when you hit a PR, whether for a single or for twenty reps, you feel like King Kong and you're ready to do everything short of run for President. Right?"

Phil nodded again, and now he was starting to see how the pieces fit together.

"Most of us walk around with the idea that we think first and act second," said the psychologist, "because that just seems to make good sense. What research psychologists know, however, is that things can easily work in the opposite direction as well: You think a certain way because you act a certain way. If that sounds too abstract, consider the German expression that translates into something like, 'Eating makes you hungry.' Very often, our attitudes are brought into line with our actions.

So when you train properly, each workout leaves you eager for the next, and don't forget that some of this enthusiasm begins at a physiological level because sound training for size and strength boosts your testosterone levels, which increases your drive. If you don't capitalize on this natural momentum, you will be like the Greek fellow with the rock—always giving up ground you had fought to win in the first place.

What happens, then, in terms of the detraining phenomenon is that you can fall into the trap of forever reducing your training frequency because you "haven't recovered completely," or whatever. When you cut back your training too much, it's as if every micro ache and pain, and every residual cue of soreness gains monumental stature and before you know it, you are so focused on awaiting for some imaginary state of complete recovery that you don't train again for two weeks. Is it really a big surprise that you aren't making the type of progress you want?"

Phil nodded again, because by now his mind was racing down this path, already considering how training too infrequently would be like driving across the country at 55 miles per hour, stopping every two hours to stretch his legs—he would eventually make it, but why make it take so long? Phil was a believer and was nearly out the door before he remembered to thank the good doctor for his help getting back on track.

"You're very welcome," the psychologist said, to the vanishing figure of Phil. Any temptation the good doctor might have had to bask in this victory was dashed by the sight of his dog, in the next room, happily eating a fax as quickly as it came in.

"You watch," he said to the dog, "starting tomorrow, it's training three times a day, six days a week for you."

About the Author

When he was about eight, Randall Strossen tagged along to the basement gym where one of his uncles lifted weights—the iron bug bit then and has never let go.

After earning a Ph.D. in psychology from Stanford University, Randall spent several years as a marketing vice president with a major bank and then several more working for a major accounting and consulting firm. In 1988, Randall formed IronMind® Enterprises, Inc., with the goal of enhancing performance in the strength sports by applying techniques based on scientific psychology. IronMind® Enterprises, Inc. also reflects Randall's deep respect for the rich history of the Iron Game. In 1990, IronMind® Enterprises, Inc. began selling training equipment, books, videos and food supplements and quickly became recognized by strength athletes around the world for its unique, top quality products.

Randall edits *MILO* (a quarterly journal for serious strength athletes) and writes the monthly sports psychology column for *IRONMAN* magazine, and his articles and photographs appear in magazines worldwide. In addition to *IronMind®: Stronger Minds, Stronger Bodies*, he has written the book *SUPER SQUATS: How To Gain 30 Pounds Of Muscle In 6 Weeks*, and edited the book *Keys to Progress*, by John McCallum.

To order additional copies of *IronMind®: Stronger Minds, Stronger Bodies*, or for a free catalog of IronMind Enterprises, Inc. products, please contact:

IronMind® Enterprises, Inc.
PO Box 1228
Nevada City, CA 95959

Tel: (916) 265-6725
Fax: (916) 265-4876

Index

Sandow, Eugen   4
Sauce Bernaise Effect   97–98
Saxon, Arthur   4
Schemansky, Norbert   124, 154
Schwarzenegger, Arnold   2, 4–5, 74, 123
Scott, Larry   46, 123
Selective attention   75
Self-appraisal   19–21, 43–44, 45–47
Self-concept   42–44, 92, 110, 111–113
Self-confidence. *See* Confidence
Self-efficacy   157, 158
Self-esteem   111–113. *See also* Self-concept
Self-fulfilling prophecy   92, 163
Self-talk analysis   19–21, 134
Sex-role stereotypes   139–141
Sheldon, William H.   28–29
Sisyphus   171
Situation avoidance   20
Social facilitation   100
Social pressure   6–8, 54, 122. *See also* Conformity
Social rejection   109
Somatotypes   28–29
Specialization   92
Spirituality   166
Squats   150
    20-rep squat routine   37, 69, 79, 148–149
Stanford Hypnotic Susceptibility Scale   62
Steinborn, Henry "Milo"   3, 150
Strategy   94
    coping   128
Stress   63–65, 143
    productive   40
Strongfort, Lionel   4
Success   49, 78–79, 80–82
    experiences   34
    fear of   108–110
Suleymanoglu, Naim   78–79, 123
Symbolic modeling   23
Systematic desensitization   22, 118, 134, 135

Talent   50, 95
Taranenko, Leonid   122, 124
Testosterone levels   2, 171
Todd, Terry   3
Triplett, Norman   100
Tyson, Mike   69